Dyslexia
A Teaching Handbook

Second Edition

M. E. THOMSON and E. J. WATKINS
Joint Principals, East Court School for Dyslexic Children, Ramsgate

Consultant in Dyslexia: Professor Margaret Snowling
University of York

Whurr Publishers
London

First Published 1990
by Whurr Publishers Ltd
Second Edition 1998
by Whurr Publishers Ltd
19b Compton Terrace
London N1 2UN
England

British Library Cataloguing in Publication Data
A catalogue record for this book is available from the
British Library.

ISBN 1-86156-039-7

Printed and bound in the UK by Athenaeum Press Ltd,
Gateshead, Tyne & Wear

Contents

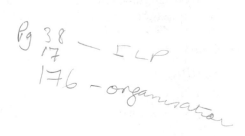

Appendices 206

Dedications
For Rosemary, Jamie and Jonathan – MET
For Gay, Rowena and Lucy – EJW

and for those unnumbered and unrecognised dyslexic children
who have never received appropriate teaching – MET and EJW

Acknowledgements
Our thanks to Sue Shaddick, who translated our random scribblings
into a coherent text; to Anne Brereton for detailed comments on the
1981 Education Act; to all our staff for their support and advice, particularly Gill Gilmour who made helpful and detailed comments.

Preface to First Edition

This book is not an attempt to provide a detailed programme of work to follow with children, page by page; there are already some excellent programmes available for this purpose. Rather, as the title implies, we wish to provide a guide to principles and techniques of teaching from a practical viewpoint. We have drawn on our experience at East Court, and have given examples from our own curriculum. We hope the reader will forgive us for this, but the many visitors we have had over the years have encouraged us to put pen to paper. Of course, every teacher will have his or her own circumstances and perspectives, and will need to draw from this book those parts which are most relevant.

Although the book is a practical one, it is based on a sound research and clinical basis, and we have referred to other sources for further reading where appropriate. However, it is a book on teaching, and we have avoided spending a great deal of time on describing the nature of dyslexia, its assessment or aetiology. These are well reviewed elsewhere.

We felt it would be helpful to provide the interested reader with detailed examples and descriptions of work sheets, word lists and other source material. Rather than put this into the text, we have presented these as Appendices. Please note that the copyright for the work sheets and work lists belong to us.

We would like to point out that we have tended to use the pronoun 'he' more often than 'she' in the text, as there are 4:1 boys to girls with dyslexic problems, and it seemed more appropriate.

Michael Thomson
Bill Watkins
May 1990

Preface to the Second Edition

The second edition of this teaching handbook is a result of experience gained over the last seven years since the book was first published. It provides additional ideas and comments to share with those involved in teaching and helping the dyslexic child.

A good deal of what we said in the first edition of the teaching handbook is still current, and therefore remains the same. Since the last edition, the Childrens Act as well as the Code of Practice have come onto the statute books. The Code of Practice, together with I.E.P.s and the implications of these, are commented upon. We have completely rewritten the chapter on Computers and Dyslexia, as this is an area which develops and changes very rapidly, with additional comments on word processing, use of laptops and spell checkers in particular which we feel may be helpful to readers. We have added some additional comments on teaching vowels, the use of word lists and updated our review of reading schemes. We have also made reference to current research on teaching by analogy and current theories on spelling development. As those of you who are involved in the highly specialised area of teaching know, time passes so very quickly. We continue to do our best but, surprisingly (or so it seems to us!), we are no wiser!

Michael Thomson
Bill Watkins
1998

Chapter 1
Introduction

Historical Context and Definition

The problem of dyslexia has been highlighted by the developing need of humans to communicate via the written word. The term 'dyslexia' was first coined and put into our written language by a neurologist, Berlin (1872) who used, as was the medical custom then, Greek etymology: thus – 'dys': meaning difficulty; 'lexis': meaning the written word. Simply put, it is a difficulty with reading or decoding the written word. However, the fact remains that despite well over 100 years of compulsory education, and latterly the raising of the school leaving age, in the UK there has been a manifest failure to achieve the universal literacy that was so optimistically planned for in the 1870 Education Act. It was into this educational arena that the concept of dyslexia was presented. It must be remembered that, in the late Victorian era, there was an implicit assumption that any intelligent child or person should gain automatic mastery of both spoken and written language. This outdated precept has remained with us until quite recently – indeed right up until the 1981 Education Act.

Initially the concept of dyslexia was used exclusively by the medical profession, who saw it primarily as a neurological dysfunction. Hinshelwood (1917) in a major ophthalmological study considered the condition as 'a congenital defect occurring in children with otherwise normal, undamaged brains, characterised by a disability in learning to read so great that it is manifestly due to a pathological condition and where attempts to teach the child by ordinary methods have completely failed'. He focused on the concept of congenital word blindness, his patient's 'difficulties' being caused *not* by defective vision but by a 'grave defect in the visual memory centre'. (The words 'word blindness' are in fact a misnomer because it is the brain that reads, not the eyes, the eyes being only receptors.) Significantly, this observation contained the germ of the later psychological concept that the problem could be related to a deficit in short-term memory store.

1

During the 1920s, Bachman (1927) mooted the idea of a maturational lag. In the USA, Orton (1925, 1937), a neurologist, made an important contribution when he put forward a theory based on the assumption that the dyslexic perceived images in an inverted, reversed or 'twisted' way caused by conflicting stores of visual information in left and right cerebral hemispheres. He used the word strephosymbolia to describe this condition. Further, he postulated a range of developmental disorders, which still hold good today. Orton considered that reading disability manifests itself in the form of letter and word confusions and reversals, severe reading and spelling difficulties, as well as difficulties with the mechanical processes of writing. Interestingly, Orton's descriptions were far-sighted because current research approaches have, in part, supported the assumptions made then.

The 1930s and 1940s saw the inquiry move away from the neurological perspectives into those of the educational and sociological areas. 'Backwardness' in reading became envisaged more as a problem of sociology than a medical issue (Burt, 1937; Schonell, 1942).

During the late 1940s and 1950s the Word Blind Institute in Copenhagen was one of the first to begin to examine the nature of dyslexia and, perhaps most importantly, to help the individual dyslexic with positive teaching. The Edith Norrie Letter Case was formulated in these times (see Chapter 3).

From the 1960s onwards psychologists and neurologists started taking an interest in the concept of dyslexia. For example, neuropsychologists questioned whether cross-modal integration of information and information transfer from one cerebral hemisphere to the other via the corpus callosum might have been the main problem. This was limited to concepts of cerebral hemisphere organisation and laterality (Newton, 1970). In 1963 the Word Blind Centre was set up in London by the Invalid Children's Aid Association (ICAA) and was both an important centre of research as well as teaching (Naidoo, 1972).

On a parallel course, psycholinguists were looking at the possibility of a language deficit at the phonological level, and linguistic coding deficits have been posited as a possible cause of dyslexia. Simply speaking, the dyslexic child is seen as having inordinate difficulty with the correct process of 'mapping' symbol to sound, a vital prerequisite for the automatic assimilation and mastery of the English written language system.

Latterly, considerable interest has been focused on the neuropsychological, biochemical investigations that have been attempted to answer many of the perplexing questions which have been raised in the research on dyslexia (see Wilsher, Atkins and Manfield, 1979).

The fact that the very existence of dyslexia has been vehemently denied by some educationalists and educational psychologists, when sizeable contradictory empirical evidence has been to hand (see Thomson, 1984,

1990; Snowling, 1987) underlies the unusual situation facing the dyslexic lobby. There appears to be a basic emotional issue at hand. This is no doubt a relic of earlier perceptions, mentioned previously, that lack of literacy was a result of general intellectual impairment.

It would not be fitting to close this brief historical survey without referring to the massive background of pressure from such worthy organisations as the British Dyslexia Association, the Helen Arkell Centre and the Dyslexia Institute and, of course, the untold numbers of parents who have, over the years, not accepted the 'official' perception that there was no such thing as dyslexia. This body of people has heightened the awareness of the general population and of the professional alike to the dyslexic condition. They are owed a vote of thanks, and they have been instrumental in the recognition of the concept of specific learning difficulty (dyslexia). It is worth recording that in the UK prior to the 1981 Education Act there was, in many cases, no provision for the dyslexic child. Certainly there was no law which either recognised dyslexia or accepted it as a condition, although a minority of British education authorities both recognised this group and made provision. Consequent upon concerted pressure from these groups, the 1981 Education Act was put before Parliament, but this was not processed onto the statute books before 1983, although the revised Education Act (1981) was adopted and, by opting for the compromise term 'specific learning disability', laid to rest much of the unwarranted controversy surrounding the term 'dyslexia'. The 1981 Education Act is examined in more detail in an addendum to this chapter.

The incidence of dyslexia (at a conservative estimate some 4% of the population) means that in a class of 25 there are likely to be 2 dyslexic children, and in a large comprehensive school of 1500 around 60 dyslexic children!

Finally, before moving on to describe some features of dyslexia, we provide a recent definition.

> Developmental dyslexia is a severe difficulty with the written form of language independent of intellectual, cultural and emotional causation. It is characterised by the individual's reading, writing and spelling attainments being well below the level expected based on intelligence and chronological age. The difficulty is a cognitive one, affecting those language skills associated with the written form, particularly visual-to-verbal coding, short-term memory, order perception and sequencing.
>
> (Thomson, 1984, 1990)

Features of Dyslexia

'Dyslexic children are characterised simply by making so many mistakes for so long.' In other words, a child does not just 'grow out' of dyslexia – although, as we shall suggest in the chapters that follow, the problem *can* be ameliorated by a structured educational process. The point must be made at this juncture that it is likely that during childhood development many children will pass though what appears to the lay person to be a classic dyslexic phase, i.e. as the children progressively mature from birth towards the first days at school they will at times present most of the symptoms that are dealt with later in this section. This, it should be firmly borne in mind, is completely natural and is nothing less than an outward indication of cerebral maturation and cognitive development. It is at this early stage that perplexed parents may well be concerned that their child is 'dyslexic', when in fact the child is only exhibiting the normal processes of growing up. 'Lucy', aged 4;6 years, produced the classic dyslexic sequencing problems – writing from right to left and spidering across the page. This was her attempt at copying from a work card. Her problem was not that of the dyslexic; rather it was her impatience to get going, and thereby missing out on the dot given by her teacher on the place to begin copying!

Her parents sensibly saw this exercise for what it was. However, it does illustrate the many pitfalls that face both professional and lay person alike.

Taken out of an educational setting, dyslexics will function quite adequately. Indeed, they may well excel at specific tasks, e.g. mechanical understanding may be very well developed. A brief anecdote here seems pertinent. At East Court some time ago we had a young man who presented with many of the features that we shall enumerate below. He was, in one word, *disorganised*, both physically and cognitively, was overactive with a 'free-wheeling' brain that appeared to be rather like a slot machine when the arm is pulled. His attention span was that of the proverbial 'class sparrow' – yet one of his many 'pluses' was the intuitive conceptual mastery of anything mechanical. The craze for remote radio-controlled cars was rampant, and one of us got hooked! A car was duly bought, and endless hours were spent 'assembling' it. However, the rear axle gearbox was not assembled in the correct manner, even after the full cognitive power of the principal concerned was applied! The young man, Master 'M', was called in to help. Not only did he go straight to the point of inaccurate assembly, but overhauled the car to boot. We might add that, at that stage, he could not read the instruction book and yet was able to demonstrate high order mechanical skills. The pictures were read without difficulty. The point here is that it is all too easy, especially in an educational setting where there is an emphasis on helping the 'disability' (specific reading disability), either to ignore or to dismiss as being of low currency the student's untold positive skills.

In listing a brief 'overview' of features we are very aware that the teacher wants a checklist which can be realistically used in a school setting. Equally, the list must be helpful to those specifically trained to teach the dyslexic. Our aim is to provide a system of indices that will aid.

There are many associated features or symptoms which teachers and parents can observe that provide clues to the diagnosis of dyslexia (specific learning difficulty). These include the following.

A puzzling gap between written language skills and intelligence

The individual child may well be adroit in the use of verbal language and have no difficulty in communicating his many ideas. It is only when faced with communicating via the written word that the deficit is highlighted.

Delayed and poor reading and spelling

There may be delayed and poor reading and spelling, often with persistent reversal and disordering of letters, syllables and words (d – b, was – saw, place – palace). The child may present as being able to cope quite adequately during the first few terms at school. Indeed, he may well cover up any difficulties by strengths in other areas or by playing the 'clown' or attention-seeker or, conversely, being the 'invisible' child. Given that many dyslexics have an artistic strength, the individual may well hold his own by pure reproduction, as an artist copies a still life, without the slightest idea that the arbitrary symbol carried a sound or phoneme that may or may not change depending on the letters grouped around it. The tortuous misery begins as the child faces overwhelming odds and a teaching system which may well be manifestly ineffectual, inappropriate and which will inevitably lead to the compounded failure which blights so many of our young dyslexics.

Bizarre spelling

There may be bizarre spelling: llob – doll, wyt – wait; kss – snake; and other more recognisable spelling: pant – paint, ors – horse, dog – god. This includes the child with a visual–perceptual difficulty, which means that he will have real difficulty in handling visually similar letter shapes; the child who cannot follow his speech sounds because of auditory weakness, either with the discrimination of the individual phonemes or segmentation difficulties; equally, reproduction of sounds may be beyond the child at any given stage. Receptive or expressive weaknesses may also lead to failure.

Left/right confusion and directional difficulties

The above area can make life a misery for dyslexic children. They have little or no idea of left and right position in space, although they may well be able to cope conceptually with right–left – up–down. In reality there may be grave practical positional difficulties. This, combined with a language which uses such statements as 'sit up' – 'sit down', causes great problems for the dyslexic, lost as it were in space without time or positional markers to give a touchdown.

Sequencing difficulties

There may be sequencing difficulties such as saying the months of the year in order, the alphabet and, worst of all, multiplication tables. Although able to just cope on a survival level, dyslexics are often faced with sequence – not just in their school exercise books but from the moment the day begins: dressing, organising, timetabling, presentation of work – in fact, just about everything is sequenced in our lives. Without sequence life becomes chaotic.

Poor short-term memory skills (following instructions, repeating digits)

As if to add to the tortuous misery, poor short-term memory means that the children will have inordinate difficulty holding on to information, information which they will at times desperately grasp at, only to find to their horror that it has slipped out of their grasp to leave them floundering. If this were not bad enough, the resultant anxiety will in all likelihood lead to even greater loss of capacity within short-term memory store.

If all of these gestures are put together, and the complexities of the human condition added, you have the dyslexic child facing the full might of the educational system. In the UK this means a system that has not been famous for coping with square pegs in round holes and one that has, historically, looked at the child as being at fault when something has not gone as prescribed by normal orthodoxies.

Given that this book is concerned with *teaching* the dyslexic, it is not appropriate here to describe in detail all the features of dyslexia itself. The reader is referred to Thomson (1984, 1990) or booklets from the British Dyslexia Association (BDA) and the Dyslexia Institute for fuller details.

Two case histories are now presented to illustrate some of the points raised in reviewing the features of dyslexia and in an attempt to bring the features into sharper focus.

Case 1: 'Matthew'

When Matthew came for interview with his parents, he was 9 years old, illiterate and innumerate to all intents and purposes. He spent much of his school life trying to avoid the horrors of being both teased and bullied. Assessment information using the Wechsler Intelligence Scale for Children (WISC) indicated that he was a boy of superior intelligence, having a diagnostically significant intelligence test profile. A specific weakness in short-term memory was high lighted by scores of 4 and 5 respectively in Digit Span and Coding subscores (score range 1 – 19, 10 being average). A history of sleep irregularities, minor 'sickness' and difficulties with peer interaction was evident. He was an only child and was very small for his age. His parents were at a loss to know what to do for the best. He had been sent, misguidedly, to a 'high-flying' preparatory school. On entering our study he became quite grey and clung to his mother. We naturally came forward to meet him, but this only resulted in him clinging even more firmly. It transpired that at his previous school he had been physically thrown across a classroom by a male member of staff for not learning a list of spellings by the end of the week! This had so traumatised him that it took some months at East Court before he was able to talk about the incident. At his previous school he had been with non-dyslexic peers who saw him as a 'dimbo'. He was ostracised and set extra work, so he could 'catch up'. Each Friday a class test comprising learning lists of words inevitably led to him being physically sick.

Being physically small he had no means of escape from what, for him, became a living hell. He had finally been asked to leave his school because it was thought that he 'was a child who was ineducable'. Assessment and subsequent diagnosis with a recommendation for special help had brought him to us. Although we could all 'laugh' at the experience by the time he left us as a confident, capable, quick-witted young man with a ready smile and a superb facility for humorous response, his early experience could so easily have ruined this young man.

Case 2: 'Tom'

Tom was 10 when referred, physically a robust, mature boy who had been perceived as a 'troublemaker' at his London day school. He had been labelled as disruptive. Tom was of very superior intelligence and could read adequately at the 9;6 year level. He had been receiving full-time help for some 2 years, and was confident in his ability to survive. His parents were eminently sensible and level-headed people and had given him and his sister a wide variety of stimulating experiences. They lived on a boat in St Catherine's Dock in London. They were reluctant to send him away to residential school but wanted the best for Tom. Tom presented as a confident 'rogue' of a boy who traded eye contact and gave an honest and full account of himself. He had a pleasant personality and an amazing verbal fluency with wide range of interest. The label 'disruptive' had come from him taking his pet snake to school for a general science lesson! He had by this stage nearly given up school as 'a complete waste of time'.

Science, art and geography were his favourite subjects, however! School reports indicated that he made good verbal contribution in lessons, but his written work was poor and too often was not handed in on time. He was popular with his peers because he was a born leader and had become the class 'joker'.

Tom enjoyed the interview almost as much as we did. He spoke frankly about what he saw as petty restrictions at his school and laughed at the jokes we told as well as telling us his. On joining us the 'clowning' soon lessened, but never completely stopped; he was a very entertaining young man after all. He made rapid strides in all subjects except English. Even our combined efforts resulted in marginal gains in spelling. However, he became a fast, fluent and wide reader. His vocabulary was extensive. He had no fear whatsoever of using new words to impart subtleties in his written work. Of course, the spelling of them was unorthodox to say the least! He became a pure phonetic speller, having almost complete failure even with the smallest of words – for example hear/here, where/were, dose/does etc. He became a computer fanatic, wrote complex programs and got up to all sorts of mischief – even attracting the local customs with a home-made radio transmitter which he used, unbeknown to us, when lights were out.

He left us as he had come, confident, charming and full of interest for life – spelling being the only real area of weakness. We have kept in touch with him – he was at a major senior school in Scotland where they welcomed his high intelligence and make allowances for his dyslexia. He passed all of his GCSEs, having taken English twice, took 'A' levels and now has a First Class Honours degree.

This description of two dyslexic students must make the point that, although both boys have the commonality of dyslexia (organisational problems, weakness in short-term memory, bizarre spelling etc.), they nevertheless have disparate features as well. 'Matthew' was a quiet, retiring child, the 'invisible' student with an introverted personality, whilst 'Tom' was the exact opposite, physically robust, the 'class clown', a 'troublemaker' and extroverted. 'Matthew' preferred to set his thoughts to paper; 'Tom' always preferred the verbal approach. They were, in almost every respect, like 'chalk and cheese' and yet they still had the clear underlying similarities of their dyslexia, identified by assessment.

Dyslexia as a Syndrome

In this section, the evidence for dyslexia as a syndrome, differing from other forms of learning difficulty, is examined. It is important to do this before we examine some specific teaching techniques that are geared to the 'dyslexic' as opposed to the 'remedial reader'. Whilst it is true that many teachers, psychologists, doctors, parents and other interested parties have used the word 'dyslexia' to describe a special group of children, in the UK it is only since the 1981 Education Act that the term, synonymously used with 'specific learning difficulties', has been widely used.

The word 'syndrome' implies that there is a collection of similar features and underlying causes that characterise 'dyslexia'. Our experience of running a residential school for dyslexics confirms our belief that we are dealing with a group of children having common, underlying difficulties. Naturally, due to individual differences, experiences and variations within the underlying causes, each child will not present in the same manner. Each child is individual and, to quote out of context – 'Vive le difference!' The reader is referred to Thomson (1990) for a detailed discussion of epidemiological studies and the concept of dyslexia as a separate entity from other learning difficulties.

It is of course important to place the above, and indeed our approach to dyslexia, in a developmental context. This point was made in the definition at the beginning of the chapter. In the context of teaching this means that children change over time, and that the approach of teachers must be changed to take this into account. Young dyslexics, for example, are markedly disorganised. This disorganisation is particularly noticeable in the residential school setting at East Court! Personal possessions are left lying around despite continual reminders and a very organised regime. Problems with timetables, places and activities, remembering arrangements, keeping living areas tidy, putting clean clothes out and doing up ties or shoelaces are just a few examples of disorganisation! Many younger dyslexics are non-starters in written language, with severe problems in basic alphabetic skills and reading. The older child may have some reading ability but may need more help in spelling or essay writing. Children's strategies change with time and the teaching they have received. We shall briefly review the developmental context later in this chapter.

One of the dilemmas for teachers is whether to try and remedy weaknesses, or circumvent these by providing alternative strategies. For example, early teaching programmes were aimed at 'training up' a particular weakness. This sometimes gave rise to inappropriate exercises in, for example, shape matching or figure–ground perception. This improved these skills, but not reading or spelling. In many cases underlying difficulties, e.g. weak short-term memory, remain as areas of weakness but the written language skills can be remediated. An example by case history can illustrate this point. Figure 1.1 shows the development of abilities as measured by the British Ability Scales during an 18-month period. It may be seen that IE's ability in 'Similarities' (verbal reasoning) starts off at a higher level than the other abilities (illustrating the specific nature of the dyslexic problem) and then improves steadily over the

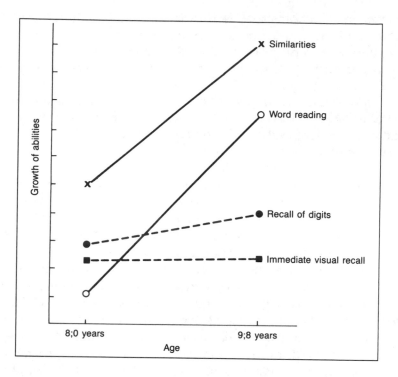

Figure 1.1 Growth of various abilities for IE

2-year period. 'Word reading' was very poor indeed when IE was first seen, but this also improves greatly over the 2-year period, illustrating the important effect that remedial teaching had upon his reading abilities. What is of particular interest is that the 'Recall of digits' and 'Immediate visual recall' subtests (which were particularly poor in IE's case) do not improve at all over the 2-year period. It is clear that the short-term memory items are still weak, reflecting the nature of the dyslexic syndrome. Our view is that teaching should not focus solely on the underlying cognitive weaknesses, in this case short-term memory, but on the written language itself. Pre-reading skills, memorial training and the like waste valuable time that could be devoted to reading, writing and spelling. This theme will be returned to at the beginning of Chapter 3.

Causes of Dyslexia

We do not propose to spend a great deal of time reviewing the plethora of evidence relating to the causes of dyslexia – this is a practical book on teaching. However, a good teacher must have a clear idea of causes if he or she is to have clear insights into teaching procedures. The implications, for diagnosis of dyslexia and teaching, are discussed in the next section. However, brief comments will be made here.

Research into the causes of dyslexia falls into two main categories:

1. The neurological, i.e. pertaining to brain functions.
2. The cognitive, i.e. pertaining to perception, memory or similar functions.

The reader is referred to Thomson (1984, 1990) or Snowling (1987) for reviews of this research. A summary developed from Thomson (1990) is presented here.

In relation to the neurological perspective, there are strong suggestions of links between cerebral hemisphere function and dyslexia, i.e. in relation to differences between the functions of the left and right sides of the brain. Basically, these theories relate to the greater facility the left hemisphere has in language, including many subskills underlying written language. These subskills include dealing with symbols, sequencing and naming, key features of reading and spelling. Studies using dichotic listening and divided visual field techniques suggest that there is some kind of association between dyslexia and 'abnormal' (or certainly 'different') neurological functioning. The word 'functioning' is stressed here, as we are not necessarily talking about anatomical differences. Dyslexic difficulties might be due to either a left-hemisphere deficit, or possibly some kind of disconnection syndrome between normal processing for auditory material with abnormal processing for visual material. Another factor which cannot be ruled out is a lag in the maturation of left-hemisphere function for language. It should be stressed that the above does not imply any form of brain damage; we are referring to individual differences in brain organisation.

In the cognitive perspective, early notions of some kind of visual–perceptual difficulties are open to serious criticism, as are some of the notions of visuomotor performance difficulties, and intersensory integration problems, at least in the form described in earlier research. However, it would appear that *some* dyslexic children might have primary difficulties in these visuomotor areas.

Reviews of eye movement research indicate that eye movement and eye sequencing difficulties are secondary to the primary problem in decoding the visual symbols into sound, i.e. the reading process itself. The eye is but a receptor. However, there is a good deal of evidence for difficulties in serial and sequencing skills, particularly where sound encoding is involved. These difficulties are usually associated with some kind of short-term memory problem.

In relation to memory, there is good evidence for some weakness. A memory capacity difficulty seems possible in dyslexics, but there are more likely to be difficulties in the short-term strategies used. Research on memory and dyslexia (see Thomson, 1984, 1990; Snowling, 1987) indicates that, in the case of long-term memory, and in the very brief sensory store, there does not seem to be a major problem among dyslexic children (although there may be some difficulty in accessing names correctly). It is in the short-term memory areas that there is evidence of weakness, where dyslexics have difficulties in remembering letter patterns, and basic sound–symbol correspondences. Here the problems appear to be in remembering series, in remembering sounds long enough to blend them together to form words in spelling, or in basic letter patterns for reading. A letter combination taught one day will be forgotten the next day by the child, which can be very frustrating for the teacher. This short-term memory difficulty shades into another area of weakness – that of being aware of the sound structure of written language, particularly in phonological coding. Phonemic awareness, i.e. the knowledge a person has that a word like 'cat' can be split into three phonemic sound units, i.e. (k)–(ă)–(t), is an important area of weakness in dyslexics. Another area links phonological coding with short-term memory, i.e. in translating visual symbols into their sound equivalents. Basically, it is argued that there are two ways to read. One is to go directly from the visual input to meaning; this is the way we read if a text is very easy – we are reading fluently, or reading for meaning, without any difficulty. An alternative way to read is to read in a so-called 'mediated' way. This includes going from visual symbol through sound coding or memory systems and then accessing meaning. This is when we read aloud, use speech to read, when the text is difficult, or we read something that contains letter patterns where we are actually decoding as we are reading. This can, of course, be a subvocal process. It is here, in this early stage of reading, that research finds difficulties in the dyslexic, not only in terms of rhyme, but also in terms of translating the visual symbols into sounds and in the short-term memory encoding systems that are needed for reading.

There is a point where perception, coding and memory overlap with each other; it is suggested that many of the difficulties in aspects of sequencing and memory relate to verbal encoding and verbal processing. Dyslexic children do not appear to have a general verbal processing difficulty in the sense of being unable to understand or use language, but have difficulties related to various strategies or to translating visual input into sound-based or verbal codes – specifically aspects of phonological and sound coding. It appears that there are difficulties in aspects of segmentation, translation of visual symbols into sound codes, and possibly in translating visual symbols into some kind of articulatory code. Here it is suggested by some authors that there is an overlap between dyslexia and aspects of speech disorders. Certainly there is very strong evidence for some kind of phonological/phonemic verbal coding difficulty in dyslexic children. This, in many ways, is quite clearly related to problems in using a verbal phonological code in short-term memory, with the consequent deficits in the reading, writing and spelling process.

Reading and Spelling Development

It is only really in the last few years that there has been a systematic attempt to relate the development of reading and spelling in children to the place where it breaks down in those with dyslexic problems. It is not appropriate in a book of this kind to go into great detail on the theoretical issues involved, but as some of them do impinge on the way in which we teach children, they may be worth a brief review here. A widely quoted model is that of Frith (1985) who argues for three stages in the development of reading. These are Logographic, Alphabetic and Orthographic and are shown below in Table 1.1.

Table 1.1 Three stages in the development of reading (Frith, 1985)

Stage 1: Logographic
Associate speech signs with symbols. Read as logograms. Shape recognition, using visual memory in environment. Particular words spoken/written. Reading logographically helps to spell logographically.

Stage 2: Alphabetic
Chunking letter sounds and morpheme identification. Grapheme/phoneme translation route, sound to letter correspondence; requires phonemic awareness, decoding novel words. Using phonological/letter sound approach in spelling creates alphabetic approach in reading.

Stage 3: Orthographic
Automatic recognition of graphemic clusters. -tion, etc. Access to lexical representations set up relating to letter-by-letter sequences. Use of lexical analogies. Use orthographic code first in reading then transfer/develop spelling.

Ehri (1991) also describes the three developments – emergent readers, phonetic cue reading and cipher sight word reading (Table 1.2).

Table 1.2 Development of sight reading (Ehri, 1991)

emergent readers:	no sound/symbol, visual aspects of word only
phonetic cue reading:	one or two specific cues, individual letters/ blends give phonic clues
cipher sight word reading:	stored in memory, spelling/phonological associations

Most stage models begin with the visual recognition of familiar words at the early stages. The next stage is usually some kind of alphabetic component which involves the use and application of phoneme/grapheme rules, in other words, the relationship between the spoken sound and its graphemic equivalent. The assumption is that sound coding or phonological processing, probably related to short-term memory, will be an important component of this stage. Phonemic awareness is usually described as being an important skill to be learnt, often developing from reading itself – that is, dealing with the sound structure of spoken language and its relationship to written language. These, of course, are important elements of teaching programmes which are described later. A third stage, after this alphabetic or sound/symbol relationship, involves the store of sight recognition words, which are then associated with a mental lexicon. Word understanding as well as orthography becomes important.

Many of these stages subsume a dual route to reading model, i.e. reading from the word through sound/symbol associations to pronunciation and finally accessing the meaning of the word or else reading directly from the visual input to meaning. Another approach is illustrated in Figure 1.2. Here 'speech' input and the 'print' input are processed interactively with meaning and the context. In many ways these are analogies to 'Look and Say' (orthographical processing) and 'Phonics' (phonological processing) although we appreciate that is simplifying the model.

Current research in dyslexia highlights the weakness that dyslexics show in the phonological area. This has important implications for teaching. One is that teachers need to teach dyslexics exactly that thing which they find most difficult. This implies having to overcome that 'alphabetic' barrier by teaching the relationship between the sound and the symbol in order that the child may recognise new words, build up the grapheme conversion links, develop segmentation and syllabic skills and all the fundamental substrate of the structured programmes which we outline later. A key feature of early development is the nature of phonological awareness and the following terms will be used in this book:

Word	Syllable	Onset and Rime	Phoneme
dog	dog	d - og	d - o - g
string	string	str - ing	s - t - r - i - n - g
magnet	mag'net	m - ag ' n - et	m - a - g - n - e - t

Thus, magnet can be divided into two syllables, two syllables with onset 'm' and rime '-ag' and 'n' and '-et', or six phonemes. Grapheme/phoneme relationships would therefore involve recognition and blending, intra-syllabic skills, recognition of cluster units and visual or whole global reading – the whole word perhaps directly into meaning or into

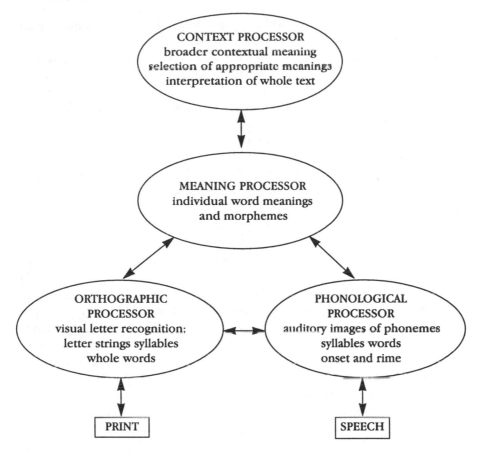

Figure 1.2 Interactive Processes in reading.

a grapheme/phoneme correspondence route and then into the meaning of the word (or with a nonsense word, into pronunciation).

Notice the word 'rime' (it is spelt correctly). This refers to the vowel plus consonant at the end of the word as opposed to two words which may rhyme but be spelt differently e.g. yacht and knot.

Sometimes these theoretical approaches have led to very specific links. Munro (1995) provides a good review of some of these but also suggests the following in the development or building of orthographic knowledge:

1. Developing (prerequisite) phonemic knowledge including recognition of rhyming words, onset and rime, segmentation, deleting sounds, matching sounds and so on.
2. Learning individual letter sound matches.
3. Working on two or three letters at once, recognising letter clusters.
4. Learning long vowels, more complex letter clusters, vowel digraphs, blend patterns.
5. Study of word structures and perhaps morphology.

The specific teaching tasks and mechanisms under each of these head-ings are essentially what this book is about.

It is worth noting that much of the work on reading development sug-gests that children understand the syllabic structure of words first and then become more involved with the phonemic structure. As teachers we tend to teach phonemes or phonogram units or letter sound links first and then go into syllable units. Perhaps we ought to be rethinking our approach. Certainly we recognise the importance of syllabic structure in teaching reading and discuss this in detail later in the book.

A slightly different but very widely quoted approach is the notion of interactive analogy in learning to read and spell as proposed by Goswami (1988, 1994). She proposes an interactive development rather than a series of stages, i.e. rather than from discrete stages, for example logographic through alphabetic, children learn by means of lexical analogy. For example, knowledge of the word 'mean' would give rise to 'heat', 'bead', 'beat', 'peak', etc. She particularly stresses the intra-syllabic division between onset and rime, i.e. the '-ap' in 'tr'ap', '-at' in 'h'at' rather than the other divisions, for example 't-r-a-p', 'tra'p', 't'rap', 'ha't', 'h-a-t'. She draws on earlier work linking rime detection to reading development and suggesting that the onset of rime awareness comes before reading, and phonological development is a consequence of developing reading and spelling. Olson and Wise (1992) found a sim-ilar effect when using computer-presented material. Here the computer would read back highlighted text where either the whole word or seg-mented feedback was given. The segmented speech was better learnt if it was 'd-ish' and 'b-oat' rather than 'di-sh' and 'boa-t'.

Treiman (1983) was one of the earlier writers to examine the impor-tance of onset and rime. She argued that rhyme awareness was an important component of early reading development and as a result of learning to read the child became more phonemically aware, which might give rise in turn to spelling skills. This of course is also linked to the work of Bradley and Bryant (1983) on sound categorisation, i.e. phonological training and letter sound relationships. A survey evaluat-ing this kind of approach to teaching was done by Snowling (1996) and some important conclusions should be borne in mind for teaching.

The first is that phonological training that takes place with children, whether this be sound categorisation or learning sound units or phonograms rather than letter-based units, produces better results in children if it is linked to real reading activities. By this we do not mean 'real reading' as in whole language approaches, but if the phonologi-cal training is associated with learning to read and spell words rather than done abstractly. This has been found by a number of authors, for example Hatcher, Hulme and Ellis (1994), Cunningham (1990) and Lovett et al (1994). The latter in particular were looking at how dyslex-ics might be taught to generalise from learning one or two words to learning other regular and even non-words. Here it was found that phonological training, in conjunction with identification strategies, did best of all.

A number of these approaches, we feel, are something that many teachers of dyslexics have done over the years. Teaching by analogy, for example, is essentially looking at word families. Developing phonemic awareness of phonological coding skills is essentially teaching the relationship between spelling patterns and speech. As is always the case, however, it is nice to have one's teaching methods and pragmatic approaches underpinned by theoretical research even if the research does follow on what teachers have known for many years!

Assessment and Teaching

The question must be asked, 'Why assess?' The answer, quite simply put, is 'To diagnose in order to remediate'. It is an attempt to observe and collect information systematically in a short period. This information could be gained in a classroom situation, under normal circumstances, over a longer period of time. The 'act' of assessment really focuses our attention as we look at a number of attributes that contribute to a successful learning experience for a given child. Assessment should be both 'functional' (i.e. help focus on what is hampering learning) and 'descriptive' (i.e. aid in identifying what should be done to further learning).

In this section we shall be looking briefly at the psychometric assessment of the dyslexic child, specifically the child of school age, and how educational assessment and the data obtained can be a powerful tool in the hands of a skilled teacher. A fundamental point, often overlooked or ignored, is that assessment is of little real use if it is not positively linked to and used in the teaching of the child. Clinical assessment has its uses in research, and without research understanding of any phenomena would be limited to guesswork and open to 'subjective' feel – there is no need to expand on the implications of this! For ourselves, we require empirical evidence to support the assessment of dyslexia.

It should be stated quite clearly that we all believe that assessment is a vital prerequisite to teaching; it allows the teacher to arrive at a baseline or datum point from which to start. It also allows him/her to develop an Individual Education Programme (IEP) if necessary. As we have already noted in the first section, the dyslexic child is often disorganised and lost in a chaotic sea of confusions. The purpose of assessment allows the 'guide' to begin from a known point.

Assessment should be seen to have three major functions:

1. Diagnosis.
2. Delineation of specific difficulties.
3. Guide to remediation.

Diagnosis without remediation seems to be at best of dubious value, at worst cruel. Remediation without assessment seems a waste of valuable time.

The diagnostic process looks at the child to determine whether he or she has a dyslexic problem, and if so what kind it is. It will rule out slow learning, major sensory deficits, primary behavioural difficulties and maladjustment as the prime causes. Teaching methods for these groups will not be appropriate for the dyslexic. Dyslexics require a specific and particular kind of teaching methodology. Implicit in the diagnosis will be the delineation of particular difficulties, such as a specific weakness in a number of given areas, e.g. auditory and visual memory sequencing, auditory blending, visual perception, temporal ordering, rhyming, to name but a few. The child might have, for example, a complete inability to learn or use grapheme–phoneme correspondence, or subtle difficulties with the processes of decoding or encoding of either (or both) auditory or visual information. Equally, they may be able to cope with task-specific items but have grave difficulties as the 'loading' and complexity of a given task increases.

Remediation without assessment and delineation can become, in the eyes of many of the children, retribution! Remediation follows from having first identified a particular learning difficulty – in this case, dyslexia. The aim must be to indicate where to start, and at what level, in terms of the child's needs: to prescribe a plan of action, a series of particular techniques that will be used and, most important of all, strategies to aid the children.

The cognitive school of thought favours psychometric testing and focuses on generalised skills and abilities using normative data, i.e. data gained from large populations, then analysed to arrive at the 'norm' for a given population. It requires that both cognitive strengths and weaknesses be assessed, and implies that the results are a measure of the above, i.e. strengths/weaknesses of the individual child. Tests such as the Wechsler Intelligence Scale for Children, (including WISC-R and WISC III 1992) (WISC – Wechsler, 1976), the British Ability Scales (Elliott, 1983), Neale Analysis of Reading Ability, Vernon Graded Word Spelling Test and the W.O.R.D. reading and spelling test which allow objective percentile scores to be used are examples of psychometric tests used. They are skill-specific tasks, and look at areas such as memory (both visual and auditory), verbal conceptualisation and visuospatial ability. From the data obtained it is possible to analyse the child's problems in terms of the question 'What strengths/weaknesses has a particular child?' A profile is thus obtained which is a personal record of a given individual's performance. The report thus engendered forms a comprehensive analysis of the child's profile and should also contain, if it is to be of real 'hands-on' value to the teacher, recommendations for teaching arrived at from an analysis of the information available. The test results will remind those who read the report that the child in question has certain measurable strengths, but also has specific measurable weaknesses which can be measured against the population norm (e.g. matched age and cognitive ability). It may well go on to suggest particular teaching strategies and methods that will positively help the particular child. One of the limitations of this type of assessment is that it does not always make it clear that a particular teaching method is the correct one. Further, it often does not cover specific curriculum content that needs to be attacked in helping the child. This is not an inherent weakness within the cognitive school of thought, but rather it is a comment on the quality of the report from many psychologists – it is difficult for many of them to keep a firm footing in both camps, e.g. school curriculum development and psychological investigation. One of the major advantages of the cognitive school of thought is that it allows the collection of normative data and, by implication, a database from which to work.

The behavioural school of thought favours task analysis or 'criterion referencing', i.e. looking at specific skills and abilities of a given child without recourse or reference to larger groups. The behavioural school questions the need for the normative approach arguing that comparing like with like is of little interest or relevance. They pose the question 'What has the child failed to learn?' and believe that the problems may be explicable in terms of environmental or contextual influence. Curriculum mastery is seen as the goal, and task and behavioural analysis as the means to answering the questions posed. To these ends, precision teaching and hierarchical analysis are employed. Reports are written, giving analyses of the problem in terms of what the child has specifically failed to learn. Inevitably, reports contain recommendations for teaching content based on findings, e.g. curriculum analysis and specific detailed goals. The limitation with this approach is that it fails to look at general points raised, e.g. cognitive skills and subskills, and in doing so confines itself to basic skill acquisition and learning hierarchies, thereby making reports that are, by their very structural philosophy, difficult to apply to more complex multifaceted skill areas.

We feel that both schools of thought have a lot to offer in their general philosophies. Of course they are, as has been suggested before (Elliott, 1983; Thomson, 1990), not mutually exclusive; both are tools to be used primarily to help the child rather than as a basis for 'schisms'. It would be so easy to dismiss one in favour of the other, and in doing so become guilty of 'throwing the baby out with the bath water'!

Based on our experiences, we favour the cognitive approach: primarily because we adhere to the school of thought which believes that dyslexia can be defined principally as a cognitive developmental condition; that is not to say that the behavioural school has little to offer. The idea of asking the basic, simple question 'What has the child failed to learn?' seems sensible. An answer should then be sought by way of detailed observation. This seems to be utterly straightforward – and does away with long-winded medical and psychological cogitations. However, the behavioural approach can result in rigidity, for example in the form of task analysis and micro teaching. By doing so, it can significantly move away from both the delights and frustrations of the more generalised approach of the cognitive school. The inherent strength of the behavioural school is that it attends to the teaching of the individual and assessment is inextricably linked to this. However, many of the questions posed are not answered fully by the behavioural approach, but are answered by the cognitive approach.

Having established that we favour full psychometric assessment, it is important to give details of some of the attendant problems of dyslexia that face the teacher of the dyslexic child. Mention must also be made of secondary features that are often associated with the primary dyslexic condition. (Detailed explanation of assessment is to be found elsewhere – see Thomson, 1984, 1990.)

Primary behavioural and emotional difficulties can cause learning failure and present symptoms similar in many respects to those of the dyslexic child. Primary emotional/behavioural problems may be of a pathological origin or result from environmental/social or other non-specific circumstances. Such difficulties will effectively bar the child from the normal learning situation, i.e. their problems will be such that their primary 'block' prevents them from effective learning. Obviously, the educational management and remediation will be different, calling for specialist counselling, psychotherapy, behavioural modification and 'token' economy – these children will require progressive management of their 'primary' cause.

For dyslexics, secondary emotional problems are often concomitant, i.e. because they have experienced, in many cases, progressive and continuous failure, they have developed secondary emotional difficulties. These difficulties may be so severe that they prevent the child from effective learning (in many respects the same outcome as with the primary cause already noted) so that they can be mislabelled by the system. The dyslexic may have adopted the 'class clown' mantle; equally he may be 'disruptive' – all are strategies adopted in an attempt to survive in a hostile environment, e.g. school. If we consider the experience of this group and the realities for them of continual failure in a core subject plus the attendant failure in other subjects requiring written communication, it becomes obvious that an educational environment is required that will allow the dyslexics to 'earth' their 'secondary' emotional response to the 'primary' dyslexia. Once this release occurs, the dyslexic can be rid of earlier 'troubles'.

The assessment of intelligence is of seminal importance. It means that an impartial and objective understanding of the dyslexic child can be reached. It provides important salient information that can be used in aiding both the description and remediation of the dyslexic. In a 'nutshell' it provides a datum line or database from which the teacher can work. The two major individual IQ tests used by psychologists, the Wechsler Intelligence Scale for Children (WISC – Wechsler, 1976; WISC III UK Edition, 1992) and the British Ability Scales (BAS – Elliott, 1983), provide a rich harvest of information, i.e. they act as both a measure of IQ in the strictest sense and a most useful diagnostic tool.

Intelligence assessment can be perceived as having four major functions:

1. To obtain a measure of the intellectual level (or IQ) of the child, in order to rule out slow learning or low intelligence as a cause of written language failure.
2. To examine the interrelationship between the child's intellectual level, chronological age and written language attainments, in order to describe any discrepancies between these.
3. To obtain a diagnostic profile on the intelligence test used.
4. To describe the cognitive functioning of the child, in order to identify areas of deficit and to help plan remediation.

Assessment using either the WISC or the BAS, and following the above rationale means that a negative bias in subjective assessment can be done away with. Under this heading is included intelligence assessment of the child based on inappropriate forms of assessment, e.g. reading/spelling or verbal tests that are used wholly to set up or group children. Equally, to judge a child solely by his character, nature or language is asking for trouble. 'He's a badly behaved boy, therefore he needs remedial help' really won't do!

Table 1.3 looks at assessment from the standpoint of labelling. Fact and fiction are detailed with reference to past, present and future. The model underlines the benefits of proper assessment.

The WISC and BAS are powerful tools when used diagnostically. The problem comes when overall IQ values such as verbal, performance or full-scale scores are bandied about without reference to the subscores, and an awareness of the implications of these.

What appears simple and straightforward, e.g. a full-scale IQ in the average range (i.e. IQ 90–110), implying that the child is 'average' and therefore not 'slow learning', can in fact be rather more complex. The case presented in Figure 1.3 shows high intelligence which is 'masked' by a wide range of subscores. Averaging produces a 'mean score', and so the information, presented without the additional vital subscores of the tests used, leads to an incorrect appraisal. A wide range of subscores effectively reduces and masks the 'real potential' of the child and so often leads to misinformation. The child is mislabelled, and all too often dismissed as having only a minor problem, when the reality, as we have indicated, is completely different. Figure 1.3 shows a profile gained from an assessment using the WISC-R. There are two profiles: one of a non-dyslexic child, the other of a dyslexic child. The two profiles are completely dissimilar because the non-dyslexic (or normal) has a steady profile, i.e. ±3, whilst the dyslexic (or ACID profile) has a 'saw-toothed' profile with a large discrepancy i.e. ±13. (The reader is referred to Thomson (1990) for a detailed discussion of these issues.)

The question often posed is 'What use is the intelligence test, and how does it help?' Initially it allows the achievement of a baseline of intellectual potential. It does *not* tell us that the child is dyslexic, but it may well be a useful tool in the whole battery of assessment procedures and give important diagnostic information. Full assessment using a wide range of tests does tell us if a child is dyslexic.

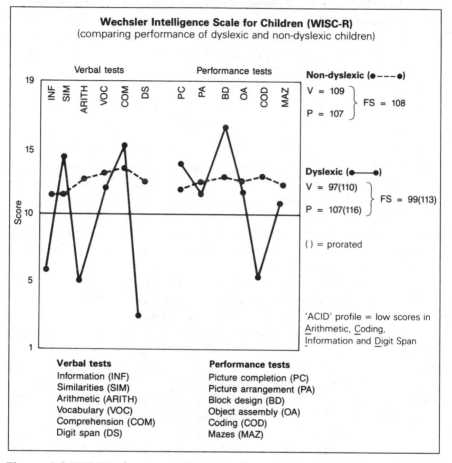

Figure 1.3 WISC-R showing a dyslexic and non-dyslexic profile. V = verbal IQ, P = performance IQ, FS = full-scale IQ

It must be noted that the psychometric tests (WISC-R and BAS) do *not* offer a magic remedy for the remediation of dyslexia; they do *not* offer a programme of work; they do *not* tell us how a given weakness will affect the dyslexic child in a classroom situation; they do *not* tell us anything about the future; they only offer an insight into the child's ability on the particular day of the assessment. The dyslexic will have 'good' and 'bad' days and, in many respects, this mirrors the profile shown in Figure 1.3, i.e. he will have 'peaks' and 'troughs'. They do *not*, if they are of any worth whatsoever, make specific pronouncements or predictions about the child's future. A word of caution seems apposite here.

Table 1.3 Assessment

PAST				
Past	*Fact*	*Parental label*	*Child's label*	*Action*
'Fuzzy'	Parental concern initially a 'free floating' anxiety What can be done? Child too often judged on attainment – specifically reading and spelling	Neurotic parent Over-anxious Too high expectation Parental pressure	Lazy Thick Stupid Wilful Slow learner	None – to seek advice from class teacher 'Don't worry'

PRESENT

Psychologist looks at child's POTENTIAL as well as attainment

Strength areas	Spatial skills Science Computer Art Mechanical
Weaknesses	Spelling, number Processing of symbolic information Poor short-term memory tables Expressing ideas in written form

OBJECTIVE ASSESSMENT

FUTURE				
Future	*Fact*	*Parental label*	*Child's label*	*Action*
A clear view of child and his or her cognitive abilities	Focus of attention on child's problem	Caring Informed	Dyslexic or specific learning deficit (1981 Act) (1993 Act)	Seek help LEA school or independently

There are a number of psychometric assessments that take basic infor-mation such as IQ levels and make wide, sweeping statements such as:

> On the Wechsler Intelligence Scale for Children (Revised), Matthew achieved an overall IQ of 109, which is at the very top of the average range. Approximately 25% of boys of his age are expected to achieve a higher score than this, whilst the remainder function at a lower level. For purposes of comparison, this places his level of ability just within the range of those boys who eventually pass GCSE's, though rather below the average for those who go on to 'A' levels.

This type of statement is felt, by us, to be wrong and it leads to all sorts of problems. For example, at the early age of 6–8 years, it is a known statistical artefact that verbally bright children – and by this we mean specifically children who have a certain fluency of language and vocabulary – will gain a high score on the WISC-R. Certain dyslexics may be within this grouping. Parents given information as to the level of IQ and predicted success at the age of 16+ invariably become both disappointed and frustrated by subsequent scores that may well be lower as a result of a combination of statistical phenomena and age increase.

So what does full assessment give? For a start, like the intelligence test, it allows the setting up of a baseline. Reading and spelling levels are important, not just as a means of telling us the actual normative reading/spelling level of a given child, but more interestingly for giving important clues as to how a child goes about the process. To these ends, error analysis is an important tool. Scoring here is important.

The Neale Analysis of Reading Ability is a well-known test of English prose where the child has to first read a passage aloud before answering questions on the text. The Neale test goes some way towards answering some of the questions raised by the assessment, e.g. Rate, Accuracy and Comprehension: Rate refers to the speed of reading, Accuracy to how accurately the text has been read and Comprehension to how well the child has understood what he has read. It is from such data, i.e. scores and error analysis, that teaching recommendations can be made. Perceptual areas are investigated at the assessment and further support the psychometric test findings. The Aston Index (Newton and Thomson, 1976) and the Bangor Dyslexia Test (Miles, 1990) provide useful pointers with implications for teaching (Table 1.4).

Criteria referencing has already been mentioned under the broad heading of 'The behaviourist school'. This has an important contribution to make because it requires clearly defined targets, and asks clear concise questions. In the assessment situation many of the features of the criteria referencing philosophy can be positively incorporated, e.g. to observe precisely what the child is doing and saying; to observe what the child can and cannot do in a given test – in the Block Design subtest of the WICS-R any of the following areas of weakness can be looked for and accurately identified:

1. Inversions of shape or pattern.
2. Reversals of shape or pattern.
3. Repetition of action.
4. Verbalisation to aid problem solving.
5. Difficulty with parts to whole (figure/background).
6. Fine motor control difficulties.
7. Observer strategies used for a given task.

Following their identification it can be assessed whether such actions are appropriate or not.

Full assessment allows a considered judgemental pronouncement to be made, i.e. whether the child is dyslexic or not as the case may be. Further, it defines and details the problems facing the child. It allows a psychologist to make recommendations with regard to the level of the child's attainment and construction by the specialist of an IEP together with suitable placement to gain maximum help. This may mean within the child's existing school via intervention help, or withdrawal, or occasionally may mean a school move.

Table 1.4 Some useful tests for screening for dyslexia

General intelligence and cognitive profile
  Wechsler Intelligence Scale for Children ⌐ 'ACID' profile, i.e. poor scores on
                                                                   ⊢Arithmetic, Coding, Information
  Wechsler Adult Intelligence Scale   ⌏ and Digit Span
  Raven's Matrices
  British Ability Scales – weak short-term memory
  Illinois Test of Psycholinguistic Abilities – language based

Attainment tests
  Neale Analysis of Reading Ability
  Schonell Graded Word Reading and Spelling
  Vernon Graded Spelling Test
  W.O.R.D. Reading and Spelling
  British Ability Scales Word Reading

Screening test
                          ⌐auditory sequential memory   sound blending
  •Aston Index ⌏ visual sequential memory – pictorial   sound discrimination
                          └   – symbolic   laterality

                                        ⌐ direction left/right
                                        │ polysyllabic words
                                        │ digit span
  *Bangor Dyslexia Test ⌏ AM, STM
                                        │ rhyming
                                        │ mental arithmetic
                                        └ months of year

The reader is referred to Thomson (1990) for details of their diagnostic use. The tests marked* are available from Learning Development Aids, Wisbech, the others from NFER/Nelson, Windsor.

Addendum: Dyslexia and the 1981 Education Act

The 1981 Education Act is as important as the 1944 Education Act, although it did not gain Parliamentary sanction until 1983. For many, the Act came too late to help and is, as many parents, educationalists and solicitors have found to their cost, a highly complex Act which is sadly open to 'wide interpretation'. The 1981 Education Act reformed the earlier general law (1980) in an attempt to define specific requirements. The Act requires the LEA (local education authority):

(i)   To carry out a statutory assessment if the request is considered to be reasonable.
(ii) Following the statutory assessment the LEA must decide whether the child, in their opinion, has Special Educational Needs.
(iii) If the answer is 'yes', then a further question is asked: 'Can the child's special educational needs be met from resources generally available to the school?' If so, then the child will be helped from within school. If not, then it follows that the LEA must provide extra resources and write a Statement.

The above three sentences appear at first glance to be clear and concise. However, as we shall see, the reality of the situation is far from clear. First, there is considerable scope for wide interpretation of the requirements of the Act. Second, 'to meet the child's special educational needs' is, it appears from many parents' accounts, beset with difficulties.

The term in Section 1 (ii) of the Act, 'Children with Special Educational Needs' includes, by definition, many varied disabilities and is very wide. The need for skilful negotiation is vital, as any parent trying to obtain help from their LEA will naturally need to be well informed in the fine detail of the 1981 Act and the 1993 Act which incorporated the Code of Practice. As a direct consequence of this need, the British Dyslexia Association has provided a very useful document: 'The Education Act 1981: Your Questions Answered' by Sterne and Brereton, as well as providing a counselling service of people very well versed in the intricacies of the Act. However, in the final analysis parents would be well advised to seek expert legal advice from law firms who specialise in and provide solicitor and barrister-at-law services. A copy of the Code of Practice (1993) is an invaluable tool.

Broadly speaking, the Act aims to provide each child with educational facilities appropriate to his or her specific educational requirements. The law looks particularly at that group of children who are seen and defined as having 'Special Educational Needs'. The Act gives parents clear rights of appeal, if, in their opinion, the provision is not met. By this is meant that the Act can form the basis for a High Court action, yet in the first instance there is no need to do this. The 1981 Act does in effect put in place two sets of appeals, starting with the Local Education Authority Appeal Committee and proceeding to the Secretary of State. One of the difficulties associated with this process is the length of time it can take (approximately 18 months). An Ombudsman at Local Government level can be of help here to make an independent judgement. It should be noted that the Ombudsman 'rules by consent' – his judgements are not enforceable. However, if the LEA disregards his recommendations then he can issue a second

1944 ED ACT 1993 ACT
1981 ED ACT *Code of Practice*

report. It is encouraging to note that so far LEAs have always heeded the Ombudsman.

Either the parents or the LEA can instigate the Statutory Assessment procedure. The local authority can inform parents that they intend to assess their child for 'Special Educational Needs' if it is the LEA's opinion that the child requires an assessment. Parents must be given details of the procedure, together with a person whom they can contact and liaise with. The 'Named Person' only has to be given to parents after the Statement is issued! However, most LEA's do give parents a contact person early in the procedure. This is normally an Education Officer from the LEA. His task is to give parents information. The parents have a right to submit their own views and this must be done within 29 days. Further evidence (e.g. independent medical reports) may, however, be submitted by parents later.

Parents also have a right to request that the Authority undertake an assessment for 'Specific Educational Needs'. The Act states, 'The Authority must comply with the request unless where it is, in their opinion, unreasonable'. To complicate matters, the Act has been interpreted by the Divisional Court as having 'two levels of disability' which require 'two different approaches'. The Department of Education and Science favoured this view in their circular 1/83 (now superseded by circular 22/89). The first category – children who are seen as being in need of help but not sufficiently handicapped as to warrant Statementing – are dealt with within their own school *without* the strength of a Statement under Section 7 of the 1981 Education Act. The school must make provision and meet their need. Unfortunately, the practice is that, all too often, there is a grave lack of provision – either through lack of assessment procedures, resource, expertise or staffing. Quite frequently a combination of all the above results in a solution which is, at best, little short of the situation that unhappily existed prior to 1983 or, at worst, is unlawful.

At first glance, the second category is much easier to define and protect by the Act. The severe dyslexic or 'Specific Educational Disability' child is clearly highlighted. However, all is not plain sailing, as all too often the highly intelligent dyslexic child 'masks' many of his or her difficulties by very high intelligence and by dint of survival strategies which present the child as 'average ability'. Indeed, it appears that it is not the 'degree of difficulty' which determines whether or not a Statement is written. It depends on the provision available either within the school or which can be provided. For instance, given that within the school there is an RSA or BDA qualified teacher and there is an 'awareness' of the need for support, then it is unlikely that a Statement will be issued.

There are, as will already have been observed, many pitfalls in what was heralded as an 'important charter' for children with 'Special Educational Needs' in 1981 when the Act was first put before Parliament for consideration. If the LEA declines to make a Statement, then the parent has recourse to Right of Appeal to the Secretary of State. Sadly, the interpretation of this depends on current case law interpretation in the court and the Secretary of State's hands are tied. Parents may alternatively appeal to the Local Government Ombudsman on the grounds of maladministration, i.e. that the authority has misdirected itself.

As far as dyslexia is concerned, most specialists in the field, including ourselves and others, for example Chasty (1981) and Crowther (1982), feel that dyslexics require a specialist form of specific skilled teaching, which may not be presently available in the ordinary classroom. Provision by an LEA may be for a peripatetic teacher or sessional help. Indeed, it may be for inclusion in a general remedial group within the school, whereas the parent or the child may have been hoping for more specialised and intense help. Specialist teaching for basic skills will include mathematics and associated subjects where the dyslexic child will have specific difficulties. Parents are advised to look for 'appropriate qualifications', e.g. the British Dyslexia Association (BDA), the Royal Society of Arts (RSA), the Helen Arkell Centre, Hornsby Centre, or the Dyslexia Institute Diploma. These are examples; there are many other courses. A 'Teaching of Reading' Diploma or Slow Learning Diploma would not, in our opinion, be acceptable; neither would a general Special Educational Needs Diploma or Degree be suitable for the specific type of teaching which the dyslexic pupil needs. What is urgently required is more widespread teacher training for dyslexic learning difficulties. Although there are a number of courses, many establishments still either choose to ignore the issue of dyslexia or provide inadequate or inappropriate training courses.

The reader is referred to Appendix XI for a diagrammatic illustration of the route for Statementing.

Code of Practice

Background

The 1993 Education Act required the Secretary of State to issue a Code of Practice. The Code of Practice gives practical advice to LEAs and governing bodies of all maintained schools on their responsibilities towards all children with special educational needs (SEN). Part III of the Act details these responsibilities. An estimated 20% of the school population will have SEN at some time in their school career.

The Code came into practice on 1st September 1994, being a requirement of the 1993 Education Act. Prior to this, the Audit Commission and HMI (1992) had voiced concerns with regard to progress since the 1981 Education Act. These concerns centred around the following points. Our comments are given in parentheses.

1. Unacceptably long delays by LEAs in processing statutory assessments of children with special educational needs – it was not unusual to find delays of years.
   (*Delay long enough and the problem will pass through the system!*)
2. Lack of accountability in resourcing children with special educational
   needs.
   (*Fuzzy, unfocused teaching programmes.*)
3. Vague statements of little actual use.
4. A dramatic increase in the resulting backlog of Appeals before the
   Secretary of State.
   (*Often the Appeal Committee could not force the LEA to make provision. Equally, there could be a conflict of loyalties with regard to
   the Appeal Committee members, i.e. county or child? Impartiality
   was questioned (Chasty and Friel, 1991).*)

From 1 September 1994 LEA schools and all other agencies who help
with pupils having special educational needs, including the Health
Service and Social Service, must implement the advice contained within
the Code of Practice.

The Code itself

The Code of Practice is subdivided into six parts:

1. Introduction: principles and procedures.
2. School-based stages of assessment and provision.
3. Statutory assessment of special educational needs.
4. Statement of Special Educational Needs.
5. Assessment and Statement for under-fives.
6. Annual Review.

In effect, the 1993 Education Act and Code of Practice attempted to
focus clearly on the needs of the child with regard to this acknowl-
edged 'most challenging' area. The fundamental principles of the Code
1.2 are:

• Pupils who may have SEN at any time whilst at school must be
  addressed. A continuum of needs and provision will be assessed.
• SEN children have a right to a broad and balanced curriculum including the National Curriculum.
• The needs of most pupils will be met in mainstream without statutory assessment or issuing of Statement of SEN. Further, children
  with SEN should be educated within mainstream schools.
• Some children who may have SEN prior to formal schooling will
  require intervention of LEA and Health Service.

- Parents' knowledge, views and experiences are vital and will contribute to effective assessment. A partnership between parents, their children, schools and LEAs and other agencies.

Identification of SEN and clear assessment as quickly as possible is considered to be very important. Equally, provision for SEN children with help from the most appropriate agency, normally within mainstream school, will be sufficient in most cases and no statutory assessment will be deemed necessary. A time limit of 26 weeks is set where a Statement is considered necessary. Clarity and thoroughness must define the child's educational and non-educational needs, together with provision of facilities and arrangement of monitoring and review. An annual review is implicit. The wishes of the child should be considered in light of his/her age and understanding. A multi-disciplinary approach combining close co-operation between all involved together with a satisfactory resolution should be aimed at.

Adoption of a five-stage model is posited. The first three stages are school-based and will, when needed, call upon external specialists. At stages 4 and 5 the LEA will share responsibility with schools. The Code of Practice details five separate stages:

Stage 1   Class or subject teachers identify or register a child's special educational needs and, consulting the child's SEN co-ordinator, take initial action.
Stage 2   The school's SEN co-ordinator takes lead responsibility for gathering information and for co-ordinating the child's special educational provision, working with the child's teachers.
Stage 3   Teachers and the SEN co-ordinator are supported by specialists from outside the school.
Stage 4   The LEA consider the need for a statutory assessment and, if appropriate, make a multi-disciplinary assessment.
Stage 5   The LEA consider the need for a statement of special educational needs and, if appropriate, make a statement and arrange, monitor and review provision.

Although the Code of Practice does not insist on these five stages, in reality we have never come across any deviation from this model.

The Code of Practice is best read comprehensively as it prescribes some 170 pages covering in fine detail all the many points arising. It covers LEA and independent education – indeed, any child requiring SEN help comes under this document. It is not explicit in detail in the criteria for statutory assessment – it makes the point that it can't be. It is left to individual LEAs to make the decision. Specific staff SENCOs will have responsibilities for making provision for children under their care. This in practice will range from 'nominated, responsible person' to SENCO through to special needs teams in the largest of schools.

The overall philosophy is to support children within the mainstream system without recourse to the issue of a Statement. This will be stages 1, 2 and 3. Individual schools will be responsible for the allocation and provision of resources to facilitate this. Clearly, the Code of Practice is aimed at giving the individual child appropriate, high quality, effective and precise help so that he/she can work in unison with those responsible for providing such help. Those involved with the Code of Practice are required to make efficient utilisation of resources.

To summarise these procedures:

- Early identification.
- Clear and detailed assessment.
- Careful planning prior to intervention.
- Clear, objective record-keeping; at regular intervals.
- Use of gathered information to facilitate individual educational programme of work and accurate communication of information to other staff involved with child and parents. (This will help inform those involved with Annual Review and Transitional Plan for movement on to senior school).
- Engage child and parents in discourse to maximise gains.
- Child and parents have responsibilities to air their views.
- Accountability of LEAs, Health and Social Services to work within clearly defined guidelines and specified limits.
- SEN Tribunals to resolve disputes.

In effect, a whole new set of requirements are to be implemented by the Code of Practice.

1. Statements must be precise in detailing the needs of the child and the provision to be made.
2. The child has a right to make his/her views known – he/she *is* to participate in decision making.
3. An Individual Educational Plan (IEP) must be drawn up for all pupils from stage 2 onwards.
4. Schools must have a register of all children with SEN. Equally, a 'special educational policy' must be written and available – giving information as to the arrangements and persons responsible.
5. A named person must liaise with parents to offer advice and give information. This person should be independent of the LEA.
6. Statutory re-assessment at the age of thirteen plus – senior school transition. This ties in with the Transition Plan which must be written for children over 14 to prepare them for the transition from school to adult life.
7. The setting up of an independent system of appeal – the SEN Tribunal – independent of local and central government.
8. LEAs must have regard to the Code of Practice when disputes arise.

9. OFSTED Inspection will look at effectiveness of school's policies and practice with regard to the Code of Practice.

The Code of Practice and dyslexic children

The Code of Practice, HMSO 1994, Section 156 defines special educational needs in the following manner:

> A child has *special educational needs* if he or she has a *learning difficulty* which calls for *special educational provision* to be made for him or her.

Dyslexia (specific learning difficulties) is defined as:

> Some children may have significant difficulties in reading, writing, spelling or manipulating number, which are not typical of their general level of performance. They may gain some skills in some subjects quickly and demonstrate a high level of ability orally, yet may encounter sustained difficulty in gaining literacy or numeracy skills. Such children can become severely frustrated and may also have emotional and/or behavioural difficulties.

A child has a *learning difficulty* if he or she:

a) has a significantly greater difficulty in learning than the majority of children of the same age.
b) has a disability which either prevents or hinders the child from making use of educational facilities of a kind provided for children of the same age in schools within the area of the local educational authority.
c) is under five and falls within the definition at (a) or (b) above or would do if special educational provision was not made for the child.

A child must not be regarded as having a learning difficulty solely because the language or form of language of the home is different from the language in which he or she is or will be taught.

Special educational provision means:

a) for a child over two, educational provision which is additional to, or otherwise different from, the educational provision made generally for children of the child's age in maintained schools, other than special schools, in the area.
b) for a child under two, educational provision of any kind.

As quite a few of our children have been Statemented since 1983, we have considerable experience in the processes which have led up to the issuing of Finalised Statements. Initially, that is after the 1981 Education Act came into force, we were optimistic that the Act would help many dyslexic children, The reality of the situation was sadly a hotchpotch of chance. It seemed that the area the child lived in had greater effect than the strength of the Act, inasmuch as some LEAs grasped the power of the

Act with both hands and acted both effectively and efficiently in making clear decisions based on the individual child's best interests, regardless of other expedient factors. These children and their parents gained considerably from the Act. The child's problems were identified, an action plan of specific help was engendered and careful placement in close communication with parents was provided. For those lucky few, help was at hand and clearly was given to the satisfaction of LEA, parent and child.

As it happened, unfortunately, for many the Act made little difference – in fact it raised hopes unrealistically. We were all positive and hopeful that provision for the dyslexic child would improve. For the majority of parents with dyslexic children it meant asking formally for the Statementing process to begin. Many of these parents had already had full independent psychological assessments completed either by various agencies (e.g. the Dyslexia Institute) or by independent psychologists. It was clear that the 1981 Act had opened the flood gates for requests for help and provision. The reality for many parents was either that their LEA acceded to their request but was snowed under, i.e. full psychological assessment could take a year or, in some cases, far longer; or they deemed it unnecessary to undertake an assessment on the grounds that there were other children who had far greater difficulties. Some LEAs were overtly hostile to the idea of dyslexia, even though it was now quite clearly defined within law.

A number of parents, with the backing of pressure groups such as the British Dyslexia Association, took their LEAs to task and spent both time and money on seeking a proper judgement, not clouded by bias or hostility. This meant in effect that a whole series of set piece confrontations had to be worked through before the Secretary of State became involved. Invariably, LEA Tribunal Appeal was inadequate and, in the words of the Audit Commission and HMI, many were quite unsatisfactory affairs. We have both experienced the open hostility of such meetings and have been left feeling something of the awful frustration and anger in the face of such bias which unnumbered parents have had to cope with.

Even at High Court level, some cases were lost on points of law rather than the inherent clear needs of the child which any educationalist could have seen. It seemed to us that it was a lottery of where you lived rather than your child's needs. Some cases were won when there was clear evidence that provision from within the LEA resources was quite adequate, whilst others were lost when it was clear that the child had been dealt a dreadful blow by an educational system that is held up to be 'the best in the world'!

It would not do to list the many instances where both child and parents have been fobbed off with inadequate provision and LEAs have paid little more than lip service to the spirit and law of the 1981 Education Act. These are catalogued in law reports, factual accounts by parents and agencies and are available.

The Code of Practice is, in part, a new start and an attempt to put behind some of the less than satisfactory aspects of the Education Act 1981. It should be clear that the spirit of the 1981 Education Act was very good, indeed we all welcomed it in 1983. It was the interpretation and use of it by some LEAs which resulted in the formulation of the 1993 Code of Practice, which aims to be far more precise in its guidelines. Time will, of course, tell, but we are hopeful that it will aid children and parents in their right to receive appropriate education.

We see the following possible areas of difficulty.

1. 'The needs of most pupils would be met in mainstream without statutory assessment or issuing of a Statement of SEN.' This could lead to biased perceptions based on financial or political expedients.
2. Parental knowledge, views and experience are vital – (what is reasonable?).
3. The Code of Practice is not explicit in details on the criteria for statutory assessment. It makes the point that it cannot be. It is left to the individual LEAs to make the decision. Let us all hope for enlightened individual LEAs.
4. Funding of the Code of Practice. The DfEE considers implementation should be cost neutral. This is not substantiated by others (Johnson, 1995).
5. The need to have cases heard at SEN Tribunals within six months of an appeal being filed. The sheer volume of cases lodged may make this difficult to achieve.
6. Finally, both HMI and OFSTED will monitor the Code of Practice, and Special Educational Needs Tribunal will remain independent and will have the last say. Our experience so far with Tribunals has been more positive than the old LEA Tribunals, although time will tell!

Individual Educational Plans

One of the aspects of the new Education Act and the Code of Practice is the necessity to develop Individual Educational Plans. A major purpose of these plans is to set up goals and targets in order to evaluate children who are Statemented. Another intention, of course, is to act as a plan for the teaching approach which will be taken for the child.

Sometimes we feel that these plans can take up an inordinate amount of time and effort so that if one is not careful one can spend all one's time drawing up goals, targets and plans rather than actually getting on with the teaching. We also feel that once one defines a child as having a dyslexic problem this implies a certain kind of approach to the teaching anyway. However, we have found that plans are useful and in any event they are necessary for the current Education Act and so we have included some examples in Appendix I. It should be noted that most IEPs tend to focus on just one or two difficulties. Obviously if one wanted to produce a plan for every difficulty a dyslexic child had, one would essentially present a book such as this as part of the plan. These examples, therefore, just focus on one or two particular priority areas and are plans that we developed for children on a termly basis. It will be noted in the plans that we have written down some targets and stages for National Curriculum levels. These may be more appropriate for non-English plans. We find that the National Curriculum targets for written language plans for dyslexics tend not to be that relevant. For example, we might say that some of our children would be able to reach a certain level in respect of understanding different kinds of fiction, being able to respond to them differentially, being able to write different genres and so on, but the reality is that their actual reading attainments are nowhere near that level. This often makes it inappropriate, therefore, to look at dyslexic children's written language difficulties in respect of National Curriculum levels, a point we shall expand on in the following section.

Dyslexia and the National Curriculum

Our comments here are mainly confined to the relationship between English and the National Curriculum, although it may be worth noting that some of the comments are applicable to other subjects also. For example, we shall be making a point about the discrepancy between a child's understanding of what is required in English and his knowledge of literature and the ability to read and write it. The same could be said of, say, Science or Humanities where a child may be perfectly capable of covering aspects of the curriculum and doing very well on them but cannot be assessed properly because handwriting is poor, or may not be able to access the National Curriculum because he is unable to read set books. As we have said elsewhere, this implies that one has to develop special material which is accessible to these children. For example, if one is undertaking work on the Vikings and Romans as part of the History National Curriculum, one needs to present them with worksheets which can be read, help them to read the required material and also to write about it. For dyslexics the key is to access the National Curriculum in such a way that they do not fall behind in their knowledge of the subject matter.

Another important consideration is the notion of a foreign language. Many dyslexics find a foreign language inordinately difficult as they are still struggling with their own native tongue. Much research seems to suggest that there is an important difficulty in the relationship between sound and symbol, phonological awareness and sound structure in learning to read, write and spell, which are of course elements of spoken language too. When this is combined with new spelling patterns and word recognition clusters, one can see how learning a foreign language can be a kind of exquisite torture for dyslexics devised by someone who wanted to add a refinement to the original torture of learning to read, write and spell in English!

At East Court we operate a 'modified mainstream curriculum'. This means that we access the National Curriculum appropriately as briefly outlined above, but also that we do not teach a modern language. Our experience is that French is a particularly difficult language for dyslexics to learn as the sound structures, particularly vowels, are very different. The way we get round the problem at school is by saying to children and parents that you will not learn a foreign language for three or four years but when you return to your mainstream school at 13+, you can start a modern language if you so wish. We recommend that this is not French as non-dyslexic peers will have had two or three years already learning French and therefore they will be too far ahead, but they could start another language such as Spanish or German. We gather (not being linguists ourselves) that Spanish and Italian are relatively regular and easy to learn, and certainly German, although it has long syllables, if one is good at syllable analysis (which one should be having gone through an East Court education) it reasonably easy to get to grips with. We understand that the most regular European language is Finnish, but there does not seem to be a great demand for this in European circles at the time of writing!

We expect that many of our readers would have had the experience of having to write not only IEPs (see p. 34) but also reports for Annual Reviews and in general on the child's progress. These inevitably require the teacher to make comments on the National Curriculum in terms of Key Stages and Attainment Targets. It is notable that the start of the English National Curriculum comments that the appropriate provision should be made for pupils who require aids to writing such as Braille, signing, adapted equipment and so on, but there does not seem to be much allowance made for children with dyslexic difficulties. We find that it is very difficult to comment on our children's progress within the constraints of the National Curriculum as you get very odd anomalies. For example, we are told that an average performance for Key Stage 2, that is, eleven-year-olds, would be Attainment Target Level 4. In terms of reading this describes the child as being able to respond to a range of text, showing understanding of significant ideas, themes, events and characters; beginning to use inference and deduction; being able to refer to text when explaining their views and locating and using ideas and information. Most of our eleven-year-olds, we feel, could do that – in the abstract – if only they could actually mechanically read the text concerned! Certainly they can understand genres, themes, respond to characters and are well able to use inference and deduction. However, due to the fact that they may be reading at around the eight year level, they are unable to read texts which explore those themes in any great detail. What is one, therefore, to write on a report? We tend to make extra comments – for example, we might write under Attainment Target 2 (Reading) that the child could be at Level 2 in terms of being generally accurate in reading simple text, but at Level 4 in terms of responding to the range of text, understanding of significant ideas, etc.

In relation to Attainment Target 1 (Speaking and Listening), this is not a major problem for dyslexics. Of course, some dyslexics do have interesting variations in speech. For example, the following are comments that have been made by students: 'In the Middle Ages there was a lot of death around'; 'I felt a tingle go down to the peak of my toes'. Quite clearly these would not boost one's levels on the National Curriculum!

Reading, of course, is a problem. We feel that the National Curriculum should ideally have been divided into reading accuracy/ mechanical/phonological reading or some such as against comprehension/understanding/semantic aspects of reading. We have given some examples above, but of course the problem for us as teachers for the older children going into the later stages of Key Stage 2 and into Key Stage 3 is how to develop Level 6–8 in terms of critical response to poems and plays, and general literacy as opposed to reading and spelling competently. This often requires oral work and also generally being aware as a teacher of dyslexics that it is not just simply the reading accuracy and spelling one is looking at, but one also needs to look at understanding of poetry, characterisation, different linguistic features in writers' styles and so on.

Attainment Target 3 (Writing), again, could ideally have been split further, e.g. handwriting, spelling, writing style and essay development. To put all these together is sometimes not easy because, as in reading, we are often in the situation of having to make comments that the child's writing is so poor that one can barely read what had been written, but if only one could decipher it it is actually at a much higher level than would be imagined. Similarly, a child may write quite well but the spelling is so poor that it is difficult to judge. For example, at Level 4 one could argue that 'ideas were often sustained and developed in interesting ways and organised appropriately for the purpose and the reader', but that 'spelling, including polysyllabic words that conform to regular patterns, is generally accurate' certainly would not apply. Nor would comments about full stops, capital letters and question marks. However, to say that a child has not reached Level 4 does seem to penalise him/her unfairly. Commenting on these points, rather than giving a bald AT Level, seems reasonable to us.

Chapter 2
Making a Start

This chapter outlines the procedures and consideration involved in setting up a dyslexia unit, and provides guidelines to the principles of teaching dyslexics.

Setting up a Dyslexia Unit

In Chapter 1, we looked briefly at the assessment of the individual and made it clear that assessment is a fundamental part, i.e. a keystone, in the prescriptive teaching of the dyslexic. This section will look in some detail at the whole question of setting up a unit, and all that it implies. It will pose a number of questions that it will attempt to answer. It assumes that the question, 'Is there sufficient need for specialist help to be provided in such-and-such an organisation?' has had a positive response. Further it will question the term and philosophy of 'remedial' as it has come to be perceived in the educational setting of the mid 1990s. We will consider the implications of setting up a unit and ask some basic questions, which we shall then attempt to answer in some detail.

Why?

The question 'Why?' must first be answered. Most schools will have a sizeable minority of children with general non-specific learning difficulties. Within this section, there will be subdivisions of varying needs. These may range from children having a mild learning disability but not needing 'special school' placement, to children having a primary emotional difficulty (Emotional and Behavioural Difficulties (EBD)) which precludes them from benefiting from 'normal academic teaching'. Within this disparate group there will be a subdivision or group which can be defined as having specific learning difficulties and which will require clearly defined specialised teaching. They will *not* require 'more of the same', nor will they 'grow out of it' given time. They will, like any child gain enormously from specific specialist teaching of the type appropriate to their needs. This will mean that they have no real difficulty with the conceptual content of their education, only with the intricacies of decoding written symbols and getting their ideas down on paper. Their 'bête noire' will be the handling of symbolic language. In many cases, the provision can be 'tacked on' to existing remedial facilities, and will dovetail into the established set-up. It is rare that any school either has no provision for the 'failing child', or cannot call upon help and must set to work on helping the individual, as it were, from scratch. Assessment will have highlighted a need. In the majority of cases, help will be forthcoming, albeit of a rather generalised kind. In this section we shall confine ourselves to that group of children who can be accurately defined as dyslexic or suffering from a special learning difficulty, and for whom there is little or no specialist education provision.

Source of students

Will the group of students come from within the school, i.e. have they been highlighted by more accurate assessment, increased awareness or the like, or will this group come from new arrivals? It may be that a school is looking to an area of the specialist field of education in combination with existing children from within the school. This may be for two reasons:

1. The provision of help for existing pupils.
2. The provision of help for existing pupils but also looking towards new arrivals to fund the extra costings of employing specialist teachers, etc.

Staffing

Of course, staffing of a new unit or department will need to be carefully considered. Fully trained specialist teachers were, in the past, exceedingly difficult to come by – mainly because the whole concept of dyslexia was vigorously denied by the Department of Education and Science (DES) and the training of teachers was undertaken only by a number of specialist organisations. We are glad to note that since 1989 when we wrote the first edition of the book, things have improved. There has been a pleasing increase in the number of teachers who have gained recognised specialist qualifications. The question of staff is important because it is they who will 'make or break' any newly established department or unit.

Will staff come from existing staff by promotion or will they be newly appointed? One of the problems associated with promotion is, unfortunately, the general assumption that anyone can 'do' remedial teaching.

We have often observed poor, bored and fundamentally 'bad' staff being taken on to 'make do and mend', with the result that the new venture is destined to fail miserably, both in terms of measurable academic success as well as being seen in a poor light by other staff. The importance of employing staff of the right calibre cannot be stressed strongly enough. Any reasonable teacher can impart knowledge of their specialist subject to a child who has no learning deficit. It is the exceptional teachers who are required to have command of their subject and also to be able to stimulate and teach the specific learning disabled child. The teachers will need to know not only their own subject area but also to have a thorough grounding in both cognitive and educational psychology, in addition to having a specialist knowledge of dyslexia and how it affects the child.

Timetabling

Having established that there is a need for a new department or unit, the next question must then be one of timetabling – the integrated day or the individual withdrawal system? Both have their advantages. The integrated day means that the dyslexic will be taught in tandem within the normal timetabling schedule. English may be taught, for example, during the first or second period of the morning. When the non-dyslexics have English, the dyslexic group has parallel 'Special English'. The special teaching will, in many cases, have the same aims and goals but will follow a parallel course .

With regard to optimum numbers for an integrated day, class sizes with a maximum of 6–8 for English lessons are favoured. Although this seems a luxury, and indeed is in many cases, it nevertheless means that each child can be attended to as an individual and given specific educational input. Larger class sizes do not work for the dyslexic because they call for a generalised approach and this, as has already been explained, manifestly does not work.

The advantage of the integrated approach is that the child does not miss any lessons, and gains made within the 'special lessons' can be easily observed and monitored by teaching staff. (More of this later in this section.) Equally, the children can, because of the small numbers involved, make spectacular gains. After all, it is the task and intention of the specialist teacher to progressively bridge the gap between age and attainment. This gap, ever widening, must be closed if the dyslexic is to make the grade.

One of the strongest reasons for small group teaching vs the individual approach is that it allows dyslexic children to see themselves as members of a group, not as isolated individuals. After all, for many dyslexics their experience will have led them to believe that they are the only one in the class, school or world with this perplexing condition.

They will feel isolated. In a small minority of cases dyslexics may see themselves as 'precious' or a 'freak'. Small group teaching soon does away with this unhealthy state of affairs. Another positive advantage is that of peer interaction and group dynamics. It is our perception that the one thing that dyslexics want above all else, once they have mastered a specific skill, is competition. They revel in healthy competition. After all, for many they have never ever been first in anything and, given half a chance, they want to join the club of winners. Equally, a small group has not only group identity and cohesiveness, it also has certain prestige and protection – in many respects rather like a club. Any teasing can be dealt with by the group, whilst the individual receiving individualised help, in a vacuum, is left to feel further isolated when teasing occurs.

Of course, withdrawal of either the individual or individuals has its advantages. On the one hand, the timetable is not disrupted in any way. On the other hand, minimum fuss is created by the odd one or two dyslexics disappearing or not turning up for a given lesson. In addition, 'one-to-one' tuition has many well-documented successes. It makes the child 'special', and allows for individual help and all that this implies. There is an argument for individual teaching, and this centres particularly around the younger child who may well benefit initially from personal individualised help on a one-to-one basis. However, working in a 'middle school', we feel quite strongly that we must deal with realities. These realities will, in the majority of cases, mean children joining senior schools where they will have to face the realities of large group teaching. To protect children from this until they are 11+ or 13+ years would, in our opinion, be cruel and lead to many problems when the children attend their senior school.

The question of tutorials in addition to group teaching must be raised. Our feeling is that they are vital, having a number of important features and spin-offs. Timetable space can normally be found, especially in the senior school. For example, when non-dyslexics go to modern languages the dyslexics could attend tutorials. Ideally, from experience two children at a time, or even three, can work well. Tutorials should be special times where a more informal approach can work to good effect. The implicit message is that you have time for the individual, and to these ends an everyday item such as a kettle can be put to good use – the offer of a cup of coffee, for example, makes a welcome break. Tutorials are a time for specific skill teaching, going over areas which have been causing trouble during the preceding week and for the introduction of new areas. Equally, they are a time when valuable individual therapy can be undertaken. They may range from a few minutes discussing a problem to most of the period being spent in trying to 'earth' a particular problem or 'block' what is effectively stopping the child from learning. It is important to keep a notebook, to record as well as to act as a reminder to take action of any particular points. Communication of information to specific staff, who may well be unaware that they are causing a particular problem for the individual as a result of the teacher's approach, or to the staff in general, is a vital part of running any successful department/unit. There should be a time at staff meetings for such items.

Before looking at the practicalities of setting up a unit, brief mention of additional help after school must be made. Obviously, help for the individual dyslexic is not at question – it is accepted and supported by those helping the child. What must be questioned, however, are some of the practical solutions. Some dyslexic children, having spent part of their day in 'relentless agony', e.g. non-specific English teaching and subjects where heavy emphasis is placed on the written word or note-taking, e.g. biology and history, will, as a result, be very tired (in some cases, exhausted). To be faced with then going for extra lessons, often from well-meaning but untrained teachers, seems at best to be of little benefit, at worst cruel and a thoughtless 'revenge'. We see a lot of children who have had the full horrors of this type of 'help'. For some children this is the only answer. The children, with support from their families, cope well with the extra load of extracurricular help. Indeed, it can be a positive life-line. Naturally, the specialist teacher who gives this help carries a heavy responsibility to the child, and must not fail; otherwise the worst fears of the child and parents will be realised with concomitant trauma. This option seems to us to be, at best, a compromise – one which will help some children, particularly the dyslexic who is coping, but needs intervention help on a regular basis. For many of the children we see, it is not sufficient either in extent or intensity. As a result the child is confused and the organisational problems mentioned in Chapter 1 (under 'Features of dyslexia') cause progressive movement towards chaos. Of course, appropriate help within the school day is the ideal, and one which the dyslexic lobby has been actively seeking. It is pleasing to note that an increasing number of local education authorities are making positive moves to alleviate this gaping weakness in the educational system.

Where?

The question of 'Where?' must now be addressed. It is of course paramount to have a base for specialist teaching. The actual physical features are the key to how a department or unit is perceived by other professionals. Equally, it underlines the official recognition and standing of the set-up. It would be wrong to suggest that a department is but the physical situation – indeed, many famous departments were initially set up in the most unusual of places. For example, one of the author's early 'Special English' departments, as it was known then, had no real base other than his Aladdin-like study. Use of odd rooms was the norm, but it did not hamper the positive help that was given to those early dyslexics. Enthusiasm, growing knowledge and, most importantly, a good basic structure which worked, saw the department go from strength to strength. However, an attractive base is important.

We have visited some schools, who shall remain nameless, to discover odd cupboards or indeed odd tables in the library which pass as departments! Both staff and children alike have been isolated and dismissed by a basically hostile staff. The fundamental mistake has been the lack of communication and understanding. Other staff need to know about the new proposals. Dyslexia via the back door will not do!

Ideally, there needs to be a special base or centre, a room for example – the important thing is that it is known by both staff and children alike, is titled and has a door which is always open. The room must be 'special' on a number of counts:

1. It must be clean, vital and colourful with bright paint or posters, work etc. on the wall.
2. It must provide a relaxing environment.
3. It must act as a refuge in times of stress.
4. It must have something special which makes it more than the ordinary classroom (kettle etc.).
5. Most importantly, it must have a unique identity.

On the first count, a lick of paint, even if done by you or the children, will overcome the tired image of so many of today's depressing classrooms. Posters from travel agents or any 'freebies' will give a fresh air to any room. On the second count, little need be said other than it may be possible to arrange for a special comfortable chair or chairs which can be used either to relax in or for the 'earthing', or counselling, chat. On the third count, some of the dyslexics really do need a refuge, a place where they can get their breath. For this reason, it is important that the room is the dyslexic's territory. A 'no go zone' is not to be advocated, rather a haven which allows others to visit but only when invited, thus enhancing the image of the special unit or department. This leads us to the fourth point. A kettle or a toaster works wonders. The kettle becomes rather special in many respects, like the 'medicinal' bottle of brandy kept in the office or at home. To arrive and be invited to have a coffee or tea makes the attender special and, importantly, gives him time to breathe. Further, it carries with it the implicit assumption that the person is valued. On the fifth count, it is most important that the room should have its own unique identity. A crocodile head, a skull or a warrior's helmet will make that statement. The feared workplace becomes the 'den'.

The target

The next question to attend to is what we define as the 'target', i.e. are you aiming your help at the right population, and is the help you intend to give them appropriate? The need for assessment and diagnosis as reviewed in Chapter 1 must be underlined because without it any efforts will invariably be misdirected.

Intensive help

Will the department or unit give intensive help over a relatively short period? This may mean that the child will be withdrawn from the normal curriculum on a full-time basis, but only for a period of, say, half or one term. The implications of this type of intensive help need to be realistically weighed up, because in effect you are taking the child away from the normal school curriculum and imposing a teaching situation which could well lead to 'overloading'. Equally, in some cases the expectation of staff in such situations becomes dull or blunted. They do not have the balanced perception as a result of having only one sort of child. It is important for any staff, especially at the secondary level, to experience, if at all possible, the non-dyslexic child in tandem so that a realistic balance may be obtained. Equally, the non-specialist needs to be aware of the special problems that face the dyslexic. This goes further to underline the point already made about the importance of good communication between staff and departments.

There is a group of children who benefit enormously from this type of intensive help, but in the main, the dyslexic will require continuous ongoing support, albeit the extent of help will dramatically decrease as the student progresses through senior school.

The teacher's role

What is the teacher's role in all this? Implicit in any equation is the role of the 'manager', in this case the teacher. The need to have specialist staff trained for the specific task has been briefly referred to: this means a person who has that extra quality – difficult to define objectively but well recognised by other professionals and parents alike. It is this immeasurable quality which sets apart the skilled and successful teacher. For the dyslexic child who has in most cases a negative experience of the educational system, it is vital that the teacher who contracts with that child to help and nurture him does in fact 'deliver the goods'.

Broadly speaking, the learning process for the dyslexic can be considered to be broken down into three stages. Each stage will consist of a combination of processes which will all link together to form the whole (Table 2.1). The 'earthing' period is so very important and cannot be rushed. We all pay lip service to the notion of taking time and not rushing a taught point. This is particularly stressed in training and PGCE courses, and yet we are all guilty of rushing through a given point with some of our children trying to hang on, others falling exhausted by the wayside, whilst we arrive at the end of the lesson smug in our belief that we have delivered the goods. The reality is that we have been guilty of one of the cardinal sins of teaching. Certainly we will not have helped the newly arrived dyslexic. We will have confirmed his suspicion that we are, as one boy put it, 'just like the rest'!

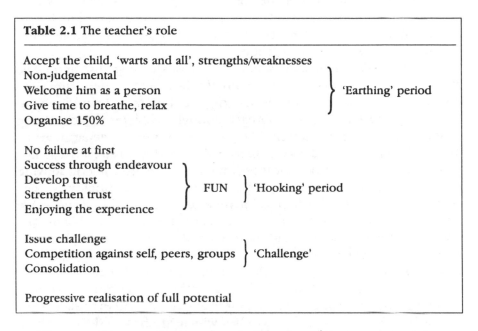

Table 2.1 The teacher's role

Accept the child, 'warts and all', strengths/weaknesses
Non-judgemental
Welcome him as a person   } 'Earthing' period
Give time to breathe, relax
Organise 150%

No failure at first
Success through endeavour
Develop trust   } FUN } 'Hooking' period
Strengthen trust
Enjoying the experience

Issue challenge
Competition against self, peers, groups } 'Challenge'
Consolidation

Progressive realisation of full potential

We must give our charges time to breathe. This, in our experience, does not take long for the average dyslexic, but occasionally, as in the case of Matthew (see Chapter 1 - Case 1), it can take a considerable amount of time – time well spent we might add. Lessons for the first term may have to be radically altered – indeed, occasionally it is best not to try and teach at all in the formal sense. This will come later and will be successful. However, do not worry, but look on the time as a sound investment. The children must be accepted at first 'warts and all'. Some of their learned behaviour may be inappropriate, but remember that they may be testing you to confirm their long-held negative prejudices. Therefore, it is vital that you do not confirm these by a simple mistake or a thoughtless action or word. Of course, there must be ground rules, and these must be known to all. Anarchy is no part of the structure! At East Court we have only one ground rule: 'think of others'. Give them a regime that is firm but fair. Children, after all, like to know the rules of the 'game' so that it can be enjoyed. Defining the parameters from Day 1 makes such sense that it seems almost redundant to mention it.

Nevertheless, we have visited some well-meaning departments which appear to have lost sight of this important tenet.

It is so easy for us to be unconsciously judgemental in our appearance and approach to dyslexics. We must be on our guard at all times. A word or witticism which older, established members of the group enjoy and respond well to, can stab at the heart of the 'hurt child'. Our experience is that, given support, these children progressively overcome this and go on to acquire a sense of proportion, a ready smile and an ability to laugh at themselves as confidence and acceptance of both their weaknesses and strengths grows. Then a natural balance, long missing in many cases, is re-established. This balance may have been lost since the dyslexic's first experiences at school.

Equally important is organisation. The dyslexic's cognitive and physical organisational problems have already been mentioned. However, the need for efficient and supportive organisation must be underlined. The newly arrived dyslexics will have enough problems without being expected to organise themselves in the Special English department or unit. Left to their own devices, chaos will inevitably ensue. Most senior schools have a system of education which involves the child in moving from one lesson to another. Books etc. must be carried; briefcases, bags etc., depending on the fashion at the time, are used for this purpose. We know of one boy's attempt to master his organisational problems. His plan was infallible, and would have worked if he had been physically stronger (built like a Russian weightlifter!). He reasoned that if he took all his books, indeed anything which might be remotely beneficial to his needs, he would be in control of the situation. He progressed from a normal school briefcase to the largest briefcase we had ever seen, ever onwards to a holdall and then to a bag which surely would have gained him a place in the *Guiness Book of Records*! The chaos which ensued was the bane of his teachers but, in large part, worked for him inasmuch as he spent longer and longer trying to find homework/prep at the beginning of the lesson. This often resulted in general class merriment and the teacher blowing a fuse, before he was let off through lack of time. The whole affair came to an end when one of us stepped in and advised other strategies.

In it important that non-dyslexic staff are made aware of this area of weakness and not to confuse it with general idleness. With the best will in the world, many dyslexics just cannot get themselves organised when they first begin receiving the process of help. Therefore it is incumbent upon the teacher in charge to be organised. As time progresses, and the student begins the process of efficient learning through specific help, so he will be in a better position to get organised. It must be remembered that for dyslexics, every action and sequence of actions does not come automatically, and the simple act of living may well be taxing their organisational skills to the full. It is of course through structure, both within the social and academic setting, that self-organisation comes. We expect to organise '150%' when our children join us, but for them to take progressive responsibility for this until, by the time they leave us at 13+, they are in control of their own destiny. This will imply, for the majority, that they will require some additional support if they are to go on to realise their full potential. This support may be in the region of, say, one tutorial per week by the time they get to the sixth form.

Some time has been spent on the 'earthing' period because we know this to be a seminal point. Ignore it at your peril! The hooking period is, in many respects, just as important, but is really self-explanatory. One point does, however, need to be made – the element of 'fun'. It has been our sad experience to see teaching which is, by any standards, sound but is without the vital element of fun; without fun life can become very boring. If you are bored, then you can bet the child is bored. The reverse is also true!

Before moving on, mention must be made of the main role of any teacher, i.e. the progressive realisation of the child's full potential. We underline 'full' because it is often assumed by those who should know better that dyslexics, having been affected by their difficulties and often making a late start, will somehow not go as far as their non-dyslexic peers. There is a danger of accepting this misperception and, in doing so, failing the child. Dyslexics will, given proper help, have a number of positive advantages over their non-dyslexic peers. The main one will be the ability to work hard – a result of having to put in two or three times the effort for the same result. This is often overlooked by staff. Indeed, there must be nothing more depressing and confidence sapping for dyslexics than to receive a piece of work which makes little acknowledgement of factual content but is sharply critical of spelling, punctuation and sentence construction. If the dyslexic is given support, together with increasing high expectations as they progress, then the future can be very bright. It is our experience that many dyslexics will do well at 'A' level, since they know the realities of sustained hard work on which they have honed their skills in completing their GCSEs.

We all benefit and thrive on praise and acknowledgement; dyslexics are no exception to this rule. Indeed, it is important for us to distinguish between observed and measured success. The first refers to the actual effort that the child has made and is not so concerned with the actual outcome. Naturally, we all want the very best that the child can achieve. The skilled teacher will, with commensurate skill, know what this is for a given child. Measured success is, as it suggests, the actual measure of degree of excellence of a piece of work. For the dyslexic, progress through these two stages will follow, and equal weight must be given to both. Success in one small step in a planned programme will require praise.

Marking

This brings us to the bête noir of many teachers – marking. The purpose
of marking is to provide feedback and to fulfil the implicit contract
which both the writer and the marker have undertaken. It is said that a
tick represents a smile, a cross means wrong or a frown. For many
dyslexics, marking is the despoiling of their best efforts and confirms
their worst fears. For the teacher it can be a tedious, unrewarding task.
Nobody gains anything from the exercise.

The best marking is a joint process when both teacher and child are
together and can work their way through the piece of work. Points can
be made so much easier via the spoken word, and misunderstandings
can be corrected. It is our policy, where possible, to follow this positive
system. However, there are times when it is physically not possible to do
this. It is a rare luxury for many.

Our advice is to mark what is correct, making positive comments.
After all, we are trying to have a positive dialogue. Of course, errors
must be attended to, especially in English where written accuracy is the
eventual goal. Let us confine ourselves to English at the moment. There
is nothing to be had from full marking of a piece of work, i.e. correcting
every spelling and punctuation mark. This seems so obvious, but the
point needs to be made. All that happens is that the work is changed, as
it were murdered, drenched in blood by the over-use of the dread red
pen! Neither party gains – it is a negative experience. The red pen
should be banned, or at least issued under licence! Mark words which
are within the child's grasp; confine correction to no more than a few
words. The opening paragraph or first few sentences should be marked
carefully. Try and find something which is pertinent to the teaching programme which is in use at that time. Do mark the rest of the work, giving ticks and positive comments. Make concluding comments legible,
and confine these to making salient points in the form of listings: 1 – 3,
notes, comments etc. Remember that the child often looks only for the
mark – 4/10 etc. It is for this reason that we tend not to encourage this
style of reward, particularly in the younger groups, as it encourages a
brief glance, a brief thought and is then forgotten. Our feeling is that
every piece of work should act as a base or springboard for the next
stage. To these ends we advocate a system of marking which works well
for us. Words which are incorrectly spelt, but which in the opinion of
the specialist teacher are within the grasp of that child (i.e. given a test
of individual words they would stand a good chance of spelling it correctly), are double underlined e.g. <u>howse</u> for the child to self-correct.
Self-corrected spellings are then handed in for further scrutiny. Words
which we correct because they are considered to be too difficult for that
child are single underlined and the correct spelling is *clearly* written in
the margin! These words are to be copied out three times and entered
in the Dictionary section of their Blue File (see p. 66). This acts as a rein-

forcer as well as a listing of words which have been mis-spelt. These words are used to fill the child's 'Ten difficult words list'. In this way new words are generated for the child's spelling vocabulary.

Training

Staff training in a department or unit is extremely important for a number of reasons, not least of which are the input of specific skills, and the appraisal of new methods and ideas that are germinated through developing awareness of the dyslexic's learning process. Communication between department staff and other staff is vital. Without it, little can be gained. Staff in other departments should be asked for, and provided with, subject word lists, e.g. the science department provides a list of specific science words which are duplicated and issued to the dyslexic unit staff for specific teaching as well as to the dyslexics to aid them. This is the type of positive support and help which should be encouraged throughout a school (see Appendix V for examples).

It is important that staff members of a department should have support from the departmental head in terms of in-service training. For example, the head of department may make a given point, e.g. marking. It may seem obvious, but to a new member of staff simple information giving can make a very real difference. Equally, departmental 'think tanks' for a given problem, or workshops, can act as powerful cross-fertilisation between members of staff, both in the department and within the school. So many staff have good ideas which beg for dissemination. We want to emphasise the point that staff training is an ongoing exercise – ignore it at your peril! Conferences give the teacher a chance to catch up on the latest techniques and ideas, and allow wide and free-ranging discussion between teachers from a wide variety of backgrounds. They also have the benefit of enhancing self-esteem, awareness and worth of the individual. Lastly, the above are important professional tenets that give prestige to both teacher and department.

Resources

Part of the process of starting a department or unit is the provision of resources. Wisdom dictates that there is a hierarchy of need which must be attended to otherwise loss of efficiency results. From experience, if it is assumed that you have a special place or base, and enlightened staff and the will on both sides to succeed, then secondary resources need not be too extensive. They will range, depending on the need, from basic teaching equipment, i.e. flashcards, teaching books, dictionaries and readers, to the very latest in electronic wizardry – computers, word processors, video equipment etc.

A listing is given below of what are considered by us to be essential resources together with some suggestions based on an unlimited budget. Before this, it should be stressed that the teacher is the most valuable resource, a point that is often overlooked in today's generally depressed educational system.

Naturally, any department will have already chosen a source structure prior to thinking about what resources it will choose. In many respects this will dictate much of the resource material. A word of caution is needed about the actual source structure, because it is our experience that each of the different systems available has a lot to offer. However, none of them provides the whole answer in one package. When starting, it is wise to choose one system and, in the first instance, to stick to that, otherwise confusion may occur. As the department/unit becomes more established, so other source structures can be used. At East Court we have developed our own unique structure – the 'East Court system' – which fulfils our needs exactly. However, to try and transplant this to another situation would not work. Rather, it is incumbent upon each school department/unit to work towards creating its own identity from the source structure it chooses. Such source structures may come from Alpha to Omega (Hornsby and Shear, 1974) the Bangor system (Miles, 1990) or the Gillingham–Stillman (1969) system (see pages 58 and 90 for further details).

Basic resources

Flashcards:	These will include individual letters, letter patterns and phonogram units
Worksheets:	Initially from source material or make own to cover curriculum
Dictionary:	Regular and additional e.g. Electronic Spellmasters
Readers:	Individual and schemes} Appropriate to age and interest. High interest/low reading level
Games:	To reinforce skills
Word lists:	Regular Irregular Commonly occurring everyday words
Assessment materials:	Minimum attainment tests, as well as specific ability and perceptual tests
Reference books:	Assume school library will have general reference books. Need for specific staff reference section and possibly reference with high interest/low reading level

General resources

This list assumes that the basic resource list materials are to hand.

Reading workshops:	SRA, Wardlock, Heinemann
Spelling workshops:	Blackwell
Synchrofax:	Audiopage
Language Masters:	
Computers:	
Word processors:	

Printers:
Typewriters:
Edith Norrie Letter Case:
Aston Teaching Portfolio:
Wooden alphabet letters: 'Feely' letters
Extensive range of readers:
Departmental or unit
reference library:
All language structures:
Comprehension books:

Computers must be high on the list of resources because they offer so
very much. They are a technology with untapped resources and each
month a whole new range of possibilities is discovered. Computer development is moving at such a pace that it is impossible to categorise all the
possibilities. Needless to say, as a resource their potential is little short of
amazing and they offer a very bright future to the dyslexic. Word processing is but the tip of the iceberg. We predict that in the not too distant
future, a generation of computers will be developed which will enable
the dyslexic to speak into the microphone, whilst sorting of grammar,
syntax, structure and style will be undertaken prior to the issuing of the
perfectly finished article! Chapter 8 details computing, but mention of
computers as a very valuable resource must be made at this juncture.

As an adjunct to computers, typewriters must also be considered. At
East Court we make extensive use of them, for a number of reasons, not
least of which is that they provide a valuable life skill and allow the
teaching of keyboard skills – a much needed subskill of computing and,
in particular, word processing. Second-hand manuals as well as electric
and electronic typewriters are easily come by quite inexpensively. It is
surprising how many parents and firms arc only too willing to donate
their outdated models!

Assessment records

An important area that is often neglected is that of attainment records. Any
department/unit worth its salt will have detailed attainment records. They
act as an important measure of success and allow easy access to objective
information. It is surprising how often we need to refer to attainment information to answer questions from parents, colleagues and LEAs. Formal
assessment records allow this process; indeed one of the added benefits is
they also allow the question 'Is teaching successful in terms of measurable
gains by objective assessment?' to be asked. In addition, it allows the keeping of on-going records which can be used in longitudinal research.

At East Court we have two forms: one is a pocket folder which
contains all correspondence together with the full psychological assessment. The other is a specially made up record card which lists the
various tests which we use (Figure 2.1).

Figure 2.1 East Court attainment record

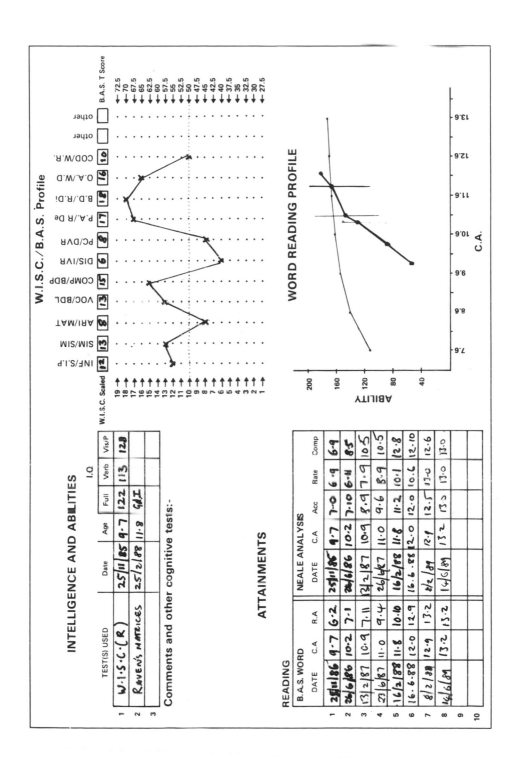

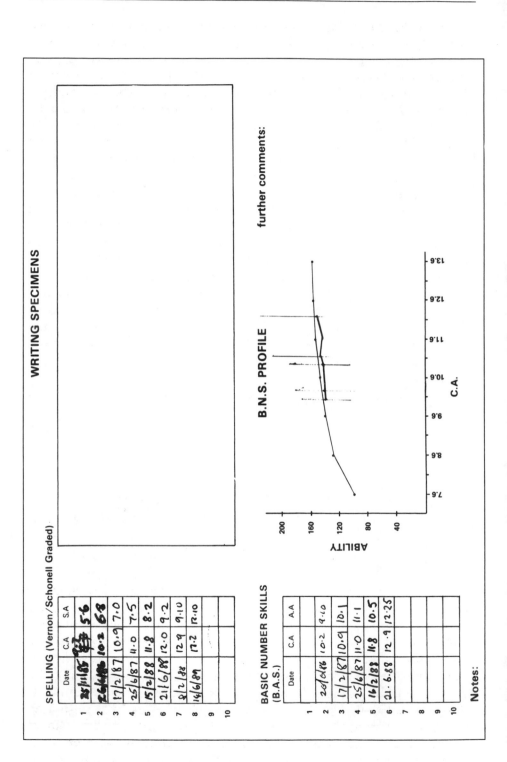

WRITING SPECIMENS

B.N.S. PROFILE

further comments:

SPELLING (Vernon/Schonell Graded).

	Date	C.A	S.A
1	25/11/85	8.3	5.6
2	26/6/86	10.2	6.8
3	17/2/87	10.9	7.0
4	25/6/87	11.0	7.5
5	15/2/88	11.8	8.2
6	21.6/88	12.0	9.2
7	8/2/88	12.9	9.10
8	14/6/89	17.2	12.10
9			
10			

BASIC NUMBER SKILLS (B.A.S.)

	Date	C.A	A.A
1	20/6/86	10.2	9.10
2	17/2/87	10.9	10.1
3	25/6/87	11.0	11.1
4	16/2/88	11.8	10.5
5	21.6.88	12.9	12.25
6			
7			
8			
9			
10			

Notes:

The children at East Court are assessed soon after they join us. Normally, this occurs at the end of September, their first month. This is followed by reassessment at regular intervals, namely February and June of each year. Assessment twice a year provides us with the information that we require and allows an objective insight into the child's measured normative attainment. This information is important but, it should be stressed, is not the be-all and end-all; rather it acts as a guide to how a given child is attaining on a given day. The 'good' and 'bad' days which can so affect the dyslexic have already been mentioned. It is wise to bear this in mind when finding either massive gains or dismal progress.

A number of attainment tests are made use of. These include the British Ability Scale Word Reading Test, the Neale Analysis of Reading Ability, the Vernon Spelling Test and the France Tests of mathematical skill. In 1989 we used the Vernon Spelling Test and still do on occasions as it is, in our opinion, a well-constructed and useful test. However, we are progressively changing over to the British Ability Scales, and most recently the Wechsler Objective Reading Dimension (WORD), which is most useful as it gives percentiles and predicted reading ages based on IQ, and allows statistical analysis of data to enhance understanding of the child's levels and potential. WORD allows us to compute levels based on:

a) Performance (actual)
b) IQ (potential – norm based)

T.S., child aged 10y 8m. Full Scale I.Q. 117

	Expected Attainment (based on I.Q)		Observed Attainment (from assessment)	
	Quotient	Age	Quotient	Age
Reading	110	14.9	79	8y 3m
Spelling	109	13.3	76	7y 10m

It may be seen that the discrepancy between T.S's expected and observed quotients are 41 in reading and 43 in spelling. There are significant at the 1% level.

In addition, we have recently dropped the handwriting specimen in favour of a speed processing test devised by Walter Bramley at the Dyslexia Institute at Bath. This test permits arrival at a measure of the child's speed of processing, i.e. how quickly he writes in normal circumstances, and it also allows the measurement of an improvement in this skill as the child progresses through the school (see p. 163). The British Ability Scale Word Reading Test is a test of the child's ability to decode discrete words. There are no contextual clues. This is a normative test similar in many respects to that old faithful, the Schonell Graded Word Reading Test. A reading age is arrived at together with a word reading profile. As will be seen in Figure 2.1, the line plots a reading profile of the average non-dyslexic child as age increases. It allows the plotting of children's progress graphically and is a ready indicator of where a child is and how much progress he has made.

The Neale Analysis of Reading Ability, a test of the child's reading skills, comprises passages of English prose which have to be read aloud before questions are asked. Accurate marking of this test means that three scores can be arrived at, namely Accuracy, Rate and Comprehension. It is surprising how, as children are taught specific skills, it is often observed that Rate declines markedly whereas Accuracy often makes slow progress. The exception is Comprehension, which improves quite dramatically as the result of new-found skills. This underlines the dyslexic's ability to handle quite difficult conceptual information with alacrity. It is the process rather than the cognition which causes difficulties.

As mentioned the WORD spelling test is increasingly used and will eventually replace the Vernon. But at present the Vernon Spelling Test is used because it gives a reasonable picture of spelling ability, and scoring procedures are based on normative data. This can often be a depressing experience, especially during the early stages, because regular spelling rules and patterns are being taught, whereas tests such as the Vernon and Schonell move rapidly from simple, regular words to irregular words. However, mention must be made of the bonus effect which results from early depression of test scores. This bonus effect means that as the children progressively gain mastery over irregular word patterns, i.e. as they progress from one stage to the next, so spelling scores make surprising gains.

Initially, we used the British Ability Number Skills subtest to measure mathematical ability. This, as the name implies, is a test of basic number computation, e.g. addition, subtraction, division, multiplication etc. and tests the individual's ability to handle a number of mechanical processes. As our teaching is sequential, progressive and culminative, we found that the children soon mastered a given, specific technique and consequently gained good score profiles whilst still having considerable difficulties with stringing together a number of processes to arrive at an answer. This is, in effect, what 'real' maths is about. As a consequence we have now dropped this test and taken on, after much debate and advice, the France Test of Maths. This has the positive advantage of giving a maths profile based on normative data as well as allowing further analysis of given individual maths competency. Most importantly, it is felt by our maths department to be a much finer assessment and attainment test. It has relevance to the real world, for example, it allows addition, subtraction, multiplication and division as basic processes as well as operation, measurement and money, extension, fractions and measurement of diagrams.

Principles of Teaching

It is generally accepted that dyslexic children have a number of measurable differences from their non-dyslexic peers. This was highlighted and discussed in Chapter 1. This being the case, it implies that the dyslexic will require a different system of teaching which will take into account such differences. Some assume that what works with younger non-dyslexic children who are taught normal reading and spelling orthodoxies, will in fact work just as well for the dyslexic. It is reasoned: 'After all, they present like younger pre-readers', so the incorrect assumption is very often made that 'more of the same' will solve the problem. This could not be further from the truth in the case of dyslexic children. However, one immutable fact remains, i.e. dyslexics must, if they are to make progress in the educational system, tackle and progressively master the intricacies of the written language system.

Those involved with teaching dyslexics need to take cognisance of the index of deficits that was outlined earlier. Teaching will need to circumvent these deficits, while making full use of inherent strength areas of the child. The underlying acceptance of the structure of the English written language will be taken as read. It is no good, as some have advocated, inventing a completely new structure which dismisses the realities of the English written language system.

Broadly speaking, three main areas of input and output are keystones in the concept of teaching: the auditory, visual and kinaesthetic modalities. It may be that the dyslexic has difficulties in any one of these areas. This will mean that a number of measurable weaknesses will impinge on the primary learning process. For example, problems in the verbal area mean that attendant difficulties may be found in auditory reception, or the reproduction of sound segments. Slight kinaesthetic problems in this area may mean articulatory difficulties, whilst other areas could remain unaffected. Equally, problems in non-verbal areas may well mean difficulties in handling visual information. There are, of course, implications to be made from such findings, e.g. 'visual dyslexia' may require a phonic emphasis to teaching, whilst 'auditory dyslexia' may well require the whole-word approach.

Naturally, the teaching approach used will need to take such factors into account. For the dyslexic teacher, the precept of awareness to these possibilities must figure large. Equally, written large in every teacher's textbook should be the following eight words: 'THERE ARE MANY ROUTES TO THE SAME OBJECTIVE'.

Nevertheless, there are a number of important tenets which we need to be aware of:

1. A need to be aware of the many problems facing the dyslexic.
2. The underlying structure of our language must be taken into account when teaching.

3. Multisensory approaches work best.
4. A broadly based phonetic system of teaching is required.
5. The principle of 'overlearning' is implicit in any teaching structure.

Teaching schemes

The teaching approach will be based on information to hand, and will vary depending on the initial frame of reference used. There are a number of different approaches which can be used effectively. Perhaps the first used was the Gillingham–Stillman multisensory approach in the 1930s. It is interesting to record that the fifth edition of their teaching textbook was undertaken in 1969 – a mark of the continuing success of their approach. Basically, their system involves the student in relating speech to visual symbols. The interrelationship between auditory, visual and kinaesthetic modalities is implicit in the teaching of this system. Weakness in any one of these areas subsumes that teaching can be undertaken via the other unaffected modalities. Their message is clear: 'teach to strengths'. Implicit is the assumption that the integration of information via unaffected routes can lead to development of written language skills. Subsequent research evidence would suggest that their basic premise may well be questionable; however, it is our experience that their system and structure work extremely well.

Another long-established method, the Fernald Tracing Technique (Fernald, 1943), needs to be mentioned here, because it also utilises a multisensory approach and in this respect seems very similar to the Gillingham–Stillman system. However, there are a number of important differences, e.g. essentially, it is a modified 'look and say' method. It requires that the child use tracing as a medium for learning. No attempt is made to analyse words into their component parts. We have found this system to be of considerable use when teaching word lists of 'irregular words' to the youngest groups. These lists are what we deem 'Survival' lists, i.e. commonly occurring everyday words which are needed just to survive! The emphasis is on the learning of the whole word and component sounds are not used or, if they were, they would make little sense at that stage.

Another system used is that of 'matching task to learner', advocated by Johnson and Myklebust (1967). They suggest that dyslexia can be subdivided into two main areas: auditory and visual. Auditory dyslexics will need specific help in the retrieval of letter names, sequencing and sound blending, and Johnson and Myklebust suggest that they should be taught using a whole word method. Function words, according to them, need to be taught in context with some additional training being given in auditory analysis and synthesis. Phonic rules, they emphasise, will need to be taught very carefully.

For the visual dyslexics, the emphasis is shifted and Johnson and Myklebust suggest that they will need to be taught via a 'synthetic phonetic' method. This means that the construction of words and units from their constituent parts will need to be taught. Individual sounds will be blended together to form words and, in turn, sentences. Sight words are taught only in the context. The problem with this 'tidy system' appears to us to be that few dyslexics are clearly either auditory or visual. The majority have difficulties which cross the two frontiers – indeed, the assumption is erroneously made by Johnson and Myklebust that dyslexia is a clear-cut entity, e.g. either auditory or visual in nature. We have included Johnson and Myklebust's perceptions because their idea of 'matching task to learner' seems to be eminently sensible.

The Bangor Dyslexia Teaching System (Miles, 1990) is another example of a structured teaching programme. Phonetic teaching methods are key components. The system argues that the 'look and say' methods employed by teachers are not effective for the dyslexic. The system assumes that the teacher will have a thorough grounding in the complexities of our written language system. Emphasis is placed on the children producing, with the guidance of their teachers, their own work book. This is normally an exercise book which is divided into ordered sections, e.g. consonant blends, tri-blends, vowels, vowel digraphs, diphthongs and so on. This system has been formulated by the Dyslexia Unit at Bangor University. The programme was written by Elaine Miles to meet the teaching requirements of the Dyslexia Unit in a local school. It was subsequently published on the basis of the unit's experience with the programme. The strength of this programme is that it was devised by and for the teachers, has a thorough and well-supported theoretical background, is highly structured and, most importantly, works.

The 'Alpha to Omega' programme (Hornsby and Shear, 1974) is perhaps the most widely used. It was first published in 1974 at a time when there was really very little teaching material available for the dyslexic. It provides a good structure and guideline which is specifically designed for helping the dyslexic child. The strength of the programme is its very detailed and structured language programme. It follows a phonetic sequence, with strong emphasis on following the spoken language of the child. It starts from basic alphabet skills and makes no assumptions. The programme is divided into three sections with test materials to assess the effectiveness of each taught part. In addition to and as a supplement of the programme, flashcards are provided, which contain individual letters, letter combinations, root words, suffix and prefix, games and exercises. The flashcards, in our experience, are really an essential aid, and fulfil the potential of the language programme.

The Hickey Programme was published three years later (Hickey, 1977), and provided a very detailed, systematic structure. It was most detailed, and called for specific training, usually provided by the Dyslexia Institute. It was based largely on the earlier work of Gillingham and Stillman and was specifically tailored for the British market, e.g. Americanisms had been taken out and English language substituted.

The programme had been devised by Kathleen Hickey while she was Director of Studies at the Dyslexia Institute.

The Aston Teaching Portfolio, published in 1982 (Aubrey et al, 1982), provided what was, in effect, a very detailed and useful source of teaching material. The premise is that, having used the Aston Index screening test, the information gained could be used to devise a programme of work that would be tailored to the individual's specific needs; it would take into account both strengths and weaknesses. The programme rationale is based on the concept/philosophy of matching task to learner. Like Johnson and Myklebust (1967), it looked at auditory and visual modalities, but emphasis was placed on the assessment checklist which acted as a guide to the teacher using it. Each task was broken into its component parts and remediation took into account each stage which a child would, it was reasoned, pass through on his or her way to written English proficiency. The advantage of this system is its great flexibility.

The Helen Arkell Dyslexia Centre booklets* are based on a structured approach. Emphasis is placed on the use of the Edith Norrie Letter Case. It is a multisensory technique, building individual letters into words by using small letter cards, voiced/unvoiced vowels and consonants. The child has to follow his spoken word to do this. In this way the child begins to analyse and build up phonemes, syllables, and words, and is so encouraged to become aware of speech sounds and process (see page 99 for further details). We have found that the Edith Norrie Letter Case is of particular use with the youngest children, who have the greatest difficulties. They enjoy using it, and find it a comfortable friend which aids them in a way that they understand and find helpful. This group has particular problems in following their speech sounds naturally, and has fairly serious auditory confusions – f/th, v/f, w/r etc.

Each of the schemes and programmes briefly reviewed here has its uses. We would advise, however, that one system be chosen initially, especially if a new unit or department is being established. However, the eventual aim should be to become familiar with each of the above programmes so that each system is seen as a useful resource – to be utilised as and when needed. For example, it may be that input from the Gillingham–Stillman programme with regard to multisensory teaching of consonant blends can be adopted and used to good effect whilst underpinning of this may be enhanced by use of the Bangor Teaching Programme together with some additional material from 'Alpha to Omega'. In this way, a good breadth of input is given selectively. This will of course imply the principle of overlearning – a vital weapon in our armoury. The danger inherent with the concept of overlearning is that of boredom – a dreaded disease! This is particularly applicable to the young, highly intelligent dyslexic. A wide range of teaching programmes

---

*The booklets can be obtained from the Helen Arkell Centre, Frencham, Farnham, Surrey GU10 3BW

is needed, so that we are able to teach from a strong position, i.e. we are aware of the various programmes and can dip into any of them that appear to be appropriate for a given child at a given stage. Indeed, since publication of the book, our Word Lists, Appendix VI, p. 227 have been widely used by others and we are constantly being asked for permission to use them. Feedback suggests that they can form the basis for both reading and spelling tasks, as well as being used for speed reading, syllable analysis etc.

We are not 'hidebound' to follow any one programme slavishly. Naturally, we expect expertise across a wide range of programmes from the staff. However, we would suggest that all of the programmes reviewed here have something in common – as shown, for example, in Table 2.2.

Multisensory teaching

The concept of multisensory teaching technique has been briefly reviewed under the Gillingham–Stillman programme but, because it is a fundamental tenet in teaching dyslexics and its basic philosophy is incorporated into most programmes, we feel it is pertinent to make comment about the philosophy behind the concept.

Essentially, the term 'multisensory' means that a combination of the three main channels of input and output is being used. Humans have five main receptors:

Table 2.2 A summary of structured teaching

Some written language programmes

Gillingham–Stillman
Alpha to Omega
Bangor Teaching Programme
The Hickey Teaching Programme
Fernald Tracing
Aston Portfolio
Helen Arkell (Edith Norrie Letter Case)
Matching task to learner (Johnson and Myklebust, 1967)

Implications of structured teaching

Phonetic
Multisensory
Cumulative
Sequential
Progressive
Small steps
Logical
Overlearning

1. Sight   ⎤ main receptors called
2. Hearing ⎦ into interaction by the
3. Touch   ⎦ multisensory approach
4. Taste
5. Smell

The major 'outputs' relating to written language are:

1. Speech – articulatory (kinaesthetic)/auditory.
2. Writing – kinaesthetic/visual.

Three of these reception channels are used interchangeably and together to enhance individual learning acquisition. Ideally, all five areas should be used, but unfortunately no-one has devised a programme that utilises tasty and 'smelly' letters! Imagine for one moment, the learning curve of the 'chocaholic' faced with chocolate-flavoured letters!

Visual, auditory, kinaesthetic and tactile interrelationships are utilised in multisensory teaching. The general idea is to train all these modalities and to strengthen the links between each of them. The aim is that there should be an automatic production of letters, letter patterns and sound in the processes of reading, spelling and writing. Cross-modality processing of information is progressively established by multisensory training, whether it is visual-to-auditory transmission or sound-to-motor programme.

The multisensory philosophy concerns itself mainly with a phonetic approach. The learning in 'phonograms' or sound units is fundamental. This implies that the individual will follow a progressive, sequential and cumulative process which will allow them to make inroads into the language structure. It must be remembered that, for the dyslexia child, our written language will have to be learned, in many respects rather as a foreign language is learned, with the one major exception that the dyslexic child will have already gained proficiency in the spoken language. We should mention that, although the idea of multisensory teaching is not new, it is a relatively new idea in the UK and is in large measure confined to the dyslexic field. Although current models of the reading and spelling process emphasise 'visual-to-sound coding', 'sound awareness' or segmentation problems, it is important to recognise that this is often just a change of terminology. There is certainly evidence to suggest that multisensory teaching procedures work (see Hulme, 1981; Bryant and Bradley, 1985; Thomson, 1989). What differs is the interpretation of the underlying psychological mechanisms that give rise to their efficacy. Fortunately these need not worry us unduly as teachers, although we need to be aware of the arguments.

Again, it must be remembered that the dyslexic child has been described as presenting much in the way a younger child does. This, in many ways, supports the concept that they are developmentally delayed. The major advantage of the multisensory concept is that it promotes in the children an appreciation of phoneme sequences, relating them to printed letter sequences and synthesising them to form words. It allows them to grasp the correlation between letter form, i.e. spatially presented letter forms and sequences, and their relations to sequence in time, i.e. temporal ordered phoneme sequences (spoken language).

Overlearning

The principle of overlearning is another concept. In the teacher's hands it is an aid to the dyslexic child because, without it, dyslexic children just do not 'anchor' information in memory systems. We find that unless some time is spent each lesson going over material already taught, 'memory fade' occurs. The result of this is that something apparently fully understood and internalised at the end of yesterday's lesson is retrieved as a confused and often jumbled mess. This comes as a surprise to non-specialist teachers, who see the child as bright and articulate. It therefore follows that the principle of overlearning is a fundamental tenet. Repetition, recapping and reinforcement of already 'learned' material is vital, and allows the dyslexic to master a point properly before new information is taught.

Aubrey et al (1982) recommend that at least a third of each session should be devoted to revision of earlier work. Although we agree with the concept of overlearning, we feel that to devote at least one-third of each lesson to revision would dramatically retard teaching programmes. We advocate the practice of recapping/revision for no more than a few minutes each lesson. This would follow completion of the 'Ten difficult words list'. It soon becomes clear whether taught material has been internalised, and if it has not then a decision needs to be made as to whether reteaching should take place then and there, or a note made for this at the next opportunity, ideally the next day or as soon as possible. A lot will depend on your plans. Given that new material subsumes mastery of earlier information, then it is clear that reteaching (recapping) will need to be undertaken. It is obvious that a point already taught will need to be consolidated before new information can be overlaid.

Implicit in the idea of overlearning is, naturally, an awareness that any new material will need to be presented in a clear, concise manner, and that it will need to be presented frequently in a number of different ways. Understanding of the concept of recognition–recall, relearning–recall needs to be made clear. This allows the child to develop a clear strategy for learning. Recognition of the information implies an understanding of the basic concept – recall of this implies ordering of salient points into a formulation which must be communicated to another (the learner becomes the teacher in the process). Relearning of information basically calls for recapping of already learned information – again, recall promotes consolidation and subsequent mastery of information. Obviously, it is very important for the teacher of dyslexics to be very organised in approach. Rote learning and recall as the main method just do not work for the dyslexic. The giving of long lists of information or strings of information which are ill-sorted will confirm the worst for the dyslexic, i.e. 'can't learn, won't learn'. In fact what is manifestly wrong is the presentation of information in a way which the dyslexic cannot effectively utilise. The key for the dyslexic is to present the concept in a clear, specific way. Once conquered, then generalisation can and must follow. The point is made again that 'more of the same' will *not* work. New and novel ways of inputting information must be sought and implemented. The idea is to work from a firm ground, e.g. something in which the dyslexic has total understanding so that success is almost guaranteed. It is best not to spend long on this before moving to new ground and not to labour a point – remember to divide information into component parts using a logical step-by-step approach. The reward of success provides the motivation to 'have a go' at new and unfamiliar information. Reference to the role of the teacher (see page 44) must be made, because this plays a major part in the equation. Fundamental to the above is the idea of being very clear in what we are trying to teach. Criterion referencing is helpful in this respect, although we prefer the idea of 'targeting' or 'focusing'. What do we want the child to learn? We would prefer that they acquire a basic skill rather than a non-specific generalised concept. There will be time for the latter approach later, once a specific skill has been acquired. To attempt this generalised approach prior to specific skill acquisition inevitably leads to failure.

A checklist of tenets

The teacher's role in helping the dyslexic child is, of course, fundamental. Here some comments are made concerning practical suggestions as to how this can be undertaken in a classroom setting. A list of key items which you feel are important in your classroom teaching should first be made, based on your children's needs. This should then be pasted into your register so that you are reminded of the basic tenets at the beginning of each day.

1. Keep making statements about your personal parameters for your classroom. Make the point that you, like the children you teach, are an individual – a special person, not like the rest of the staff but an individual.
2. Accept child, 'warts and all'. Don't make any assumptions about what the child knows or is.

3. Be non-judgemental at first, but clear in what you do and do not want.
4. Let the child know that you are interested in him as a person, i.e. interests and tastes etc. Spend time learning about the child.
5. Let the child know he can ask questions without fear of ridicule or judgement. 'Stop me if you are unclear on any point. Don't sit in silence.'
6. Encourage open discourse about areas of weakness, group discussion and support.
7. Plan lessons carefully, remembering that small sequential steps are required for maximum learning potential.
8. Work from concrete to abstract; make sure that you have a firm base or foundation. Check constantly to monitor taught points; work from one area at a time then make sure that the link between areas is understood; there is a need to link new experiences to past ones.
9. Make sure children understand any assignment, especially ordering and planning.
10. Don't overload short-term memory by giving too much material at a time. Don't rush homework and prep giving at the end of the lesson – make sure the child clearly understands what is required.
11. Nodding heads do not necessarily mean understanding. They *could* mean:
    (a) a kindness to you; doesn't mean understanding;
    (b) so bored just nodding off;
    (c) fear – unless I nod I may be picked on!
12. Remember PMP – 'practice makes perfect'. The principle of over-learning really does work.
13. Teach planning strategies and study skills so that the child may benefit from help. Importantly, give time for assimilation and practice of skills.
14. Extra time for copying from blackboard, taking notes.
15. Make allowances for 'good' and 'bad' days, but don't allow sloppy or substandard work, i.e. know your children and their ability.
16. Reading aloud is a very difficult task and will need a lot of practice. Do not spring it on the individual child.
17. Do not compare an individual's work with another's, especially if there are only one or two dyslexics in a group of non-dyslexic children. Compare the child's best work with today's attempt, for example.
18. Test child's aural knowledge, especially in the early stages. Do not rely on written communication until he or she has the necessary skill.
19. Realise that homework will require a longer time to complete and help in organisation of same. Parents can help here.
20. Be positive in marking – see page 48.

21. Avoid, at all costs, the trap of giving long lists of words to learn, especially different spelling patterns. Do not write 'sp' in the margin. This does not help the child. Do not mark every wrong spelling – frustrating for both teacher and child!

22. Aim to teach key concepts rather than getting the child to read long text. Target key facts. Organise, teach, recap, test.

23. *Never* use terms such as 'stupid', 'slow' or 'lazy' out of context. They can wound permanently!

24. Make sure that you write clearly on both the board or work, especially if the child has to copy. Check prep is accurately noted, e.g. page 26, ex. 12 may be written as page 12, ex. 26 or page 29, ex 21 etc.

25. Make sure the timetable is clearly understood, with 'hieroglyphic' codes making sense.

26. Teach punctuation carefully, and keep recapping. Terminology can be a problem.

27. Make lessons FUN. Enjoy yourself, and it is more than likely that the children will do so as well.

28. Leave time to breathe!

29. Spend time recapping on already taught material before moving on to new points. This acts as a reinforcer as well as providing a link to new and unfamiliar work.

30. Look out for specific skill area deficits, e.g. incorrect letter formation, which may be causing many peripheral problems.

31. Be prepared to laugh at yourself and with your children.

32. Keep referring back to your basic prime tenets.

Teaching philosophy at East Court

At East Court we are, in many respects, very privileged in having a highly select band of children in an ideal educational setting. It may be helpful to the reader to outline our approach to teaching. First, because of the particular nature of dyslexia we place particular emphasis on a phonetic approach. Asked 'Why?', our simple reply would be 'Because it works!'

Secondly, we apply the philosophy of analysis, which subsumes the acquisition of learning strategies, because we have a narrow band of dyslexic children who have two main features in common, i.e. (1) high intelligence and (2) severe dyslexia. We are able to utilise their very good conceptual skills, i.e. the ability to apply pure logic to a problem.

In many respects we have, as far as is possible to apply, a homogeneous group of children who respond well to the above approach. We know this to be empirically true (see Thomson, 1988, 1990 for our research evidence). Our basic system is the 'Blue File'. This forms the base of our English programme, because all English work is filed in this A4 Lever Arch file. This file has the East Court name printed in silver letters on it (to make it special) and is issued to all children on joining the school. The files will remain with the children throughout their time at East Court. The concept of filing is paramount to our whole teaching philosophy, i.e. we must be organised; to be organised implies that we will need to file information. This is a powerful model and accommodates our entire approach. Indeed, there are positive advantages to the concept of filing. Perhaps a reduction of items to be carried around from class to class is one of the greatest benefits. Equally, it stops the age-old problem of 'dog-eared' exercise books which do not promote or support the idea of pride in presentation of work. The Blue File is subdivided into 14 different sections:

1. Star check
2. Word list
3. Tutorials
4. Spelling rules
5. Phonics
6. Spelling test
7. Composition
8. Grammar
9. Comprehension
10. Reading workshop
11. Dic./Voc./Alpha (dictionary work, vocabulary and alphabet work)
12. Calligraphy
13. Private study
14. Computer work

Of course it would be potentially possible to make further and further subdivisions, but this would fail because of the inherent complexity. Indeed, it could be argued that the above list is too complicated and confusing. However, it can only be stressed that it is a listing which works. In the end, this must be our final arbiter. Remember the maxim: 'If it works, fine: if it doesn't, then it is not right at that time or stage.' Each subdivision is numbered – for ease of filing or work. For example, when comprehension work has been completed and is marked (this may be in a tutorial for the older children), we put the appropriate number equating to the divide, thus 9 = comprehension. This makes filing easier, particularly for our younger children.

Although we are positively in favour of an ordered and structured approach, this does not imply that we are either formal or dogmatic. Rather it means that there must be constant awareness of the dyslexic's fundamental problems with order. For the younger members of school, chaos is always waiting in the wings. It is for this reason that our whole approach is one of order and structure. It follows, then, that each section of the Blue File allows the staff and children to utilise a structure that supports this concept. We will now go on to give a brief explanation of how each section is used. The detailed description of the work in many of the sections will be covered in other chapters and sections, e.g. word lists, spelling rules, phonic spelling and spelling tests will be found in Chapters 3, 4, 5 and 6.

Star check

Star check contains any English work which has been considered good enough to be awarded an Academic Star. The standard is based on the child's intra-individual efforts, i.e. work which is outstanding for a given child at a given stage as opposed to 'pecking order' marking. Academic Stars are handed in to the office with a recommendation for a star. We then give the work out at assembly on the following day. This supports the concept of immediate positive encouragement for the children.

Word lists and tutorials

Word lists are those lists of spelling which the individual child will be working on at the beginning of each English lesson. This is detailed on page 141. There will be word listings ranging from single CVC words through consonant blends to polysyllabic words (see Appendix VI for specific examples). Under tutorials will be filed work completed during such tutorial times. Further revision of learned points will be contained here, as well as new work where it is felt that a tutorial is the best way to introduce a particular point. It should be remembered that some of our tutorials will have up to three children at a time, so that the tutorial can be a good time to introduce new information. We make a point of ensuring that in each lesson or tutorial, a record of work completed is filed. This has two positive features: (1) as a record of work and (2) to act as a reference for future work and to log what has been accomplished.

Spelling rules

Spelling rules, as the name implies, contain rules: both spelling (see Appendix VII), as well as lists of rule-oriented guides, syllable division etc.

Phonics, spelling tests and composition

The phonic section is the largest section in the Blue File, especially for the new entrants, i.e. the youngest group. Anything remotely connected with phonics is filed under this section. Spelling tests, as the title suggests, contains an ongoing record of spelling. This may include anything to do with spelling, e.g. dictation etc. Composition contains stories, compositions and essays. This subdivision is made because it seems to help the children. 'Stories', as the name suggests, is a simple story format, whilst 'compositions' implies a more formal approach. Essays are normally used in the child's final year and are formal and of good length, e.g. three to four sides of A4 paper (see Chapter 6, page 166). It should be noted that, whilst three terms are used to describe one broad process, we nevertheless teach the concept of planning right from Day 1, e.g. linear planning and 'brainstorm' strategies (see page 166). As the children progress through the school, so the emphasis shifts progressively away from phonics to the more formal aspects of written work.

Grammar

The grammar section contains work on formal grammar and punctuation. For the younger children, this may be kept quite simple, e.g. nouns and adjectives, whilst the leaving group may well attempt a fuller range of grammatical nomenclature. Many of the children find the more formal aspects of grammar very difficult, and yet they are able to write grammatical sentences by carefully thinking about what they are saying. It is for this reason that we do not force this issue – feeling that it is, in many cases, a situation where diminishing returns apply and, in the end, time could be better spent on more productive teaching.

Comprehension

Under comprehension there may be Common Entrance comprehension work, which the older groups attempt in the last year, or comprehensions similar to second year secondary level linked to GCSE. Younger groups tend to stick to reading workshops – SRA etc. However, we have a large collection of English comprehensions which are used. Many of these are kept on computer disk, so that printout of a selected comprehension can be easily obtained.

Reading workshop

Reading workshop, as the name suggests, contains work from the Reading Workshop. Use is made of SRA (Science Research Associates), Ward Lock and Longman systems. Each has something to offer. Basically they require the child to read a short, printed text before completing written assignments. These may take the form of short, multichoice questions which require a letter answer, e.g. A, B, C or D. Syllabification and some analytical questions are also given. The aim of these systems is to expand the child's written language skills.

Dic./Voc./Alpha and calligraphy

Dic./Voc./Alpha needs some explanation. Dictionary work, e.g. use of, or exercises in, the dictionary are filed under this section. Equally, vocabulary work is filed as well as any alphabetic work. Much use is made of Alpha and Voc. Work by the younger groups. Calligraphy is, in some respects, a misnomer because it is not really formal calligraphy but an extension of English work. Given that some of the children have no writing style at all when they arrive, it seems obvious to us to input specific writing skills so that a given individual can progressively master a chosen skill: this in itself may well be a subskill of an integrated process which leads on to mastery of the total process. Calligraphy then, is really in effect 'old-fashioned' hand writing skills. Noticeable gains are made in this field as well as allowing children the luxury of enjoying mastery of handwriting (see Chapter 6, page 158).

Private study and computer work

Private study, as the name implies, contains any work which has been completed in private study and cannot be filed under any other specific heading. For example, 'holiday work' tends to be filed under PS for the reason that it cannot usefully be broken up and filed separately. Computer work which is related to English – by this is meant work completed during English lessons, e.g. word processing work or a computer game and resultant English work – will be filed under this section. This does not contain any formal computing work. This will be kept in the child's computing file, which is retained in the computer room.

The implicit assumption is that the Blue File is an ordered and highly structured system of filing which allows the children to be in control of their own efforts, e.g. correct filing of work under the correct heading. It implies that the child can understand the concept of section divides and use them. Certainly, at first the youngest children do need a lot of help, advice and direction, but once understood and mastered it allows them greater control over their work. It stops the dreaded 'dog-eared' syndrome. The idea of using an exercise book can be quite confusing for a child to use as a file or reference book. The advantage of the Blue File is that the child is clear in his or her formulation. This avoids the confusions which characterise the exercise book, i.e. working from the front for classwork and from the back for notes.

General Classroom Procedures

Organisation

A major problem facing the dyslexic child, as noted earlier, is that of organisation, and it is crucial therefore to provide this organisation for the children. Initially, this must be so supportive that the teachers, helpers and parents must all conspire to see that there is a dramatic reversal of previously learned experiences, i.e. compounded failure – failure promoting further failure because of erroneously made assumptions that, if the child has been taught a point, he has mastered it. This is the downward spiral to despair! The model (see Table 2.1, page 45) details this, together with the stages which we feel the child will need to progress through as specialist teaching is undertaken. The stages may seem obvious to most of us – yet sadly, all too often, the important component, i.e. 'fun/play', is manifestly lacking in a system that places high emphasis on early success. For many dyslexics prior to receiving specialist help, their experience is one of endless drudgery and compounded failure, especially in the core subjects of English and maths.

The dyslexic's disorganisation usually takes the form of cognitive and physical muddle which relates to planning work. It is for this reason that a sensible and supportive system has been adopted of help specifically relating to classwork, e.g. files for classwork – the Blue File and its filing system have already been detailed.

Small group teaching

Another important point is the concept of small group teaching. It is clearly taken for granted that this is a beneficial situation for dyslexics, and one which educationalists all support. Some people argue for a one-to-one situation and posit this as the most efficacious situation. We do not wholly subscribe to this school of thought, believing that small group teaching provides a useful and positive source of enjoyment and interaction among peer groups. Equally, the children do not experience the isolation which many dyslexics feel, where they are either withdrawn from lessons or given help at the wrong end of the day. Given that a reasonably homogeneous group of dyslexics can be arrived at, i.e. age, IQ and attainment are accounted for, then it follows that once a child has mastered a skill he can partake in gentle competition, as the children progressively spread their wings.

The children at East Court are organised into groups of five or six for written language, but in addition they also have one-to-one or one-to-two tutorials during the course of the week. In addition to this, there are other written language-oriented lessons. These include calligraphy (handwriting), reading workshops, library periods, typing periods and 'extra English'. For the younger children, phonetics are given precedence, together with language development and extensions. Handwriting also plays an important part, whilst with older groups the emphasis is upon the acquisition of more traditional English skills, i.e. English literature. This may be Shakespeare or other classics, e.g. Lord of the Flies etc. It will be noted that we follow a modified curriculum. This means that weighting is given to our prime aim, that of attending to the children's specific language difficulties (dyslexia). Certainly, our experience is that this allows us to tailor teaching to the children's needs. In essence, then, we support a child-centred approach.

In another setting the above organisational procedures may well be difficult, but in our experience a ready workable compromise is often arrived at, given the necessary determination and support from staff colleagues.

Visual aids

The importance of classroom visual aids must be mentioned here. It goes without saying that they are an important adjunct to teaching. It is very depressing to visit either schools that have few visual aids on classroom walls, or schools where those that are presented are faded and 'tatty'. For dyslexic children, visually presented information in the form of wall displays acts as an important subsidiary back-up and helps them to consolidate taught information. Having taught a skill, reinforcement, which is visually presented, enables the child to have ready reference and also acts as a prompt. Spelling rules, syllabification, mnemonics, grammar etc. can be displayed to good effect. Word processing work devised by the children to aid themselves and others is popular and well received. Often, dyslexic children need reminders of the technical or subject-specific terms used. Visual displays play an important part here.

Matching task to learner

Under this section of classroom procedures the idea of analysing a given child's profile will be looked at, and how this profile gives us information with which we can work, e.g. the concept of strengths and weaknesses. The idea of matching task to learner is important because it allows the formulation of a campaign of help and support for a given child whilst continuing to work on strength areas (Table 2.3).

The problem facing the specialist teacher is that of finding the correct level to begin teaching at, as well as being aware of the many possible deficits dyslexics have. It is for this reason that check lists of component parts of English can be of considerable use. Of course, it is vital to hold a healthy mistrust of lists. All too often, having filled in a whole section to our smug satisfaction with affirmative ticks the need for further over learning, revision and retest at regular intervals can be dismissed if care is not taken. Certainly, lists can act as useful reminders or guides, but they need to be used with caution.

Table 2.3 Matching task to learner	
Weakness	*Tasks*
Short-term memory	Chunking; letter/phonogram units; overlearning mnemonics
Visual–motor deficits	Letter tracing, writing patterns; copying exercises, following speech and phonic approach
Blending difficulties	Following speech; Edith Norrie Letter Case; word building, teach through visual; re-visualisation; looking for letter patterns, tape recording
Sound discrimination	Sound matching; speech therapy; word pairs; similar sounds; nonsense words
Phonological (auditory memory, phonetic awareness)	Multisensory; tracing of letters; words; SOS syllables; blends
Visual channel	Auditory approach; train visual skills through phonetic analysis, blending
Auditory channel	Visual approach; train auditory, whole word, rules from letter patterns; Fernald multisensory

How often have we heard of the child who states quite categorically that he has completed stage 2 or 3 of a given programme, and therefore an assumption is made by child and parents alike that he has mastered it. If only this were the case! An outline of our own written language structure is given in Chapter 3 (page 91).

Error analysis

Error analysis is another important model because it allows us to pinpoint a specific area of difficulty which a given child is experiencing. This is an area of the behaviourist approach which is, to our minds, positive and aids in the formulation of programmes to help specific children. Of course, in error frequencies it must be borne in mind that methodological difficulties can be run into – because it is all too easy to become obsessed with the categories of error and to look for a multiplicity of types, thus adding confusion. A word of caution, therefore. Error analysis can lead to the teacher coming to the conclusion that errors may not be mutually exclusive. Error types, for example phonetic or ordering, may well both occur in a given word. Equally, confusion could arise as to whether an error should refer to the letter, syllable or unit, or word. To give an example of this, an error saw/was can be filed under visual spatial difficulty (i.e. problem with remembering the order of the letters) or equally well as a difficulty in speech production, either phonological or articulatory.

Sometimes the younger dyslexics will have so many problems that their writing will be full of errors. To complete a full-scale error analysis on this would highlight so many problems needing attention that many possible confusions would have to be dealt with. When this happens sense must prevail and detailed understanding of teaching structure will suggest the order in which the problem can best be attended to. It follows that most teachers are, intuitively, constantly completing error analysis. This will be on an informal basis, for example noting down particular errors that a child produces then planning teaching in terms of a particular level to start at. It may be that a given child has specific problems in following speech sounds – sound/symbol correspondence. It should be noted that this acts in two ways: (1) it reminds us of the deficit, (2) it acts as a record and enables us to plan teaching. A checklist of basic sounds compiled by Cotterell (1978) is presented in Table 2.4.

Table 2.4 Sample checklist of basic sounds

a	bl x	scr	v	sc(sk)	aw	ir	ace
b x	br x	shr	w	sk	-ly	oa	act
c	-ck	sph	x	sl	ea(e) x	-oe	age
d x	cl	spr	y	sm	ea x	oi	all
e	cr	squ x	z	sn	ee x	oo	ape
f	-ct	str	ch	sp	er	or	ark
g	dr x	thr	sh	st	ew	ou	arm
h	dw	a-e x	th	sw	ie x	ound	art
i	fl	i-e x	wh	tr	igh	ow	ask
j	fr	e-e x	qu x	tw	ai	ow	each x
k	-ft	o-e				-oy	ear x
l	gl	u-e				-ue	east x
m	gr					ur	eat x
n	-mp					-y	ice
o	-nch	ai					oak
p x	-nd	air					
q	-ng x	alk					oar
r	nk	ar					oil
s	-nt						old
t	pl x						
u	pr x						

From Cotterell, 1978.
Note: a number of letter combinations, suffixes, etc. are omitted in the example. Items with x are observed errors.

In the example shown in Table 2.4, the child appears to have learned most of the basic sound/symbol correspondence in terms of letter sounds and names. Consonant blends, however, are causing problems, particularly those which require voiced/unvoiced distinctions. Revision or possible reteaching is called for – not forgetting the principle of overlearning. The 'e' sound is also causing problems. He has a confusion of the various representations of this sound. Work will be needed here. Finally, he will require the teaching of the simple rule of English orthography, i.e. 'u' always follows a 'q'. Error analysis is only one system that can be usefully employed to help the children. Another, which we have briefly made mention to under assessment, is the prescriptive or criterion-oriented assessment approach which is utilised in the Aston Teaching Portfolio. The Portfolio follows a 'cook book – menu' approach, e.g. it attempts to identify difficulties in auditory or visual modality functions, i.e. auditory and visual perception, not basic modality reception, eyesight and hearing. It includes areas such as short-term memory and sequential skills, the identification of sounds, blending or discrimination. Basically, it looks at the problem in terms of the dyslexic having either auditory or visual deficit. However, teaching is prescribed utilising a combination of visual and auditory techniques, with emphasis being placed on a strength-oriented approach.

Given that a child has difficulty in auditory recall, discrimination or sound blending, it is suggested that a more appropriate way to teach would be via a look/say approach using pictorial aids, diacritical marks etc. This approach utilises the child's strengths and leads to positive learning success and building of self-confidence.

For the dyslexic with a visual deficit, whereby he confuses letters, letter combinations or words, e.g. visually similar letters (u/n, m/w, b/d etc., dr/br, saw/was, skip/skeg and stop/step), then it usually highlights a weakness in visual short-term memory or synthesising the meaning of what is presented visually. He may have grave difficulties in learning anything by the look/say approach. For this child, a phonetic approach is called for, especially in the early stages. It follows that the dyslexic with an auditory difficulty will have problems in synthesising sounds into words and analysing the basic sound elements, as well as transferring the learning of sounds to the important skills of word attack. Such a child will inevitably be experiencing difficulties in perceiving the subtle sound similarities and dissimilarities in words. It is as though decoding processing facilities have not become fully efficient and fluent. This child is dysfluent in this vital area. Difficulties will range across the whole area; indeed short vowel sounds in the middle of words will be a particular area of weakness as well as initial and final sound similarities. For these children the whole word/sight word approach will elicit the best results, certainly in the initial stages.

We would stress that, in our experience, certainly for the children at East Court, we tend on the whole to find a mix of the above two main types to be the best approach. Given a clear and well-marked distinction, it does make the challenge easier; however, it is normally the case that the children have a mix of both.

Table 2.5 looks at error analysis particularly from the standpoint of reading and spelling process, and is illustrated with specific examples of visual difficulties. Errors are listed with examples, followed by type of problem, then teaching cards from the Aston Teaching Portfolio are highlighted as a means of helping the child.

Table 2.5 Reading and spelling error analysis (based on the Aston Portfolio)

Reading	Spelling
Auditory channel deficits	
Substitution of sounds	Omits endings -ed, -s, -ing
Poor sound blending to make words	Use synonyms house/home
Knows name not sound of letters	Omits second letter in blends – fed
Mispronounces words, e.g. chimney as	for fled, mid for mind
chimley	Substitutes t/d, f/v sh/ch and confuses
Wild guesses where there is no relation-	voiced, unvoiced pairs and high
ship between words seen and read	frequency sounds
If stuck on word, may not be able to	Does not hear subtle difference
sound it out	between sounds and leaves out vowels,
Poor 'phonic' attack	plsh/polish
Substitutes words a/the	Identifies beginning or end of word
Uses synonyms mummy/mother	but not the middle, and this may be
	missing, e.g. md for mind
	Confuses vowels, bit/bet
	Wild guesses, no relationship between
	the sounds and letters representing
	them, and the spelling – raul/urchins
Visual channel deficits	
May invert words or letters	May visualise the beginning and ending
May reverse words, letters or phrasing	of the word, omitting the middle –
and word by word reading	hapy for happy
Rate of perception slow	Spells phonetically – site/sight (cannot
Loses place or skips lines and parts	re-visualise)
Adds words which are not there,	Mix capitals and small letters cAt
occasionally changing the meaning	Inverts letters u/n, m/w
May omit and read through punctuation,	Reverses letters, words – on/no
distorting the meaning	Gives correct letters in wrong
Makes guesses or says words that look	sequence –teh/the
similar or start in the same way –	
surprise/surface	
May confuse order – place/palace	

Consider a card from the Aston Portfolio where a reading error, e.g. reversal, 'dis/biscuit' is seen as one of visual discrimination. Using the Aston Teaching Portfolio it is necessary to look under 'Problem' thus:

Card content: Section – this breaks the process into four main headings, namely:
1. Assessment
2. Reading: visual skills
    Reading: auditory skills
3. Spelling
4. Handwriting

Under 'Reading: visual skills' is found 'visual difficulties in reading', which gives the instruction to go to the Dark Blue section cards. The Dark Blue section lists a number of 'menu-type' areas, i.e. card 3 asks the question 'Can the child discriminate between letters?' and card 4 says 'For children with reversal problems'. Card 3 makes 16 suggestions as to how the child can be helped, whilst Card 4 makes 11.

For the inexperienced teacher, this approach is a sound starting point. For the experienced specialist teacher it acts as a useful tool, a reminder of the many ways of helping the child. It also, most importantly, emphasises the idea of 'many routes to the same objective.'

Example lesson plans

Under classroom procedures, it is appropriate to give some specific examples of actual lessons. Two lesson plans are presented: one for a younger group (8 years), and one for an older (13–14 years), leaving group. The lessons comprise 40-minute periods with a 5-minute changeover. Children move from one specialist teacher to another. It will be observed that all English lessons have a basic structure which is followed fairly uniformly. To begin with, 'Ten difficult words lists' are given. The actual process is described on page 141. This is followed by perhaps two or three different specific tasks which will be followed by a game to finish the lesson. A model lesson plan is included here in the box. We stress the need for structure and flexibility: structure – the skeleton, order; flexibility – the approach. Without these two, confusions and chaos attend. The idea of structure permeates all of our teaching; indeed, it is pleasing to note that the National Curriculum and Assessment Performance Unit are advocating this education approach. The Code of Practice requires each child who has a Statement to have an Individual Educational Plan. This seems to us to be a most sensible and pragmatic approach, and one which we have been advocating, and in fact undertaking, for many years. Without a target to aim at we cannot focus our energies. It will therefore come as no surprise that we strongly advocate the use of lesson plans. The lesson plan in the box is followed by detailed discussion of how we would go about teaching according to the plan (see also page 34 for examples of IEPs).

English lesson plan: youngest group

1. (a)   Ten difficult words list
   (b)   heading up of paper
2. Spelling rule no. 2 (already written in Blue File but not fully taught):
   (a)   recap on concept and advantages of learning this
   (b)   look up in Blue File
   (c)   check terminology used, e.g. 'syllable', 'consonant', 'vowel', 'suffix'
3. Computer game utilising rule 2 (spaceship landing)
4. Test
5. Game 'Stand up, sit down'

For the youngest groups a lesson is always started with the 'Ten difficult words list' (see page 141 for details). This may initially take a disproportionate amount of time, and we are both familiar with the extremes of frustration on endeavouring, as we term it, to 'push wet string across a table', i.e. get the youngest and most disorganised group to complete their 'Ten difficult words list' in a 'reasonable' amount of time. Left to their own devices, this would invariably take up the entire lesson! However, this exercise is seen as a sensible investment of time because, once the process has been mastered, then it can be perfected and used throughout the time the youngsters spend with us. Lists can be completed after quite a short period of practice within 3 or 4 minutes – time well spent, and our research evidence points to the efficacy of this approach.

The next task is heading up. Some of the children will need considerable initial help here – making errors of spelling own name, days of week and month, especially if it is February! The concept of spacing and techniques of spacing is important here, because children are often confused as to where to start and where to finish, and consequently run out of space (again a long-term investment).

Blue Files will already be on the tables, so the children turn to section 4 – Spelling rules. As they will have already copied this into their Blue File, it is a matter of retrieval – again a useful exercise. The rule will also be presented on the classroom wall – a ready reference: so the children will now have Spelling rule 2, the '1,1,1' rule, before them. The teacher recaps on the value of the rule – pictorial analogy is often useful here, e.g. the building of a word and the fitting together of two bricks, the dovetailing of a wooden joint etc. The benefits of mastering Spelling rule 2 are that, once this is done, over 350 words will be spelt correctly. The rule also gives insight into the structure of words, e.g. concept of base word, syllable, suffix.

Now the teacher works through the terminology to make sure it means something to the children – make this fast and fun, e.g. 'Ten pin bowling' game. Here, all the children stand up and you attempt to 'knock them down' by catching them out. If the child cannot answer with a quick response they sit down – the last one standing is the winner. This encourages quick thinking! The same should be done with other terms used in the rule, e.g. consonant, vowel, suffix. As many suffixes can be named as possible – jot these down on a board to act as a guide. This can be followed by using the rule (see Chapter 5, page 149).

A number of computer games have been devised by us to aid consolidation of taught points. One of these reinforces Spelling rule no. 2. It involves making choices of whether to double a letter or not, and requires the child to land a spaceship at one of two bases, i.e. double or not double. Two children can play this game – one as pilot, one as captain/director. This game is very popular, especially because it is seen as a 'skive'. The fact of the matter is, in reality, it calls for great concentration!

While two children are using the computer within the classroom, the other children can be having a game which involves choices. The children are asked to fill across the top of a sheet of paper:

Base word = Stop   Suffix = ing

1 Syllable	1 Consonant	1 Vowel	Suffix begins with vowel	
✓	✓	✓	✓	4✓'s = double the final letter, i.e. STOPPING

The idea of using this particular format is to encourage the children to be logical and sequential, e.g. the rule is known as the '1,1,1' rule, i.e. with words of *one* syllable ending in *one* consonant after *one* vowel, the suffix begins with a vowel. The idea of Sherlock Holmes is normally introduced at this juncture, as it seems to make the whole thing more fun. Here the children become 'great detectives' in search of the secret of English. Four affirmative ticks = double the final consonant, otherwise don't (see also Appendix VII).

Given time, a short test calling for the spelling of base words and suffixes, and the application of the rule, can be given before drawing the lesson to a close with a game. The youngest children seem to thoroughly enjoy the game of 'Stand up, sit down'. This calls for following directions quickly. Normally one thing is said whilst giving the opposite direction with the arms, e.g. say 'sit down' whilst lifting up arms. The last person remaining standing wins. Great fun can be had by all! The game only takes a few seconds to complete, and acts as a powerful spur to keep actively working throughout the lesson.

For the older, 'leaver' group, i.e. children who have been at the school for 2 or 3 years in the main, the emphasis is on honing up skills already learned, as well as introducing more formal aspects of English, e.g. essay writing and comprehensions skills.

The final year group are taught by us, and we look upon this year as our 'pre-stressing' year because we expect our children to make the leap from being fairly substantially supported to becoming autonomous as they progressively take charge of their work load. Considerably more will be expected during this time in terms of output. Indeed, work load increases dramatically. Essay lengths will move from two sides of A4 to three and four sides as the year passes. The average is three sides of A4 in 60 minutes. This excludes the lesson where discussion and essay planning are introduced. A typical Tuesday morning (essay day) English lesson is presented in the following sections.

Lesson plan for older children

1. Ten difficult words list.
2. Essay plan – set title.
3. Example of past work – for discussion.
4. Overhead projection slides where essay plan is presented.

Point (1) has already been covered (see page 77); point (2) is detailed starting on page 166; point (3) an example of a piece of work completed by a former student is included below, 'warts and all'. We find that actual examples really do help. Discussion of weak points is followed by analysis and proofreading – both important study skills.

Example of pupil's work for class discussion

The volcano
I lived in a small village near a large land scap. The land scape was as far as the eye can see. Lots of flowers grow along the scape. Pink, green, yellow and due. The wind brushed pased my Face. The dirds sang joeful and the sun deated on my Fash. In the winted the landscape is all whiht and black.

Error analysis
* Misuse of words, conceptual image
* Tense
* Word endings
* Language/vocabulary
* Reversals
* Suffixes
* Wrong use of past tense
* Wrong use of capital letters

Point (4) of the first list is followed by an overhead projection slide in which an essay title and plan is presented.

Essay plan

'Five seconds left!'
Introduction: After 5 seconds death occurs. Ask the question why? when? where? who?
Countdown – one second at a time, e.g. 5–4–3–2–1.
During the 5 second countdown to death you will have the opportunity to recount your entire life or important parts of it. Aim to detail main events or thoughts. Flashbacks! Hopes for future escape, but now face the reality.

Seconds left   *Consider the following points*

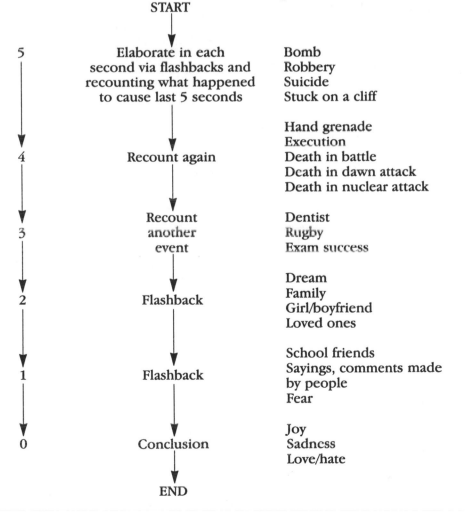

Seconds left		Consider the following points
	START	
5	Elaborate in each second via flashbacks and recounting what happened to cause last 5 seconds	Bomb Robbery Suicide Stuck on a cliff
4	Recount again	Hand grenade Execution Death in battle Death in dawn attack Death in nuclear attack
3	Recount another event	Dentist Rugby Exam success
2	Flashback	Dream Family Girl/boyfriend Loved ones
1	Flashback	School friends Sayings, comments made by people Fear
0	Conclusion	Joy Sadness Love/hate
	END	

It will be seen from the title that the main story is recounting the person's life during the 5 seconds left before his untimely end. Each second prior to his death will be the opportunity to recount a different era from his life (a clever use of time).

The plan is written with the central part of the story presented with the decreasing seconds 5–4–3–2–1. Each second can have a bubble to recount a particular flashback as described above. The idea is to write an essay to detail your thoughts, emotions etc. prior to your untimely end. This will contain an introduction, explaining the situation, followed by a 5 second countdown to death cleverly linked with the person's past. The end occurs as the person faces the reality of death.

Following this, a general discussion ensues. It is important to stress to the children that 'chainsaw massacre' and 'Rambo'-style essays are not acceptable! Again, the importance of defining parameters is stressed. It does away with a lot of wasted effort, both on the side of the child and the teacher.

Chapter 3
From Spoken to Written Language

Introduction

It is a tenet of language development that spoken language precedes written language. For most children who have difficulty in reading this means that emphasis needs to be laid on vocabulary, language development, reading for meaning or comprehension. This emphasis, however, is not appropriate in the early stages of teaching the dyslexic. The key problem is the gap between spoken language understanding and its written form. Whilst the end product is obviously reading for meaning and writing to communicate, the dyslexic child needs help with the mechanics of written language. The implication for the teacher is that dyslexics need to be taught the relationship between the sound patterns of English and their written form. This relationship, particularly in terms of the phonological and short-term memory skills involved, is precisely what dyslexics find difficult: remembering the sound–symbol associations, being aware of sound structures, generalising these to other spelling patterns are all part of these skills. It is necessary to teach the relationships explicitly, and this involves a 'phonic' approach. There is really no avoiding the teaching of the alphabetic system. This is the basis upon which reading and spelling are learned.

As a result of this we are left in a position of trying to teach a skill that is fundamental to the dyslexic's weakness. To take an analogy to perhaps an absurd length, it is rather like trying to help a partially sighted person to see better without glasses! Attempts to circumvent the process of teaching 'phonics' are doomed to failure. This is because the alternatives offered, such as visual memory for spelling, language development approaches or 'real' reading, i.e. choosing an 'interesting' book, do not work with the dyslexic because they still draw on skills that are weak in the dyslexic, and they do not take into account that dyslexic children may learn *differently* from the non-dyslexic.

83

The difference between reading and spelling tasks needs to be borne in mind. Reading at first sight seems more of a pattern recognition task, and therefore more visual. Research does support this commonsense view, but reading also involves using phonological or sound-based skills. This applies particularly to reading words that are unfamiliar at first glance, or generalising from letter–sound combinations to other similar word families, e.g. 'old' to give gold, bold, older and so on. Regular words, in particular, can be read phonetically, and later orthographic skills are dependent on earlier alphabetic skills.

Spelling, however, is more of a production task, and research suggests that the memory of sounds is accessed and then assembled or blended to form words, and is much more of a sound-based or phonological task. In other words, to spell we need to keep the 'sound' of the word in mind and link this to the correct letter patterns. There are, of course, many letter pattern options available! Once this match has been made (correctly or incorrectly) the letters must be put together to make the word, by assembling the units. This must then be written down in the correct order, and also by remembering the initial sound/symbol(s) correspondence.

Below aspects of 'phonics' or phonetic teaching are looked at – first at the linguistic knowledge needed by the child, and then at classroom procedures.

Linguistic Knowledge required by Child and Teacher

Many training courses for teachers of dyslexics insist on a thorough grounding in linguistic principles, particularly in aspects of phonology and written language structure/orthography. However, the disturbing fact remains that most PGCE courses pay scant regard to the reading process. Some courses give only mention of the need for reading, with the assumption that graduates will somehow 'know' how this complex process is arrived at by the majority of the population. Indeed, every student we have seen, and we have seen large numbers from a whole range of PGCE courses, confirms our suspicions that little is practically being undertaken, and lip service to the cause would seem to be the continuing depressing reality. It is not our intention to provide a detailed review of this here; the reader is referred to Crystal (1987) for basic linguistics, to Heaton and Winterton (1986) as appertaining to the dyslexic and to Smith and Bloor (1985) for simple phonetics. It must be commented, however, that the important aspects which should be known are as follows:

1. Knowledge of basic terminology, e.g. vowels, consonants, phonemes.
2. An understanding of phonemic structure of English, including aspects of syllabification and stress. This would include, for example, some simple phonetics.

3. A thorough knowledge of orthographic rules, regulations and conventions, for example spelling rules (see Chapter 5, page 146) or word derivations.
4. The basics of syntax (grammar) and some semantics (meaning).

It is useful to outline the linguistic knowledge that children ought to have. This is important for a number of reasons. Initially, to help the child understand the phonics that he or she is to be taught. Providing an analysis of the written language system can give 'meta-awareness', i.e. an explicit knowledge. Secondly, it provides a way of recognising that written language is not always spelt the way it sounds (and vice versa), but that most English is regular and does have recognisable sound/symbol links. Providing a logical and systematic attack on written language is a great help for many children. Finally, and not by any means least, understanding the terms used is a great motivator and confidence booster. A child who has failed, and is convinced that he or she is no good at written language, can know things that his or her National Curriculum peers or parents may not know. He or she can feel specially privileged and can 'show off' the new found understanding – very important to build up lost self-esteem.

The teaching of sound analysis skills by the teaching of rudimentary phonetics starts with the alphabet. Children should be taught both *names* and *sounds* of the letters: sounds to help build up basic words and in word attack skills, and names to help in spelling, recognition or orthographic units and in dictionary work. The teaching of the alphabet will include the recognition of *vowel* (a,e,i,o,u and y) and *consonant* distinctions. In the early stages it is important to recognise the difficulty dyslexics will have in perceiving sound structure within words. This phonemic awareness difficulty means that dyslexics have great difficulty in recognising individual component parts of letters, particularly the vowel sounds. For example, in recognising the difference between pin or pen in reading and spelling, or the position of the 'sh' in fish or shop. Once the alphabet has been taught by sounds and letter names, many routines will need to be developed to help children classify and recognise sounds within words. One common example might be asking a child to put CVC (consonant, vowel, consonant) words under appropriate vowel headings, or to recognise commonalities in words, both by visual inspection and rhyme, or by blending and producing new words through changing one or two letters only, e.g. span can be changed to plan, flan or to spin and spun.

The next stage is to introduce long and short vowel sounds. The 'a' in lake is described as saying its name or being *long* ('long name'), whereas the 'a' in cat would be saying its sounds, or being *short* ('short sound'). The introduction of long and short vowels can be supplemented by the diacritical mark – the macron and the breve. Thus ā is long name 'a' and ă is short sound 'a'. This can be made more accessible to younger children by talking about Mr M (macron) and Mr B (breve) with suitable illustrations.

Classification of sounds of all kinds is particularly useful. One example linked to a spelling rule might be that of the (k) sound at the end of words. Here if there is a short vowel sound before, (k) is spelt 'ck' as in 'lick'; if there is a long vowel sound it is spelt 'ke' (the magic 'e' pattern) as in 'like'. Then '-ck' and '-ke' can be put into two columns at the top of the paper. The child is then given words to listen to and to decide whether the vowel is short or long. He or she is then required to put the word under the right heading (see Appendix II for examples of worksheets/procedures). This technique of organising and classifying sounds can be used in many different ways in many different language structures.

Once long and short vowel sounds have been covered, focus is shifted to consonants. The notion of a *consonant blend* needs to be introduced, along with flash cards of blends and key pictures, for example br – brown, cl – clock etc. We use the 'Alpha to Omega' flash cards, although any will do as long as the clue blend and card remain consistent. Obviously the linguistic system has to be simplified for children. For example, a consonant can be defined 'phonetically' or 'phonologically'. The former relates to mode of articulation, and the latter to use in the structure of spoken language. Our operational definition of a consonant blend is 'two or more consonants put together to make one sound.' This would not please a linguist, but draws crucial attention to the difference between pronouncing 'fr' as in frog as opposed to individual sounding out of the two letters to make 'fu–ru'. The definition also includes those trigraph blends, e.g. str, shr etc. and subsumes sh, th, ch, which are often called digraphs.

There are three other major 'linguistic' terms that are used with children – sound pictures, syllables (including syllable types) and vowel combinations. These will be discussed below, but the reader should note that the order in which these are taught is discussed in the next section. In addition many other guides to sound/symbol relationship, orthographic conventions and spelling rules can be taught explicitly (see next section and later chapters). Again, none of these descriptions would satisfy the linguist purist, but are operationally practical and very useful in teaching and, most importantly, they work!

As a preliminary to teaching *sound pictures*, it is necessary to discuss with children the fact that, although most words are spelt as they sound, i.e. they are regular, some are not. A sound picture represents a way of writing the pronunciation of a word. A sound picture is written in brackets (the picture frame), and the vowel sound needs to have a diacritical mark over it. Thus (ă) represents the 'a' in cat. Some writers use /ă/ as a representation; again the important thing is consistency – Table 3.1 presion mark (see below). This needs to be added to complete a sound picture in multisyllable words.

Readers may feel that the presentation of letters not actually spelling a word, e.g. (mād) for maid, would confuse dyslexics. Our experience is that if this is taught carefully it does not confuse. It also allows the child to master a specific skill. Analysis of words in this way is very helpful for reading and spelling. It is usually presented in the form of a detective or scientist trying to discover the secrets of words.

Syllable analysis is also a very important part of the learning process, especially as dyslexics have particular difficulty with segmentation of sounds, sequence and polysyllabic words (see Thomson 1984, 1990; Snowling 1987). Syllable analysis involves dividing words into units or 'beats'. In the initial stages children tap or clap out the words into their syllables. A useful clue and rule guide is that all syllables in English contain a vowel and that syllables can sometimes be felt by putting your hand underneath your chin. When your chin moves down this is a syllable! Children can learn to beat out the rhythm of syllables. The next stage is to examine the vowels and see whether they are long or short and undertake analysis based on the six types of syllable. Initially, we introduce only the 'open', 'closed' and magic 'e' syllable, and then go on to the other three types which are more complicated. Children then can read words and analyse them into their syllable types, classifying them as shown in Table 3.2. They can then be encouraged to spell them out syllable by syllable in the words, work out what kind of syllable it is and write the appropriate spelling pattern for it. This technique is very helpful for learning to read unfamiliar yet long words, both for confidence and developing sophisticated word attack skills. It is also very helpful for spelling. Table 3.2 shows the six kinds of syllable, with example words analysed into their syllable types. This system is based on Steere, Peck and Kahn (1971). Page 112 describes an alternative format for analysing the syllables using 'keys' of consonants and vowels and provides further examples of using syllable analysis.

The final 'linguistic' term useful for dyslexics is the concept of the vowel combination. Unfortunately, terminology and definition of vowel sounds

Table 3.1 Some examples of 'sound pictures' and diacritical marks	
Sound pictures	*Spelling*
(ī)	as in like
(ŭ)	as in cup
(răt)	as in rat
(slōp)	as in slope
(bōt)	as in boat
(ĭn'vīt)	as in invite

in phonology is even more complex than consonants. They can be defined by position of articulation, vocalisation, primary vs secondary, consistency through articulation and so on. The common terms in teaching dyslexics are 'vowel digraphs' or 'diphthongs'. Neither of these is strictly correct. A 'vowel digraph' like 'ai' saying (ā) in rain is fine, but what about 'igh' saying (ī) – neither *two* letters nor only vowels! Similarly, a diphthong is where there is some audible change of quality, or glide. A glide is where the vowel sound changes intonation during its pronunciation.

A diphthongal glide may be found in 'boy' or 'cow'. Practically, the notion of a vowel digraph or diphthong is taught and as in the syllable analysis these vowel combinations are sometimes called 'dippys'. These include those shown in Table 3.3.

Table 3.2 Six types of syllables

Syllable type

1 The <u>open</u> syllable (o)
   <u>me</u> <u>no</u> o'pen cry'ing fi'nal
   The vowel is open at the end of the syllable; it is 'unprotected' and often says its name; it is 'allowed' to as there are no consonants 'shutting it in'

2 The <u>closed</u> syllable (c)
   <u>in</u> <u>lost</u> o'pen cry'ing fi'nal
   The vowel is closed by one or more consonants; it is 'protected' and says its sound; it cannot say its long name as it is 'shut in' – the consonant 'slams the door on it'; the closing in is after the vowel, not before it

3 The VCE or magic 'e' syllable (vce)
   <u>ice</u> <u>wine</u> <u>scrape</u> re'<u>bate</u> dis'<u>place</u>
   (suffix: drop 'e' – biting)
   The vowel has been opened by the magic 'e' and says its name; the 'e' unlocks the door and allows the vowel to say its name

4 The -<u>le</u> or consonant -le syllable (-le)
   ta'<u>ble</u> pad'<u>dle</u> stee'<u>ple</u>
   (suffix: drop 'e' – strug'gl'ing)
   A consonant occurs before the -le – -ble, ple etc., the (1) sound is thus spelt -le with a consonant in front of it

5 The <u>diphthong</u> or vowel digraph syllable (dip)
   <u>wait</u> <u>snow</u> au'gust main'<u>tain</u> de'<u>stroy</u>'ing
   Here, one of the vowel combinations (see pages 88–89 forms the syllable

6 The <u>R combination</u> syllable (rc)
   <u>bird</u> <u>ford</u> de'<u>ter</u>'mine <u>cur</u>'tain
   A vowel combines with an 'r'; the vowel comes first – ar, er, ir, or, ur
Some examples of syllable analysis;

o rc	dip c	o rc c vce
a'corn	spoon'ful'	re'or'gan'ise
c rc o c	c vce	c -le
trans'for'ma'tion	stag'nate	crum'ble

Table 3.3 Vowel digraphs

Spelling (vowel digraph)	Sound picture	Example word
ai ay	(ā)	rain play
ee ea	(ē)	seed read
igh y	(ī)	night fly
oa ow	(ō)	boat blow
oo ew ue	(ū)	food stew blue
ow ou	(ow)	cow sound
oi oy	(oi)	boil toy
au aw	(or)	August paw

The reader will note that the vowel sound pictures are not accurate in linguistic transcription, e.g. the vowel in rain should be /eɪ/, and in hope /əʊ/. Furthermore, some are stretching a point vis-à-vis sound, e.g. (ū), food, although these are found as shown in many sources of written language structure.

Of course, the situation is more complex! Appendices VII and VIII show other vowel sound choices. These vowel sound choices are usually taught after the most common sounds shown in Table 3.3 are mastered. Here we are moving even further away from sound transcriptions and it is here that we draw the line! No further attempts are made to represent spelling phonetically. Taught at a simple level they can be a real and positive help. Syllable analysis for complex words is very useful for reading and spellings (see Chapters 4 and 5), but we do not recommend 'sound picture' analysis beyond fairly simple words, and really only for alphabet, consonant blend and basic vowel sounds (including magic 'e'). Beyond that the move is being made into a phonetic alphabet. The reality is that children need to acquire current, modern, written English, and it is that which we must teach.

Written Language Structure

Chapter 2 made the point that one of the key features in teaching the dyslexic is to cover, in a sequential and systematic way, language structure. A recurrent theme of this book is the importance of a thorough grounding in the area traditionally known as 'phonics'. Of course, the final aim is communication by reading and writing as well as appreciation of good literature. 'Literature' here includes any books or written material that can free the imagination, extend ideas and develop thinking! We shall examine these later, but much of our time will be spent in the techniques of teaching written language structure. It is our firm belief, supported by experience and research, that this underpins all the later developments, and cannot be circumvented in the dyslexic. The non-dyslexic acquires 'phonic skill', sound–symbol generalisations or orthographic conventions apparently automatically from reading (as if by osmosis!). The dyslexic does not acquire these skills easily and must be *taught* them, explicitly, with plenty of implicit experience also!

Structure is also important because, despite appearances, written English is in fact mostly regular, i.e. with regular sound–symbol patterns, and only 3% are so unpredictable that they would need to be learned by rote (Hanna, Hodges and Hanna, 1971). Crystal (1987) comments that 75% seems an agreed figure, but that the 400 or so irregular spellings are among the most frequently used, and an impression of irregularity is gained (see Appendix IV for a suggested basic list). It is fruitful, therefore, to teach these regular phonic structures, as most of the written English may be generated from it. One difficulty is, however, that many sounds may be represented by a number of letter combinations. For example (ā) can be spelt as in mate, lady, rain, play, break, eight, they! A table showing vowel sound choices may be found in Appendix VIII. This selection of alternative sounds, and indeed homophones, is a source of continual misery for some dyslexics. One of the boys at East Court is remembered well, who despite having overcome most of his spelling difficulties still seemed to choose, inevitably, the wrong combination! Youse for use was a common fault, as was eny for any etc. Everything was spelt phonetically, or with the wrong spelling choice. He went on to obtain A grades in maths, physics and technology at GCSE!

It is not our intention to set out a detailed language structure, with lists of words and dictation exercises. This would encourage a page-by-page following of a teaching scheme when teaching should be dynamic, responsive to need, exciting and fun! In addition, there are many detailed guides to written language structure (see page 58 for a brief review). However, with the above comments in mind we would like to outline, briefly, a general written language structure, and a suggested order of acquisition/teaching. Once again, it should be stressed that flexibility is important as well as response to an individual child's difficulty and needs.

Written language structure – a framework

The particular starting point for each child will vary, although it is useful to reinforce and briefly go over previously learned materials and provide immediate success prior to new ground being broken. This structure acts as a guide or framework; some work may be done in different order, particularly when responding to children's errors, as in free writing for example. Of course, the techniques used to teach the particular structures may vary from child to child. This order of teaching is based on the order of acquisition in spoken language, ease of teaching/learning for the dyslexic, and experience in teaching.

Individual letters, names and sounds; vowel/consonant distinctions

This order of learning avoids teaching letters which are similar in shape or sound:

e	f	b	u	r	
k	p	n	v	y	
a	l	i	h	s	g
c	t	d	m	j	
z	o	q	w	x	

Simple CVC (consonant–vowel–consonant) words may then be introduced. Once basic sound–symbol relationships have been established short vowels can be taught as units. Sound blending and categorisation can also be used at this stage, i.e. putting the individual sounds together to make words, and classifying vowel sounds.

Consonant blends

Commonly used consonant digraphs follow, taught as a whole unit (one sound).

sh,   ch,   th (voiced)

Blends are added, namely: bl, br, cl, cr, dr, dw, fl, fr, gl, gr, pl, pr, sl, sm, sn, sp, st, sw, tr, tw.
Words with CVCC patterns (e.g. lash) and CCVC (e.g. flag) can be introduced. At the start of teaching consonant blends these should be introduced at the initial position, i.e. frog, chip, plan etc. This can be taught as CCVC pattern. Word lists with this pattern are shown among those provided for reference in Appendix VI.

It is helpful to teach blends with a clue picture, e.g. cl/clock, sp/spoon. We happen to use the 'Alpha to Omega' cards, although any consistent scheme will do. Three letter blend at the initial position can come next: scr, shr, spl, str, thr.

Consonant blends in the final position are a little more difficult, and can follow the above, e.g. fi<u>sh</u>, lo<u>st</u>. Again, reference lists are provided in Appendix VI and can be taught as CVCC.

Open and closed syllables can be usefully taught at this stage, provided word analysis is undertaken on simple words such as magnet, poem etc. (see page 112 for further details of syllable teaching). The point here is that once CVC words and consonant blends have been taught, simple, regular multisyllable words may be introduced, provided they are carefully controlled. Source lists may be found in Appendix VI. Later on 'end blends' such as -ck, -mp, -ng etc. are required. It is useful to teach -ng, -nk, -nd as nasal blends (noise in the nose). The double consonant ending might also be taught here: -ll, -ff, -ss. These are often taught as a spelling rule, i.e. words of one syllable with one vowel ending in (l), (f) or (s) usually double the consonant, e.g. fluff, puff, boss. There will always be exceptions, e.g. bus.

Long (single) vowel sounds using silent 'e'

Magic, silent or lazy 'e' is taught along with the five vowels, with single consonants first, then blends (mat/mate), slop/slope). At this stage it is useful to extend the notion of sound pictures, and also to introduce the VCE syllable. More difficult, but regular, words can be taught – bagpipe, lemonade, congratulate. Once again the reader is referred to some suggested lists in Appendix VI.

Vowel/consonant 'blends' such as ar, er, ir, or, ur

These come next, although these can be subsumed under earlier stages. We tend to teach the r combination syllable at a later stage (see page 88).

Simple plurals

Simple plurals, such as adding s, cat/cats and hissing plurals, fox/foxes. Some early suffixing rules can be introduced, but these are often better at a later stage (see page 146).

The 'w' rules and soft c

Before moving into vowel combinations some work of the 'w' rules, i.e. w changing the vowel sounds as was (wŏz), word (werd), and war (wor) can be useful, although this can be very difficult for dyslexics, and because there are not that many words affected we do not spend too much time on it. Some of the common words can be 'rote learned', More important at this stage is work on hard and soft c, thus:

ce			ca	
ci	(s)	but	co	(k)
cy			cu	

as in cell, city, cycle   cat, cot, cub

This can be taught in conjunction with (k) at the end of words (long vowel is -ke, bake, short vowel -ck, back) although care needs to be taken not to overload. Soft g (j) can also be taught here.

Vowel combinations

Vowel combinations are an important, yet difficult, part of the structure. Table 3.4 illustrates the basic vowel sounds, based on a general guide as to the spelling of the vowels, i.e. the middle and end spellings. Another useful clue is the old saying 'when two vowels go walking, the first one does the talking!'. This is not the whole story for vowel sound choices, however. Appendixes VII and VIII show further examples, and references.

Table 3.4 Vowel sound medially and finally

Sound	Middle		End	
(ā)	ai	rain	ay	play
(ē)	ee	seed	ea	sea
(ī)	igh	sight	y	fly
			(y with consonant blend)	
			ie	pie
			(ie with single consonant)	
(ō)	oa	boat	ow	snow
(ū)	oo	food	ue	blue
(or)	au	pause	aw	claw
(oi)	oi	boil	oy	boy
(ow)	ou	sound	ow	cow

Suffixing and prefixing

From this point on the order and timing of teaching requires even greater flexibility and response to need, but suffixing is an important next stage, i.e. the teaching of word endings such as -ed, -er, -ing, -ly. The suffixing rules that it is useful to teach are shown in Chapter 5 (page 146). Similarly prefixing and 'compound' words need covering at about the same time.

Syllable division and analysis

Syllable division and analysis using the six kinds of syllable will be required (see pages 88 and 112). This can be done by teaching them all at a later stage, or covering 'open', 'closed' and 'VCE' only at an earlier stage, and gradually introducing the remainder as the child progresses. We favour gradual introduction parallel to teaching reading/spelling.

More complex or rarer word patterns

These can be introduced and include ch pronounced (k); ti and si as (sh), or tion as (shun) and sion as (z'hn); ph as (f). Sometimes these words can be introduced earlier, for reading as 'survival reading', i.e. reading necessary for early reading and reading notices etc. There are many more examples to be found in the sources of structure mentioned on page 58. Throughout all of the above it is important to realise that the skills of punctuation, grammar, comprehensions or 'general English' will still need to be taught alongside these specific phonic skills (see also later chapters). At East Court we have devised our own checklist, and we present this as a guide only. We have all spent many hours discussing the order etc., but have to come to the conclusion that it really does not matter to the odd decimal point where such and such a step comes. The whole point is that the document acts only as a guide. Children are not robots, neither are we, although some children believe we are and that we are stored in the classroom cupboard overnight to come out and terrorise them during the day!

A summary of teaching order is given in Table 3.5

Teaching Techniques

The initial stages of moving from spoken to written language involve the children following their own speech and transcribing the appropriate sound into its written form: thus cat becomes (k) – (ă) – (t) to make c-a-t to form cat, or (fr) – (ŏ) – (g) into frog. This involves a number of skills, the most important of which are:

1. Awareness that the 'whole' sound of the word can be split into smaller sound units.
2. Being able to detect and isolate those units.
3. Having knowledge of, and being able to access/link, the appropriate written form with these sound units.
4. Putting the units together to form words, whether in spelling or reading.

Table 3.5 Teaching order

Phonetic components	*Corresponding brief guide to associated topics*
1. The alphabet	Alphabetic order
2. Consonant sounds	
3. Short vowel sounds a,e,i,o,u	'Consonants', 'vowels' including y
4. CVC words	Syllables closed
5. (k) sounds c,k,-ck	
6. Initial consonant blends	Capital letters; full stops
7. Consonant digraphs	
8. Triple blends	Simple sentences
9. Final blends	
10. Long vowels, open syllables	Nouns, verbs, 'root' words
11. -ll, -ff, -ss, -zz	
12. One, one, one words	Suffix s – simple plurals (1)
13. Long vowels VCE	
14. Vowels modified by r ar, er, ir, or, ur	Diacritical marks
15. Hard, soft c,g	
16. Vowel suffixes VCE drop	Word patterns CCVC, CVCC, CCVCC
17. y changes	Syllable division
18. Short vowel check -ch, -tch	
19. j sounds g, ge, dge (age = y ending)	Two-syllable words CVC/CVC
20. -ed suffix (t, d, ed)	
21. ic words + ed	Open/closed syllable
22. Revise y as a vowel	
23. Wa, wo, wh, v ends	Compound words
24. Long vowel endings: ay, ee, y, ow, ue, ew	
	Plurals (2)s, es
25. Long vowels medial: ai, ee, igh, oa	
	Suffixes add -less, -ness
26. oo (ŏŏ) (ŏo)	Add -ing, -ed, -ly, -ful
27. Regular final syllables: ble, cle, dle, fle, gle, kle, ple, stle, tle, zle	Punctuation check
28. -tion	
29. ea (ē) , ea (ĕ)	Prefixes wel-, al-
30. Prefixes ad-, con- etc.	
31. qua, wa, wo, revise er, ir	Apostrophe s for omission, contractions
32. ou, ow	Plurals (3) y – i
33. au, aw	
34. oi, oy	Verbs – tenses
35. ch, que, revise (k) ends	
36. er endings er, or, ar	Synonyms, antonyms
37. ie (e) (ī)	
38. er middles er, ir, ur	Past tense

(contd)

Table 3.5 (contd)

Phonetic components	Corresponding brief guide to associated topics
39. ph, gh (f)	
40. Wild old words	Plurals (4) f – ve
41. Unaccented o (above)	
42. Revise er ends er, ar, or – OUR	Apostrophe s possess
43. Silent letters	Speech marks
44. sion, cian, revise tion	
45. eigh (a), revise i before e rule	Stress in multisyllabic words
46. ey endings	Vowel suffixes, long words
47. ou, ui	
48. ous, us	Suffix to ie – dying
49. ti, ci, si revise (special, patient etc.)	
50. Other (shn) endings	Plurals (5) oes – os

Note: the corresponding topic does not necessarily dovetail into the phonetic component

In the research literature these skills are called phonemic awareness, segmentation, auditory organisation, short-term memory and sound blending. Here some teaching procedures which can help develop the above skills are reviewed. In most of these procedures it is necessary to concentrate on regular words for consistent sound–symbol associations.

Some dyslexics have slight articulatory difficulties, and may need help in the production of sounds such as th/f, or r/w. Most will also need help early on in the rhythm of speech, i.e. in pronouncing long words and in correct segmentation/syllabification of speech. Techniques here are similar to some speech therapy exercises and programmes. The first stage is to make the child aware of his or her own speech and sound system. The child needs to listen and attend: to watch the speaker closely, particularly the lips and tongue, as well as noting non-verbal clues. Each one of these skills will need to be explained and demonstrated. In other words, attention is being drawn to the communication process right from its preliminary stages, before even arriving at written language learning.

Particularly helpful for the preliminary stages are 'sound stories'. Here children listen to a tape of sounds and must work out what they are, or what the sequence of sounds suggests is happening. Matching these with cards illustrating the events represents the preliminaries of sound–symbol association. Good examples of these, including other ideas for use, are published (e.g. by Learning Development Aids, Wisbech). Hamilton-Fairly (1976) recommends five stages in the discrimination of sounds which are needed for written language.

1. The teacher or therapist should give examples of the sound on its own.
2. The child should differentiate that sound among others (e.g. k/t).
3. The child should use the sound in nonsense words in initial and final position, with reinforcement and guidance from the teacher.
4. The child should use the sound in real words.
5. The teacher or therapist should say words incorrectly to try and get the child to notice the correct and incorrect version.

The important point is for the child to be made constantly aware of his spoken language and its consequent translation to the written language system. It is possible to point out the difference between voiced and unvoiced sounds, for example (b) as in bag, (p) as in pig, with the teaching following the normal course of phonological development.

Apparatus

It is useful for children to hear their own speech as well, and the use of a tape recorder is helpful here. A particularly useful apparatus at this stage is the Language Master. This consists of strips of card about 3 inches x 15 inches (80mm x 400mm) with a thin strip along the bottom which is magnetised and may be recorded on. The card may be played back by running it through the Language Master box. The card may also be written on. There are many procedures, but here are some useful ones:

1. Child runs card through, records a word or sentence. The card is played back, words listened to and corrected with teacher. (The advantage over a tape recorder is that a single card is used with less rewinding etc. required.)
2. Teacher writes simple word or sentence on card, and then teacher reads them aloud and records them. Child then reads card as it passes through and can match teacher's voice to the word(s).
3. Child now reads word/sentence out loud and records it. Plays back/listens, matches.
4. As above, child writes.
5. Single words, syllables or sentences are written (by child or teacher), spaced well apart. Task is to say word/syllable at the exact point (marked by arrow on the machine) that they appear. Figure 3.1 illustrates this using syllables.

Many children find the timing of this kind of exercise quite difficult, and it is useful to develop sequence of sounds as well as word reading fluency.

Part of the link between sounds and their written equivalents is the teaching of written language structure linked to 'word families'. An early example might be CVC words with different vowels. An example of a simple classroom exercise might be categorising words according to vowel sound. Thus the child could write a,e,i,o,u spaced across the page (or (ă), (ĕ) etc. if they have been taught sound pictures). The teacher then says out loud words such as mat, pin, mug, and the child writes each word under the correct vowel heading, one at a time. Another version might be for the words to be written on the board or worksheet and the child required to read them aloud and write them under the required heading. This kind of task also helps the development of phonemic awareness and auditory organisation.

Figure 3.1 Reading and developing syllable/segmentation skills using Language Master

Similar procedures can be undertaken for more difficult language structures, e.g. vowel combinations might be used such as:

(ā)

ai   ay

Here the child listens to words such as rain or play and writes them under the appropriate column. This also helps awareness of middle and end sounds, as well as introducing simple guides to spelling, such as (ā) in the middle of words being spelt 'ai', and at the end of words 'ay'. Alternatively, additional vowel sounds can be used such as:

(ā)   (ī)
ai   ay   igh   y

Appendix II shows detailed examples of these and other activities. This teaching of word structure or families is an important part of 'phonic' teaching, and is an important addition to teaching grapheme–phoneme correspondences on their own. Orthographic patterns can be made explicit, and generalised to novel or unfamiliar words. It is useful to link the above to 'sound blending' techniques.

For example, cat can be blended (k)–(ă)–(t) to make cat, or linked to teaching larger segments, namely (k)–(ăt). This can be written on flash cards as ca‿t, m‿at, f‿at; or sp‿ace, r‿ace; or l‿ight, m‿ight, fl‿ight. The child is taught to sound out the first letter or consonant blend, and then to sound the whole of the second unit: thus l‿ight would be said (l)–(īt). Children need to be encouraged to link the units by 'gliding' from the first sound into the second. For some children it helps them to be given an exercise where the final sound is single, as in 'ca t' (kă – t) or 'ligh t' (lī – t). This is less satisfactory, however, as the divisions do not follow such easily recognised orthographic units. Indeed, some researchers (e.g. Goswami, 1994) argue that the rime unit is the best 'split' of the word, viz c-at and not ca-t. See page 16 for further discussion of this point.

Many materials can be used to develop the above, ranging from flash cards or word lists with particular letter patterns to cards cut in such a way that the beginning can be changed but the end remains the same e.g.

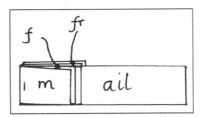

open for
f   m   fr   etc.   ail

A further very useful piece of apparatus to help children follow their own speech sounds is the Edith Norrie Letter Case (Figure 3.2). This is used extensively by, and is available from, the Helen Arkell Dyslexia Centre. It is a multisensory technique, building individual letters into words by following the spoken sound sequence from a letter case. The child is required to pick out appropriate letters. The important aim of this particular piece of apparatus is to make the child consciously aware of his or her own speech process. Indeed, there is a small mirror for this purpose, in which the child is encouraged to look at his or her own lips, tongue, position of mouth and so on, when forming the various sounds. In addition there is colour-coding for voiced/non-voiced sounds, and for vowels. This enables the child to build up words in which there must be at least one red letter (i.e. vowel). The letters are also categorised in relation to articulation. A description of the Letter Case follows, including one or two ideas for its use from the Helen Arkell Centre.

Lip		Tip				Back		
M	B	N	D	T	TH	G	NG	Q
V	P	R	L	S	C	C	Q	CK
W	F	Z	J	SH	CH	X	H	
	A	E	I	O	U	⅄	Mirror	

Figure 3.2 The Edith Norrie Letter Case. Key: bold letters for vowels; Y has a line through it to indicate use as a vowel (e.g. fly). Voiced letters – m, b, v, w, n, j, g, d, r, l, z, ng. Ech box has a number of letters, upper and lower case

In the Edith Norrie Letter Case the letters are arranged phonetically not alphabetically. The vowels are in the five middle boxes at the bottom of the case and each one is red. Children should learn that there must be at least one 'red letter' in every word, and one in every syllable; 'y' sounds as a vowel and is in the same row. The consonants are divided into 'The lip sound family'; a 'Tip of the tongue family'; and a 'Back of the throat family'. This enables the child to narrow down the range of letters to choose from. By means of a small mirror the pupil learns whether sounds are produced by the lips, tip of the tongue or back of the throat.

Starting with phonetically regular words and short sentences, the pupil spells out the sentence from the box and is allowed as much time as is needed to sort out difficult words. He or she reads it through looking for mistakes, and the teacher may supply more clues to help in correcting them, e.g. 'Say the word again and look at your lips in the mirror' or 'How many syllables are there in that word, and how many red letters have you got?' When the sentence is correct, including capital letters and punctuation, it is copied out, the pupil being able to pay attention to the formation of the letters. The sentence can be covered up and written from memory, then checked for corrections by the child. Later the letters can be removed when a couple of words have been studied so there is no control check. Memory is being trained. Even later the letters need only be used for difficult words, which are best used in context.

The apparatus is particularly useful for children who are failing to follow their own speech sounds, or have serious auditory confusions. For children who are doing reasonably well in written language after teaching, sometimes the occasional word for which they are confused can be built by using the Letter Case. Cotterell (1970), for example, suggests the use of the Letter Case with those having spelling errors such as omission (belog for belong, sak for sank), as well as omissions in initial consonant blends (tay for tray) and weak auditory discrimination (crig for grip) or vowel confusion (nat for net). The technique helps teach basic sound–symbol correspondence links, as well as building up simple words that are phonetically regular.

It is often helpful to have an adjunct to classroom work with children, i.e. work that can be set in tutorials, or with minimum supervision so that individual work may be undertaken with another child. The tape recorder or the Synchrofax machine can be used to provide work linking sound to writing help, as well as presenting the same materials in an alternative way. This can prevent boredom in undertaking the overlearning so essential to the dyslexic. The Synchrofax is essentially a talking page, and has one advantage over the tape recorder in that one exercise (3 minutes of speaking) can appear on each page, preventing searching through tapes. The example given below is from a Synchrofax work sheet, but could equally be done via a tape recorder.

Example of spoken/reading/writing work sheets for the (or) sound

The child looks at the work sheet (shown in the box) placed on the machine, and then plays the recording as follows:

Teacher's voice on Synchrofax recording: 'Spelling choices for the (or) sound. There are several ways of spelling the (or) sound. The first choice for the (or) sound is 'or' as in fork. Read the words at one (1) with me: for, corn, forty, border, morning, before, porch, important, stork, swore, born, north, export.'

(Child reads words as teacher says them.)

The second choice for the (or) sound is 'al' as in tall. Read the words at two (2) with me: all, tall, small, stalk, walk, chalk, bald.'

(Child reads.)

'Many one syllable words ending in double l have this spelling pattern, e.g. all, ball, call, fall, hall, small, stall, wall. Remember, if you can hear the (l) sound after (or), choose 'al'. I'm going to read the words at (3). Listen to each word and fill in the correct spelling choice, either 'or' or 'al'. Remember, press the stop button after each word. Then write in your choice. When you are ready, press the button again for the next word. Are you ready for the first word? (1) More.'

(Child then stops and starts at own speed for the rest of the words).

'(2) Shore; (3) wall; (4) fall; (5) score; (6) fork; (7) sword; (8) force; (9) small; (10) border; (11) tall; (12) pork; (13) record; (14) torch; (15) chalk; (16) sort; (17) sport; (18) hallway; (19) ordinary; (20) extraordinary. Now switch off the machine and have your work checked.'

(Child gets work checked by teacher.)
'Now here are some sentences for you to complete. Listen to each sentence, turn off the machine and write the spelling choices on your work sheet.

1. The corn stalk was taller than the fork.
2. He crossed the border on a stormy morning.
3. Walter was short, bald and nearly forty.
4. The horse halted at a thorny gorse bush and refused to walk any more.
5. He was born in the north before midnight.
6. The small ball will fall into the hallway.

Now have your work checked.'

Work sheet: spelling choices for the (or) sound

   'or'   'al'
   fork   tall

(1) 1. for 2. corn 3. forty 4. border 5. morning 6. before 7. porch 8. important 9. stork 10. swore 11. born 12. north 13. export
(2) 1. all 2. tall 3. small 4. stalk 5. walk 6. chalk 7. bald
(3) 1. m––e 2. sh––e 3. w––l 4. f––l 5. sc––e 6. f––k 7. sw––d 8. f––ce 9. sm––l 10. b––der 11. t––l 12. p––k 13. rec––d 14. t––ch 15. ch––k 16. s––t 17. sp––t 18. h––lway 19. ––dinary 20. extra––dinary.

Complete these sentences

1. The c––n st––k was t––ler than the f––k.
2. He crossed the b––der on a st––my m––ning.
3. W––ter was sh––t, b––d and nearly f––ty.
4. The h––se h––ted at the th––ny g––se bush and refused to w––k anym––e.
5. He was b––n in the n––th before midnight.
6. The sm––l b––l will f––l into the h––lway.

There are of course many other language structures to choose and many formats, but the above example, and indeed the whole section, should give the reader some idea as to the approaches to take.

The mixed phonetic and phonological difficulties many dyslexics have can be helped by training in articulating contrasting sounds. One useful technique is training in pronunciation, reading and spelling of 'minimal pairs'. Here words, for example on flashcards, perhaps with clue pictures, can be presented. A minimal pair consists of two words that differ by only one phoneme, or sound unit. There are over 40 important units. For example, pig – big, set – sat can be used with children to develop awareness of sound differences and their relationship to speech. Appendix XIII shows examples of common minimal pairs which could be used. Auditory discrimination cards of initial and final sounds can also be used to develop minimal pair contrasting words.

Audio-cassette material

Much of the structured programme and the procedures outlined in this book require a lot of overlearning. Particularly useful are taped programmes where a child can sit with his or her own headphones and go through a programme of work reinforcing or supplementing what the teacher has been doing. We think these are best used as reinforcement/development aids, and a child should not be expected to learn the written language structure from them without any help or guidance. In a busy classroom they can also be a great help. There are many on the market, but the following are worth mentioning:

The ARROW system of books with accompanying tapes cover letter/sound links, high frequency words and word families with a combination of reading and writing systems with multi-sensory learning. The system involves listening, reading, speaking, listening to the voice and writing. It is used widely and has great gains claimed for it – although a short training session is required.

Two other materials, available from the Dyslexia Institute, are the Units of Sound and the STARS (Structured Tape Approach to Reading and Spelling) system. Units of Sound is widely used with words ranging from simple CVC to complex multisyllable and is highly structured and organised. Words are arranged on the page in columns according to their patterns of sounds (see earlier comments re interactive analogy!) and questions are given so that vocabulary understanding is introduced into the reading process as well.

Finally, many games can be developed which practise and develop the skills described at the beginning of the section. Those games, including listening to or recognising shared sounds in words, identifying sounds at the beginning, middle and end of words and rhyming, are recommended.

Chapter 4
Reading

Introduction

Reading is often perceived as something that children acquire osmotically – a crude analogy is that of blotting paper and ink: the paper absorbs the ink, in the same way the child is seen to absorb reading. Certainly, for the majority of children reading does appear to be an automatic process; the teacher acts only as an assistant to the miracle of this complex higher cognitive process.

Without going into a detailed theoretical analysis of the reading process, it is nevertheless pertinent to detail just what we mean by reading. Of course, we all read information, be it non-verbal such as gestures or pictures, or symbols such as letters, all the time during our daily lives. Yet educationalists refer to reading as a specific process beginning with a capital 'R'. This process, which subsumes an inherent automatic understanding of the structure, order, temporal sequencing and meaning of language used. In reading, the reader simultaneously synthesises information from a number of sources. Briefly, these will include previous experience, knowledge of syntax, semantics, orthography, sound-to-symbol mapping and phonetic information. Contextual clues will help when phonetic or visual whole-word approaches break down. The reader adopts different strategies or word attack as he progressively masters a given stage.

Primarily, our concern is to get the children to move quickly from past negative experience of failure in reading to success in the process and, by implication, a positive attitude to reading. From our standpoint, this implies that we are aware of stage and process. The children will be fixed in many cases at the 'logographic' stage as described in Chapter 1, where early gross or crude visual process occurs. A look–say strategy is used. The child is likely to be confused by visually similar patterns and is likely also to make mistakes because of the inefficiency of this strategy – particularly at this early stage. The alphabetic stage quickly follows these early attempts, and comes when the child wants to use written symbols to communicate via the written word. This stage produces a growing awareness and desire to gain mastery of phonemic awareness, i.e. understanding of grapheme/phoneme correspondence: 'A' says (ă) and (ă) can be written 'A'. This is where initially the process of reading and spelling go hand in hand in a parallel manner and the link between the two is made. It is at this stage that those children who have found it an easy transition will be able progressively to utilise the newly acquired skills to aid them with the process of reading and spelling. It will allow them to 'attack' new and unfamiliar words which they have never seen before because they have a conceptual understanding of the process needed to 'decode' new and unfamiliar words.

As the children acquire new skills of reading, so they progressively move through the alphabetic stage, and for the majority of dyslexic children this stage takes the longest, and for some it is the stage which they will largely remain in.

The final stage is the orthographic, in which automatic processing takes place. It is the stage that in many respects characterises full adult literacy. Abstract representation of the printed word occurs without recourse to the alphabetic stage. This allows fluent, accurate reading. (For a detailed account of these stages/processes see Snowling, 1987.)

Our approach to teaching reading is based on the principle of following a detailed structure, one which helps the child to come to terms with the pattern or the plan. Often, dyslexic children are confused by the 'patchy' input which they have been given and cannot 'read the book for the words'. An anecdote seems pertinent. Some time ago we had a very confused yet intelligent boy who had confounded a whole succession of willing, sympathetic helpers. He was confused and angry; his parents were at a loss to know what to do for the best. He could not read more than a few simple words. He could 'read' road signs, labels in supermarkets and the odd word. It is easy to put ourselves into this position by going to Greece or Russia, where a different alphabetic system is used. Then we have to 'read' from concrete clues, i.e. picture context or situation. It transpired that our 'John' did not understand that letters were sorted into words which were placed on a line from left to right. He had been trying to read the intervals between the blocks of words! This is an extreme example of the pitfalls which blight many children's progress. In many respects this is a reflection on us all. We so easily make needless assumptions based on preconceived ideas of what a particular child can do at a certain age and stage. It often amazes us just how much information we can gain from a child while talking to him and asking direct questions about how he sees his problem. It is surprising just how introspective children can be.

Equally, a cumulative approach is implicit because a broadly based footing is vital from which a child can build and develop.

Use of Word Lists

East Court word lists

We have commented elsewhere that the major difficulty with dyslexics and their reading is in the 'mechanical' aspect of reading as opposed to comprehension and understanding what is read once the words and letters have been decoded. This makes the initial reading of books difficult if children are unable to read the words, even if the story might be interesting. This makes the provision of 'hi/lo' books of the utmost importance (see page 122).

In reading books, however, we find it quite useful to prepare difficult word lists which consist of words which the teacher feels may be difficult. These can be taken from the text that a child is going to read. Some reading schemes, for example the Headwork Readers published by Oxford University Press provide these already. In other cases teachers will need to prepare them themselves.

This means that words can be introduced to children, to be learnt before the story is read, and the list can also be used as a preparation prior to reading the passage, for reinforcement of phonic rules, in dictionary work including pronunciation, meanings, synonyms/antonyms/homonyms, grammar/parts of speech and so on. The following specific suggestions broadly follow the notion of teaching the words individually or within the context of the story.

Learning the words individually

The specific words which may give rise to difficulty can be taught before the reader is given a story. Alternatively, some work could be done on the words after the book has been read following (b) and (c) below. Here are some suggestions as to the way in which the words can be taught.

i) Put on flash cards and learn in 'look, say (correct if necessary), remember, look, say' etc.
ii) 'Multisensory' learning. Look at word, say whole word aloud, spell out aloud letter by letter, write down word saying each letter as it is written, read out aloud. Letter names or sounds could be used.
iii) Phonic analysis (regular words). Break down word into phonic structure, encourage to follow speech and use common sound/symbol correspondence, consonant blends, vowel combinations, suffixes etc. See also (iv).
iv) Syllable analysis. Break word down into beats or syllable units, analyse into syllable types e.g. closed, open, silent 'e' etc. (see also (iii)).
v) Reading by analogy. Point out similarities between this and similar words with same structure, particularly rhyming component of word.

vi) Put word(s) into sentences. Encourage use of context/inference to work out word possibilities.

vii) Listen to a tape recording of words being read and follow so that heard input and looking at words match.

viii) Type word into a computer with speech/sound facility. When the word is typed in correctly, self check by listening to computer say the word.

ix) Use the word list for speed-reading trials. These should be done in a fun way, with children trying to beat their own times.

Any of the above can be used with a wider range of words, with the difficult words included. So, for example, one could work on silent 'e'/soft 'g' words such as rage, cage, or even hedge, ledge, and have 'mage' as one of the words. Of course work on the use of the words in context, vocabulary development and discussion can parallel this work.

Use of words in the context of the stories

a) Without help. This approach requires minimal intervention. The stories are read by the children, who may be invited to ask for help if needed. It is assumed that they will be able to read the relevant level and enjoy the book even if some words may not be read correctly.

b) Without help but listening to a taped cassette of the story and reading along with it. This might be a cassette provided with the book or prepared by the teacher.

c) With help. Here it is assumed that the book will be read individually to a teacher or helper, perhaps in a paired reading situation or in class. If a word or passage is proving difficult some help can be given. This could be by: encouraging the reader to read on a little and work out the word from the context; breaking the word down into its syllables or phonic units to aid word recognition; or simply by providing the word as in the typical 'paired reading' situation.

d) Read the story in conjunction with the words (with or without tape); tick off the words as they are found and read.

e) Put the words into appropriate questions about the text. These can be given before reading as comprehension guides/expectation as to what might be in the text.

f) Text from the stories can be taken out and the words omitted to form a cloze procedure. The appropriate words can be chosen from the list.

As a precursor to full mastery of the reading process, we have devised a series of reading lists which are used extensively. These are presented in Appendix VI, but Table 4.1 shows their content. We would emphasise that these lists act only as a means to an end – they are not the final objective, rather they are stages in the process. We do not use them exclusively – indeed, they act only as useful staging posts. They allow us to control what we are teaching and to see that the children succeed at every stage before moving on to the next. In this way, a cumulative approach is maintained. A parallel link to spelling is encouraged. We have 14 East Court word lists.

Table 4.1 East Court word lists	
List no.	Type of words covered
1	One-syllable (CVC) words, e.g. cat, men, dog
2	Consonant blends (CCVC), e.g. spin, stop, twig
3	Consonant blends (CCVCC end blends), e.g. thrust, brush, chest
4	Magic e (CVCE), e.g. pine, cane, robe
5	One-syllable vowel combinations, e.g. sail, sheet, might
6	Two-syllable (VCCV), e.g. velvet, tandem, bandit
7	Two-syllable any regular, e.g. final, ugly, student
8	Two-syllable with R combination or CLE syllables, e.g. castle, hermit, ample
9	Two-syllable with vowel combination, e.g. about, window, railroad
10	Three-syllable regular words, e.g. carpenter, peppermint, infancy
11	Three-syllable with vowel combination, e.g. appointment, sunflower, readable
12	Four-syllable regular words, e.g. differential, temperature, interruption
13	Four- or five-syllable with vowel combination, e.g. exploitation, discontinue, unemployment
14	Five-syllable regular words, e.g. administrator, inconsiderate, originally

Initially, flashcards are used to aid learning of letter–sound correspondence. Generally, we do not stick rigidly to the system advocated in any one system. Rather, we tend to introduce small groups or collections of alphabetic letters which the children are expected to learn. These may be consonants, e.g. b, c, d, f, g, followed by h, j, k, l, m etc. We teach letter sound and key words, e.g. b = ball, c = cat, d = dog (see Chapter 3 for further details). At the same time, and in parallel, we also introduce irregular words. These are called 'survival' words because they are commonly occurring, irregular words which it is vital that children learn to recognise by sight, e.g. danger, gas, stop, exit etc. Our approach is a two-pronged one at this stage, i.e. basic phonetics (alphabetic) as well as look–say (logographic). We do not expect the children at this time necessarily to know or learn the spelling of these sight words, only that they can recognise them for survival. At the phonetic stage, we will be moving in parallel towards an understanding that letter/sound units can be built into sound patterns. Thus, individual letters (consonants and vowels) can be arranged to form simple CVC words.

List 1 (one-syllable CVC words) is used extensively at this stage. All children will be issued with copies of this list, and our aim will be to have them reading individual words as soon as possible.

The children at East Court will have a basic grasp of what they have to do, and they respond well to competition. First, this will be intra-individual competition, where they are aiming to read, say, the first ten words in the first column. Speed is not, at this stage, encouraged because we want to promote the idea of accuracy. Listing of names and time on a piece of sugar paper put on the classroom wall acts as a record and a spur. We must be emphatic that the idea of 'pecking order' at this stage is *not* encouraged – what is, is a measured improvement of reading skills.

The lists can be used to do time tests as the children progress. A stopwatch works wonders! In parallel with this, we encourage the children to use words from the list to begin writing sentences. It will be seen that our lists range from simple CVC words to five-syllable regular words. Not only are these lists invaluable in specific skill practice (decoding), but they are equally important as reference as well as source material. They act as language extensions because, as the child moves through the list, so language development takes place. This is not to say that the lists act as language enrichment – rather, it is a welcome spin-off. The lists encourage active word analysis, particularly syllabification. The concept of segmentation will have been covered by this stage, but these lists encourage analysis. This is where the teaching of the six types of syllable pays off handsomely. The children metaphorically don their 'Sherlock Holmes' caps as they seek for clues in the arbitrary collection of letter patterns. One of the positive spin-offs from the acquisition of these skills is that of growing knowledge and expertise, i.e. they have the mastery of a subskill which is not normally taught. The effect on the child's confidence is noticeable. Of course, the latter lists contain quite difficult words. However, some of the more difficult lists can potentially be read by even the younger children once they have a thorough understanding and mastery of earlier lists. The concept of syllable division is so very important, because it theoretically allows the children to attack new and unfamiliar words knowing that they have a fair chance of success (see pages 88 and 112). Here, oral language skills and vocabulary development go hand in hand with reading. If any one process is ignored then you are increasing the chances of failure. Reading is a 'holistic' process, which, as we have already made clear, calls for the integration of many complex cognitive processes.

Under the heading of word lists mention must be made of some of the lists used on a day-to-day basis. These lists are normally kept on the classroom wall as reference lists as well as acting as reminders of words and skills already taught. First, a 'magic e' list is presented on the classroom wall. This challenges the children to 'have a go' at reading three lists of magic e words: the first is noted as 'easy', with words such as man – mane, win – wine; secondly, words that are noted as 'difficult': mine – gate – slate – slim; thirdly, as 'almost impossible': grope – stripe – scrap etc. The challenge is to 'improve your times, high scores noted!'

Consonant blend challenge, presented as a 'Snakes' reading game, introduces an element of fun to a lesson. Words are arranged on a snake and the child is asked to read from snake to snake (Figure 4.1). Lists of vowel digraphs are read as a challenge. Again, this enables the presentation of both regular and irregular words – after all, reading involves both sorts of words!

One of our favourite lists – much enjoyed by the leaving group, and about which a whole school grapevine mythology has grown up – is that of, wait for it (lower eyes, genuflect) 'The impossible word list' (see Appendix X). This really is the ultimate challenge, yet it is a challenge which is taken up each year by the leaver group. They have to work hard at it, but all succeed in one way or another to conquer it. Of course, mastery of the six types of syllables is fundamental to this – a process that will be explained shortly. However, before doing so, a fuller elaboration of 'The impossible word list' is needed.

Our aim in completing this list was two-fold:

1. To read words that would test any adult and that are multisyllable.
2. To present words that, if they could be read, would be so difficult that any other words thereafter would seem comparatively easy!

We sought words from the biggest dictionary, then spent some time looking for words that were to form the final listing. The idea was to stretch the children yet, at the same time, to boost their confidence in their ability to tackle any word. A direct spin-off of this was language extension and vocabulary building. We not only ask for reading of these lists, but also for an understanding of what each word means. Further, syllable analysis is undertaken as well as speed reading. Believe it or not, most of the children find they can speed read aloud the entire list in approximately 15 seconds. Our record breakers break the 10 second barrier! The children delight in challenging their parents to speed read the words and, of course, they invariably win! Some children have made extra pocket money by betting parents, friends and relations!

Perhaps an anecdote would be pertinent here. Some time ago we had a boy join us for 1 year. He had been at a well-known dyslexia unit, but progress had been mediocre to say the least. The young man was obviously very self-satisfied with what he had seen as substantial progress – indeed, he boasted that he could read lists of difficult words. It transpired that these words were lists which the children at East Court who were 3 years younger than him were proficient at! The point we want to make is that, very often, the expectation of teachers are unrealistically low because they perceive the dyslexic child as having a profound difficulty which they will never satisfactorily overcome. This young man made very dramatic progress within the first fortnight of being at East Court, and subsequently became a champion at 'The impossible word list'. As a result, his confidence in his ability to tackle difficult and unfamiliar words increased dramatically.

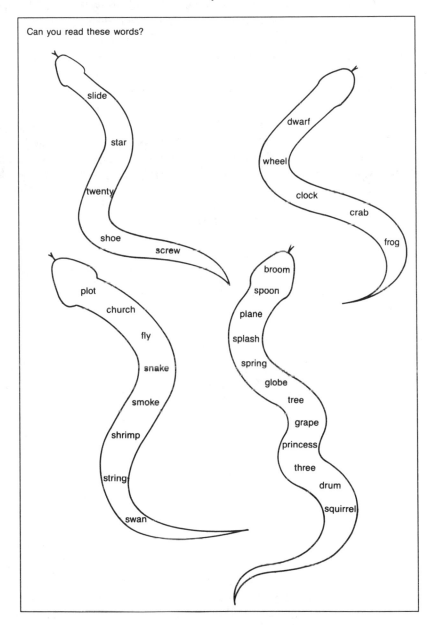

Figure 4.1 Consonant blends: can you read these words?

Syllable Analysis

Syllable analysis in the format of 'The six types of syllable' is something which was originally pioneered in North America, but which we have since adapted and developed to our specific needs. The six syllables are presented briefly under this section because they really are inextricably linked to the reading process (see also page 88). Their presentation takes the form of a quest for the magic key to unlock words. To do this successfully, a number of stages must be passed through and these stages link well to the idea of a quest. Simple drawing of keys enable the children to remember easily both the concept, i.e. unlocking words, as well as the actual code, i.e. CV or the like. There is a story for each key, which can be used to elaborate the concept – but the code is the 'neat formula' that gives mastery of the process. This allows the dyslexics to capitalise on their good logical skills. The process is ordered and logical. With proper use, there will be complete mastery over any word. The word loses its mysticism, the user is in control – 'the wizard'. The six types of syllable are presented in Figure 4.2 as a reference only.

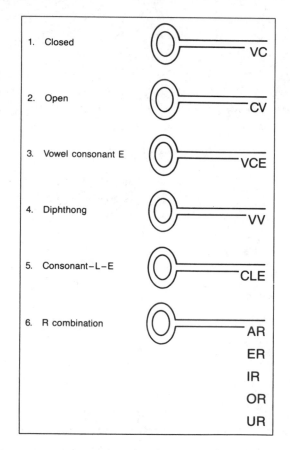

Figure 4.2 The six types of syllable (or keys to success)

The word lists which have already been detailed can be used to good effect, and we recommend that these should be used initially, especially as the child will be familiar with these when syllable analysis is undertaken. The lists provide a ready source of words which can be used prior to assembling your own list – or, equally, taking words at random from any book or source. It is important to make sure that ambiguous words, which contain difficult syllable analysis because of their structure, are not included at an early stage. Two examples of this type would be:

o c	We say 'tion' is closed because it is
sta'tion	*not* a 'dip' as defined on pages 88 and 89

c c o c c	Here, although 'm' has no vowel
ven'tril'o'quis'm	'quism' has two syllables, so we
	compromise!

However, they can be included later, as is done in the more difficult lists. These can be a point of discussion, and further evidence of the infernal written language system of English.

Table 4.2 takes one example from each word list (1)–(14) and shows how syllable analysis is undertaken. The system of labelling syllable type is a matter of personal choice. The younger children at East Court may initially attempt three types of syllables, i.e. closed, open, VCE.

This system may take some time to impart, in order that the children thoroughly understand and can use it without difficulty. We find that approximately one week needs to be spent on each type of syllable, and this would be in parallel with other activities supporting the idea. By the time the children reach their leaving year they will be fairly proficient and practised at using all of the six different types of syllable. We emphasise the oft-made point that 'practice makes perfect', particularly with syllable analysis.

More on vowel combinations

We have discussed vowels in relation to syllables on pages 88, 89 and 112, but felt some extra comments here would be helpful.

Vowels and vowel combinations do, of course, present one of the most serious difficulties for dyslexic pupils. This is because the sound/symbol links are not always the same, either by sound or by letter. For example, the sound 'a' can be represented by many different spelling combinations, i.e. 'ai', 'ay', 'ea', 'eigh', and so on. The letter combination 'ca' can be pronounced 'e' or 'a'. Vowels never seem to offer the consistencies of English language in the way that, for example, consonant blends and individual letter sounds can. Hall (1994) gives some further examples of these inconsistencies:

Table 4.2 Syllable analysis

List	Word	Syllable division	Syllable type
1	cat	cat	vc c cat or cat
2	spin	spin	vc c spin or spin
3	thrust	thrust	vc c thrust or thrust
4	pine	pine	vce pine
5	sail	sail	vv sail
6	velvet	vel'vet	vc vc c c vel'vet or vel'vet
7	final	fi'nal	cv vc o c fi'nal or fi'nal
8	hermit	her'mit	rc c her'mit
9	about	a'bout	o vv a'bout
10	carpenter	car'pen'ter	rc vc rc rc c rc car'pen'ter or car'pen'ter
11	appointment	a'point'ment	o vv vc o d c a'point'ment or a'point'ment
12	differential	dif'fer'en'tial	vc rc vc vv c rc c d dif'fer'en'tial or dif'fer'en'tial
13	anonymous	a'non'y'mous	o c o vv o c o d a'non'y'mous or a'non'y'mous
14	administrator	ad'min'is'tra'tor	vc vc vc cv rc c c c o rc ad'min'is'tra'tor or ad'min'is'tra'tor

Two types of terminology are used above. One describes vowels (v) and consonants (c); the other is c = closed, o = open, vce = vowel consonant e, d = diphthong, rc = r combination, -le = consonant le (see also page 88). vv refers to vowel/vowel and is the vowel combination. We also call this dip for diphthong or di for digraph (see page 88).

- in: *bat*, *wet*, *kit*, *got* and *cut* – the vowel says its short <u>sound</u>
- in: *bait*, *weak*, *kite*, *goat* and *cute* – the first vowel says its letter name but the second vowel says nothing.
- in: *was*, *said*, *some*, the vowel says the wrong vowel sound, i.e.: in *was* the 'a' says the short 'o' sound, in *said* the 'ai' says the short 'e' sound and in *some* the 'o' says the short 'u' sound.

- finally, consider *funny*, *my*, *bay*, *symmetry*. In this list, 'y' sounds as a long vowel sound (as in funn*y*, m*y*); short vowel sound (as in symm*e*try), or nothing at all (ba*y*).

Here are some examples of the way in which vowels can be taught under the heading of the short or simple vowel sounds and the walking or letter name vowel sounds (or short and long vowel sounds). Most readers will be familiar with the adage 'when two vowels go walking the first one does the talking', and the additional corollary to that is that the walking vowels usually (but not always) say their letter name. Thus, vowels that walk such as 'oa' in *boat* and 'eo' in *people*. An additional guide might be that vowels that 'walk' always say their long sound or name when there is only one consonant between them, for example, *kite*, *kiting*, *potato*; but are stopped from walking or saying their letter sound if there is more than one letter between them, e.g. *kitten*, *running*, *coffee*. The application of these vowel rules applies to suffixes as well, which can be combined with the other spelling rules that are described elsewhere as an additional guide. Obviously one needs to pick on those which match a particular student's way of thinking. Here are some examples of the application of the walking vowel rule to various combinations.

1. *Decoding 'boat'*. Here the rule is applied directly and the long 'o' sound produced.
2. *Suffix applications*. Use the guide on walking vowels being long when there is only one consonant between them. They need to 'stop the vowel walking' and therefore words ending with CVC or CCVC require doubling: run, running; swim, swimming whereas CVCC words do not require doubling as there are already two consonants which 'stop the vowel walking'. Suffixes not beginning with a vowel will not affect the root word. The walking vowel is particularly helpful for CVC words where the specific rule of dropping the 'e' may give problems with hopeful, safety and so on. The application of the walking vowel rule indicates that the final 'e' can be dropped if it is no longer needed i.e. kite, kiting; bake, baking. It should not be dropped in words such as hope, hopeful as there would then be two consonants together which would stop the vowel walking.
3. *Decoding of long words*. Here the student is encouraged to focus on the syllable as designated by vowel sounds (see page 88 on syllable analysis). Here the closed syllables, as described elsewhere, can be described as having had the vowel stopped from walking by consonants.

Again, these are just examples of different approaches, and as always it depends on which are most suited to a given student and which appeal to his or her way of thinking and, most importantly, which actually work!

Developing Reading Skills

Of course word lists and individual word reading are only a start in the reading process. Before going on to discuss the process of listening to children read, it is worth making one or two suggestions as to ways in which the above reading skills might be developed.

The initial introduction to what a book is cannot be assumed. It is surprising how many dyslexics, despite previous remedial teaching, are confused over basic concepts. Even older children may need to be shown the *front* and *back* of a book, or shown that the words move from left to right across the page, and up and down. The use of markers/cardboard arrows or other such indicators of direction during reading are a great help to many children even when they are quite fluent readers. It is also important to point out and give the appropriate label to features such as line, sentence or paragraph, as many dyslexics can be confused over this terminology. These early introductions to books can also include being read to, discussing pictures, sampling books for ideas or telling stories. In other words all the basic skills that pre-school children are introduced to and which may have been a complete mystery to the dyslexic when they were 4, 5 or 6 years of age.

The development of a basic sight vocabulary is really a matter of flash cards and a 'core' set of common words. A simple method is to have a box of common flash cards for all the children in a class or teaching group. These can be based on word frequency lists. Appendix III shows lists of words which, if read correctly, will cover much of the early readers found in school. These lists can be labelled 'List 1', 'List 2' and so on. When children can read the whole list without error they could be given a tick on a wall chart. When three ticks occur the list is deemed as learned, and the child moves on to the next list. (Of course the earlier lists will need to be returned to again for reinforcement and overlearning.)

In addition to the general list, a specific list or group of flash cards can be developed for each child. This might be from the book that they are going to read, or words that have been shown to be poorly recognised by the child. Particularly useful will be irregular words that may be difficult to teach via a phonic approach. This method of developing a sight vocabulary does rely on visual memory to a large extent, and can be weak in dyslexic children: indeed some may find it inordinately difficult. Here it is necessary to present, or draw attention to, basic words in context and try to encourage cloze or 'guessing' procedures. However, let the reader beware! Reading for meaning via context or cloze procedures is nevertheless dependent on some letter recognition. Dyslexics have a marked tendency to guess inappropriately from one or two letters, and all kinds of odd words may be produced. For example, 'The man rowed across the lake in his *boat*' might not be read 'The man rowed across the lake in his *goat'* by a dyslexic being encouraged to read for meaning or guess from context, but it might well be read 'The man rowed across the lake in his *coat'*. Here the misreading of just one letter has not been corrected by contextual clues.

Developing simple grapheme/phoneme and phonic analysis skills are key features of structured phonics teaching. This has been covered elsewhere, particularly in Chapter 3 (page 83). It should not be forgotten that it is important to provide these word attack skills so that common letter patterns, ranging from CVC words through consonant blends to more complex orthographic units, can be recognised. Simple and multisyllable words may then be built up from smaller alphabetic units if necessary.

The use of punctuation in reading spans both 'mechanical' and 'higher order' skills, and initially would include the recognition that a full stop heralds the end of a sentence and, at least, a pause for breath. Later on the intonation and stress in pronunciation, and the question or exclamation marks, may be introduced. It is helpful here to get children to really exaggerate, to the point of silliness, the intonation patterns in reading out loud. A lot of fun may be had in reading sentences with different stress patterns, with consequent differential meanings. The reader can make up their own and try them out with children. Table 4.3 shows a few examples of stress and intonation patterns giving different meanings in English. The fun has an underlying educational purpose.

The development of fluency can be aided by the use of the tape recorder as well. This can take the following stages:

1. Child listens to teacher read the story (derives speech patterns, intonation and prosody [rhythm of words]).
2. Child listens to teacher and follows text as well (matches above to words and sentences).
3. Child listens to teacher and reads out the text at the same time, as a kind of paired reading (see page 121) exercise (introduction of grapheme/phoneme or word production skills).
4. Child reads on own and checks text by listening to teacher.

The above sequence can be used for controlled word lists or special texts as well as general reading. We often provide tapes for the above routines in speed reading challenges (see pages 106–111).

Further tasks which help the development of fluency are 'proofreading' exercises. These might be basic letter recognition, as in crossing out named letters, or finding letters in a given order (see Attack-a-track by Lynn Lewis); or it might involve finding words in text, with context clues. The latter case, reading for errors or omissions, is a very difficult task for dyslexics, particularly with their own writing!

Table 4.3 Examples of stress and intonation in English

Sentence	Meaning
He's arrived?	Question, has he arrived yet?
He's arrived!	Exclamation, he has arrived, great!
I saw a red car	Statement, seeing a red car
I saw a RED car	Clarification, no, the car was red (not blue or green)
No! (rising tone)	Disbelief or shock
No (falling tone)	Statement of fact
Give me your book, boy	Neutral request
Give me your BOOK, boy!	No, it's your book I want, not pen, ruler etc. Critical implication
Give me your book, BOY!	'Do as you are told' statement

The development of skills in the use of context, in inference and in vocabulary involves many 'traditional' English tasks. These include 'Reading workshop' cards such as those produced by SRA, as well as comprehension exercises of which many have been published. 'Cloze' procedures and sentence completion tasks are also important for the dyslexic. A cloze procedure involves a text where words or phrases are omitted, e.g. every seventh word may be left out, with a gap or other indication of how many letters are in the word. The task for the child is to recreate the text by adding an appropriate word in context. There is not always a 'correct' answer. For example. 'I went to work by _____ ' could be car, bus, bicycle etc. The task involves reading for meaning, using context clues, using implicit knowledge about word frequencies in English, and many other syntactic and semantic skills. It is assumed that the reader is familiar with these concepts. Sentence completion tasks can be linked to phonic work by having words that complete sentences coming from particular letter or word families, e.g. 'We had egg and _____ for tea', where one of the words to choose, out of other 'ch' words, would be chips. We also find it very helpful to develop our own cloze procedures for each child, or certainly for each teaching group. These can be based on the child's attainment and reading skills. This ensures that the mechanical reading level is appropriate, but that the interest level is not too low. It is important to make sure that vocabulary, use of context or semantic level are not too easy, despite the dyslexic's poor word reading. It must be remembered that higher order reasoning or intellectual skills are *not* handicapped. We find some of the commercially available cloze procedures that the children can read are too simplistic at the conceptual level. This is equally important for choice of book – see page 122. We also ask our subject teachers to develop cloze procedures, so that, for example, a science worksheet includes language and reading development skills. Another source of cloze procedures is working with computers (see Chapter 8 for some examples).

Listening to Dyslexics Read

At the risk of being patronising to our readers it is nevertheless worth reiterating that reading is a stressful experience for many dyslexics and the approach taken to reading with them is very important. We have a marvellous video tape of a boy reading during his first week at East Court, and during his last week 3 years later. It is marvellous because the first scene shows a nervous, hesitant and anxious boy. He wipes his palms on his sleeves, he licks his lips, he keeps his head down and he is ashamed of his performance. In the second scene he grins at the camera, performs virtuoso feats of speed and pronunciation and revels in his skills. We should not forget, however, that these new found confidences are fragile.

Reading should therefore be approached in a non-punitive and supportive way. The atmosphere created is important, and yet difficult to define. The introduction of humour along with an understanding of the child's difficulty that is communicated to him is very helpful. However, we are firm believers that children need to face up to, and accept, their own difficulties. 'I can't do it because I am dyslexic' is a statement treated as a heinous crime by us both! A balance of supportiveness, understanding, but yet appropriate expectation is needed. It is also important to know the child very well. What may be a helpful comment or prompt to one child may block and destroy the confidence of another, and prevent yet another from producing a word they have just worked out.

The process of hearing a child read will involve a judgement as to whether a word should be quickly and quietly given to avoid loss of fluency or meaning or whether time should be allowed for a word to be worked out. Random guessing should be discouraged, but sensible rendering accepted. Also, it is imported to provide help and coaching where appropriate, depending on what has been covered elsewhere. For example, covering a part of a word to recognise a blend or letter pattern, pointing out a taught phonemic structure, encouraging sounding out of syllables or the use of a punctuation mark. We believe that monitoring a child's performance is important, and would regularly measure attainment (see Chapter 2). Obviously, it is important to make occasional notes of particular weaknesses and errors in order to plan future teaching and to act as an aide memoire. Similarly careful notes should be kept as to what children have or have not read, and what stage they are at in their reading. We confess that we are not great advocates of detailed record keeping of items taught and read. These often take up too much of a teacher's time, and are often a record of intent, rather than the reality of learning!

We also do not always find the classification of children's reading and spelling errors into 'auditory' and 'visual' categories particularly helpful. The main difficulty is not that error analysis does not have implications for teaching, but that classification from errors tends to be unreliable. Indeed, one of our research projects (Thomson, in press) showed that as children receive a 'structured phonic programme' their 'auditory' errors become more 'visual'. The errors made seem to be a function of development and received teaching. A discussion of visual and auditory errors may be found in Thomson (1984, 1990).

During the course of children reading it is also important to stop occasionally and discuss what has happened in the story or text so far, or to surmise what might happen next. These and other activities, such as discussing vocabulary, descriptions or style, are important parts of reading development programmes for any child, and are just as crucial for the dyslexic.

We also use the concept of 'paired reading' from time to time. Sometimes this occurs with an adult, either teacher or parent, but we also pair children together. The latter occurs normally for a short burst of 2 or 3 weeks to prevent the children getting stale. Since our last edition we have moved toward twice weekly paired reading throughout the year. This proves to be more effective than the short burst model. Certainly our children gain enormously from this, and feedback from teachers, children and parents is very positive. A more skilled reader is paired with a less skilled child, and the former is given 'training' in paired reading. We find paired reading helpful for both parties – both develop increased confidence and understanding, as well as developing reading skills. A typical 'paired reading' framework is given below.

Although the early stages of reading aloud can be a private affair with an adult, it is still helpful if children can read in groups. Obviously, it is important to make sure that the groups are well matched, but games such as points for words read correctly, vocabulary challenges or reading the next word when randomly chosen can act as a good motivator, confidence builder and attention focuser!

Mention of the use of an epidiascope, a device that allows projection of the pages from a reading book onto a white screen, must be made. Used as a useful reading aid, it helps no end. The children at East Court enjoy using it, and staff reports indicate that it aids reading development. A page of a book is projected onto a screen in a darkened classroom. The epidiascope, like an overhead projector, needs a darkened room for best results. This has a two-fold benefit: (1) extraneous stimulus is reduced; (2) the atmosphere is 'special' and allows a child to have a go without being in the limelight. Further, it allows a teacher to read and the children to follow the words as well as providing a pattern of reading that the child can follow. In many respects, it is like a television screen, but differs because it allows encouragement of an interactive process that keeps pace with the child's reading speed. The youngest groups thoroughly enjoy the experience and, most importantly, it seems to promote a number of skills needed in fluent reading. It links well to the idea of paired reading.

A paired reading framework

Paired reading has two steps: (1) reading together; (2) reading aloud.

Reading together

The helper and the reader both read the words out loud together, the helper matching his speed to the reader's. The reader should read every word. The helper needs to allow the reader a little time to lead in so that he is not just repeating the helper's reading. If the reader struggles and then gets it right, the helper can give a word of praise or some other (e.g. non-verbal) cue. The reader should not struggle for more than 5 seconds. If the reader struggles too long or gets it wrong, then the helper just says the word right and makes sure the reader says it right as well. The helper must make sure that the reader *looks* at the words. For example, one person can point to the word both are reading with a finger. It is best if the reader does the pointing.

Reading aloud

When reading together and the reader feels good enough, he or she might want to read a bit alone. A way should be agreed for the reader to ask for the helper to be quiet. This could be a knock, a sign or a squeeze. (You do not want the reader to have to *say* 'be quiet', or he or she will lose track of the reading.) The helper goes quiet right away.

If the reader struggles for more than 5 seconds, or struggles and gets it wrong, the helper reads the words out loud, right, for them. The helper must make sure the reader then says it right as well. *Then* both go on reading out loud *together*, until the reader again feels good enough to read alone, and again asks the helper to be quiet.

Finally, although we have talked about children reading, it is often helpful for children to *listen* to reading – encourages the children to relax and close their eyes; to think what might be happening next; to focus on the tone of the reading and to *enjoy* the experience.

Written Language Structure and Meaning

A good deal of time has been spent discussing the teaching of written language structure, and the phonic component in reading. This is not because 'higher order' skills of comprehension, reading for meaning and communication are not important; but because the so-called 'lower level' skills are those that require the greatest input in dyslexia. Nevertheless, we recognise that the final aim in reading is to understand what is read; to derive information from reading; to free the imagination; to expand horizons and vocabulary; and, most importantly, to engender enjoyment and a love for good literature. The final measurement must therefore be in the child's ability to receive the message. Written language structure must be related to meaning, including the ability to make inferences from text, and the interpretation of ideas from text. It must be borne in mind that some of the difficulties dyslexics have in short-term memory will affect the processing of information in reading. Our own organisation of teaching at East Court tries to take this into account by providing time for written language structure teaching as well as comprehension and other skills. A typical week's work in 'English' for our children is shown in Table 4.4.

Table 4.4 'English' timetable and emphasis for children at East Court		
Lesson	Length	Aims
English	5 × 40 minute periods	Areas covered by Blue File (see page 67, e.g. written language, structure and phonics, composition, comprehension)
Extra English	40 minutes	Literature, class reading, comprehension
Library	40 minutes	Reading own books; class readers
Reading workshop	40 minutes	Formal comprehension exercises
Calligraphy	40 minutes	Handwriting; poetry, illustration
Tutorial	40 minutes	Individual work on any of above
Typing	40 minutes	Typing and alphabet skills
Word processing	40 (average)	Composition and other written language work (see Chapter 8)

Table 4.4. gives a flavour of the relative emphasis that is placed on different written language skills, and the importance of an integrated approach, rather than the isolated teaching of phonics. As in all things, it is important to achieve a balance. Just as the isolated teaching of phonics is not appropriate, our view is that just providing books with the idea that dyslexics will learn because the books are interesting will not be enough. The so-called 'language experience' approach and 'real' reading cannot provide the dyslexic with the ammunition to get to grips with using books in this way.

Choosing a Book

The first stage in deciding on reading material for the dyslexic is the level of reading difficulty. It does not matter how interesting or exciting the book is if the child cannot read it. Dyslexics will merely have their suspicions (that they are doomed to fail in reading) confirmed if reading material is not appropriate. In the next section we discuss reading schemes and types of books suitable for dyslexics, so here the choice for the individual will be discussed.

The most obvious feature is the reading level. This implies a knowledge of the child's and the book's reading age. It is useful to colour code the books in the school library: each book has a strip of colour on the spine giving an approximate reading age in 6-month intervals up to 13+ years. In some cases these are based on information given by the publisher of a reading scheme, in others by the application of a 'readability' formula and in yet others through experienced evaluation by the teacher. Inevitably this stresses the approximate nature of the reading age codes, but it is an important start. Another help here is the reading age guides given by the National Association for Remedial Education. We also have sets of books which are called 'easy readers', consisting of those requiring a minimal reading skill. Although a reading age (whether word recognition or text reading) is again only a guide to one aspect of reading skill, it is useful information to have with which to match child to book. In practice a reading age of 11 or more means that most children's books can be tackled with some help but children with lower reading ages will need carefully chosen books matched to their reading level. Once a range of potential books has been selected by taking into account the above, there are many other factors to consider, not the least of which are the interests of the child and the relevance of the book to the child. This is, of course, crucial, but let us take that as read and focus on some specific features to be aware of in the first reading of a book. These can be broadly divided into 'mechanical' and 'higher order' reading skills and are set out in Table 4.5. The features shown in Table 4.5 can be used to help choose the appropriate level on a more qualitative basis. It is helpful for children to have their own individual book to read, as well as a class reader which can be used in group reading. Another important component is a continuation of bedtime reading well beyond the age that children might normally be read to. Dyslexics really enjoy listening to books without having to put in the effort of decoding. To these ends we make sure that all of our children are read to by care staff prior to 'lights out'.

Useful Reading Schemes

There are many books devoted exclusively to reading, its nature and our understanding of the process. The full analysis of reading is covered in these books. The process of reading calls on a variety of specialised and complex cognitive skills that involve more general subskills. The final process, or the actual 'reading task' may well call on differing processes. It will come as no surprise to readers that our approach to reading is primarily a phonetically based one. It will be obvious that any other approach, such as look–say, does not work with the dyslexic because it calls for areas of skill in which the dyslexic is essentially deficient. Equally, a phonetic approach basically utilises the route to reading which is both prescriptive and logical. Most importantly for us, it is a system which is efficient and works.

Often we are faced with the general misperception that dyslexia is *primarily* a reading difficulty. Terms such as 'specific reading disability', 'word blindness' and the like have been misused to define the dyslexic.

child. However, we can quite clearly state that dyslexia is *not* primarily a reading difficulty, because many dyslexics learn to read with a good measure of success. Indeed, many of the children at East Court leave as fluent readers with a reading age at the ceiling of the British Ability Scales Word Reading Test, i.e. +14;5 years. However, we do note that most dyslexics remain inherently slow readers, taking longer to read and comprehend a passage than their non-dyslexic peers. Equally, for the dyslexic reading aloud remains an area which causes much difficulty.

In many respects we are presented with the challenge of helping the dyslexic make sense of some of the 'code' and to 'join the worldwide club' of readers. The action of 'reading' begins as soon after birth as the infant begins to gain eye coordination, whilst the formal reading of sentences is not accomplished by the dyslexic until they have had specific skill help. For many, the process is full of contradictions, irregularities and

Table 4.5 Reading skills to take into account when choosing a book

Reading skills	Comments
Mechanical	
Recognition of 'text'	Includes left/right scanning, recognition of word/line units, top/bottom direction, pages etc. This simple stage cannot be taken for granted in the dyslexic
Basic sight vocabulary	High frequency/irregular words read Able to fluently recognise common vocabulary without sounding out
Simple grapheme/phoneme skills	Common word units recognised, e.g. consonant blends, vowel sound combination
Phonic analysis skills	Identification of word units, 'sounding' out skills, blending and syllabification skills
Simple punctuation	Recognition of punctuation and its implication in reading aloud
Higher order	
What are books, sentences, paragraphs and illustrations?	That books relate to communication, spoken language and can tell stories. Again this cannot be taken for granted
Use of context	Being able to follow the gist; expecting the next stage; what that part of the book is about
Use of inference	What the book suggests about other things; understand more sophisticated vocabulary, analogy and meaning
'Linguistic' fluency	Using punctuation appropriately; reading aloud with expression; 'skimming' for key meanings

a good measure of total confusion to boot! It is the specialist dyslexic teacher whose job it is to untangle this state of affairs and to give the dyslexic the means to actually read books. The act of reading does not start with presenting a book. Rather, it begins with a thorough grounding in basic pre-reading skills that go towards forming a whole complexity of subskills which, united, allow the dyslexic to tackle the action of reading with a fair chance of success. The process will concentrate on giving dyslexics specific skills, normally phonetically based, that enable them to decode the arbitrary symbols. The aim will be to get the dyslexic reading as soon as possible. This implies that simple books, which are so structured as to allow early success to be gained, should be given to the child. Equally, it must be generally assumed that the child wants to read. To these ends, colourful, interesting books must be made readily available to the child. The content must be interesting to the children as well as being at their intellectual level. For the older dyslexic, there is nothing more demoralising and intellectually insulting than to be presented with a 'Janet and John' book which is far below their interest level, contains short, staccato sentences, is poorly illustrated and, to add insult to injury, boring! It is little wonder that we get reluctant readers when the reality of endless hours of effort are rewarded with uninteresting books.

The introduction of the National Curriculum clearly focused teaching attention on a whole range of subjects (English for Ages 5–11, DfEE, 1988 talked about 'the ability to read, understand and respond to all types of writing'). Skills focused on can be summed up as letter and word recognition, accuracy, fluency, interpretation, understanding and appreciation of meaning – from concrete to abstract, inference, source information and use of reference.

This was followed by the 'Draft Orders for English', which aim to give greater clarity and precision to previous documents. The dreaded word 'phonics' reared its head. The wheel had turned and that which was unspeakable, unfashionable and unwanted, i.e. phonics, came in from the cold.

Reading schemes were also back in fashion. Some of the reading schemes mentioned in our first edition are no longer used, either because they are out of print or because better schemes have replaced them.

Some of the reading schemes that are employed at East Court, and that are found to work well are described below. These will not be presented in order of preference, rather in the order from youngest readers upwards. We should explain that there are many more good and relevant schemes – this is not an exhaustive or recommended list.

Bangers and Mash

This series, published by Longman, is based on a family of gorillas and their day-to-day experiences in life. The graded phonetic readers are progressive, ranging from reading ages of five-and-a-half through to seven years eleven months. It is a good series to introduce phonetics in reading. Colourful, humorous illustrations predominate and the simple text is easy to read. Quick progression through each page is encouraged. The lowest level books make the introduction of reading phonetically an easy process. Later books (15–18) reinforce earlier phonetic work. At the end of these books there are sections on 'things to do'. These make ideal books for the introduction or supplementation of work already covered. It should be noted that our younger children enjoy this series enormously.

Trog

The *Trog* series, published by Nelson, is used by us particularly for our children with reading ages between seven and eight-and-a-half years. Again, the emphasis is on large illustrations with clear text. Trog, a primitive young man in Stone Age times, has many adventures together with his grandpa. The Quicker Wits play an important part in many of the stories. The main use of these books comes with those of our children who need a considerable amount of help and will have progressed via series such as *Fuzz Buzz*, *Bangers and Mash*, and *Primary Phonics* and will be progressing through a wide range of different prints, illustrations and styles. The earlier great emphasis on logical phonetic stages is not so apparent in this series. Sight vocabulary comes into play at this stage.

Heinemann Guided Readers

This series provides our learner readers with a gradually increasing choice of reading material. The series is published at five levels, namely:

1. Starter
2. Beginner
3. Elementary
4. Intermediate
5. Upper

These books look like real books inasmuch as the layout and format is just like any other novel. The text becomes smaller than beginner books noted earlier – in fact, just like any other book. The child is clearly on his way when he gets to this series.

Information, structure and vocabulary control mean these books are carefully chosen by the publisher for a specific readership. Clear text together with black and white full-page illustrations makes them popular with our children. The illustrations can be somewhat stylised.

Headwork Readers

Published by Oxford University Press. Black and white, clear illustrations together with cracking good stories make this series very popular. This series has much to offer the reader. We make use of them for those of our students who have reading ages between eight and ten years. There are four levels in the series, Reading Age 6–10 years, interest at 11–15 years. Tales like 'A Gift from Elsa' are based on the real experiences of a Spitfire fighter pilot (MET's father). The stories are short and the text is controlled, and our children enjoy them enormously. They are a jolly good read and interest is maintained. Writing style is contemporary. The teacher resource book is considered very useful by our staff.

Collins English Library

Our intention when using this series is to give a wider choice of reading books whilst our students can make use of them from the reading age equivalent of seven years five months through to twelve years. The series has a whole plethora of titles, covering a wide range of interest which will engage even the most reluctant reader. Level 1 contains a basic vocabulary of some 300 words, whilst Level 6 has 2,500 words. Many of the titles have accompanying cassettes; a useful way of interesting and involving the student. Illustrations are black and white, and somewhat dismal – certainly stylised. Each book has its own illustrator and each brings his/her own style to the text illustrations. Some have black and white photographs.

Wellington Square series

Published by Nelson, this series is colourful and interesting. The illustrations are refreshingly alive. The stories are contemporary, relevant and, importantly, popular with both children and staff.

The starter books carry only pictures and are aimed at engaging the non-reader to become involved through looking, questioning and discussing before progressing towards the first books which carry only the briefest, comic-book style word balloons. Progressive and gradual reading development is the key to this series. The books have the advantage of being quite short, so the early readers are not daunted by a weighty tome. Perceived and actual progress by the readers as they progress is an important hidden agenda.

What makes the series so popular? Clearly, all of the above with the addition of helpful and constructive teacher resource packs. The approach is pragmatic and eclectic. The introduction in these resource packs is clear, concise and helpful. The 'photocopiable' copy masters are practical, engaging and relevant. The *Word Walls* are a good idea, as they ensure the dyslexic student becomes familiar with words which will be met in the accompanying book, thus allowing success when he/she reads. The series of books leads from fiction towards non-fiction and allows the individual to gain in confidence in the use of library books.

Ginn 'Reading 360' and 'Magic Circle'

The above series, supplemented with the Ginn *Reading 360* little books adds breadth to our reading scheme. The Ginn books are clearly printed and easily read, yet are slightly different from the *1, 2, 3 and Away* books. Speech marks are introduced, as well as other punctuation. The introduction of real events together with photography gives these books a measure of realism. Equally, the pictures and stories about them change from page to page – thus giving the reluctant reader or easily bored child the opportunity to have a new story on each page. Some of the books have very good illustrations which are both creative and humorous. They promote ready discussion. The books are popular with most pupils. They have a good mix of poetry, fiction and non-fiction. The *Magic Circle* readers are also good. When used together with the CLARD (see below) material the value of this scheme increases. This comes as cards and work books together with duplicated sheets. Between them, these cover vocabulary, questions, closed topics for writing or discussion, sequencing, crosswords and arranging information in tabular form etc.

The teacher's books which go with this system are full of useful information, further ideas and useful guidance. The 'activity books' are not part of the reading scheme but are very useful for phonetics and language work.

The Ginn *Reading 360* reading programme makes the point that the early stages of these books act primarily as discussion books. They are designed to encourage talk rather than strict reading. To these ends, the books should be utilised together with the *Reading 360* level 1 and 2 teacher's resource book. The system works on the CLARD approach, i.e.

C	L	A	R	D
Comprehension	Language	And	Reading	Development

and teachers can utilise the whole system if they so wish. One of our reservations, given the particular set-up at East Court, is that the system is perhaps best used in a school where an integrated day operates, and where there is not quite the urgency to make specific input to overcome early difficulties which the dyslexic will have, and which require in many respects detailed analysis at every stage as well as precision teaching.

However, it should be said that the reading system is, nevertheless, most useful. The illustrations in the reading books are full of detail and can act as class or small group discussion sources. Such books are very useful in developing language and vocabulary; indeed, story making and related areas can also be strengthened. The books range over levels 1 to 13. Each level has a range of readers, so a wide range of both authors and illustrators makes for interest.

'Gay Way' series (New Way)

The *Gay Way* series, recently changed to *New Way*, by Macmillan Education, is similar in many respects, and yet it gives a slightly different approach relying on a phonetic beginning with a few necessary sight reads introduced, e.g. 'The fat pig', pig, pots and pans. We find this series excellent for the dyslexic child who is experiencing difficulty in memorising 'sight' words and who has real problems with even the few 'look and say' words that have to be learned in rote fashion. *New Way* series offers a series of more advanced books which contribute a growing vocabulary, although still controlled. The books call for a combination of reading skills, i.e. phonetic attack and 'whole word' as well as contextual clue reading. These books help provide the bridge from which the child is able to explore other readers.

'Language in Action'

Language in Action provides one of the best reading schemes, because the basic premise is that the teaching of phonetics is fundamental to the teaching of reading. Although there has been considerable debate as to the rationale behind this approach, especially for non-dyslexic children, we nevertheless have always thought highly of this system. This is primarily because, in many respects, it reflects to a large extent the approach at East Court to the teaching of reading, i.e. the careful teaching of phonetic units that go to form the building bricks of reading. For the dyslexic, *Language in Action* works well. For example, each title contains the sound being taught, e.g. 'Roy and the Pointon Express', and the text focuses on this sound. Unfortunately, some of the earlier books are now unobtainable! The books with higher reading ages have a more 'psycholinguistic' approach, i.e. following from language development, and reading for meaning.

'Primary Phonics'

Primary Phonics, published by Educators Publishing Service Inc, is a collection of phonetically oriented books consisting of some 10 sets. Each set has 10 titles. The books are easily handled by the children, and are not too large (Book 1 has only 12 pages). Black and white simple line drawings are presented in a clear and attractive way. At the end of each book, on the back cover, 'phonetic elements' contains an analysis of units used in the book, as shown in Table 4.6.

Book 1 begins with simple sentences such as 'Tab is a cat' and concludes on page 12 with 'Tab is a bad, sad cat.' Book 10 has 16 pages and the last page has four lines. These books offer no compromise to other methods, e.g. look and say. They are very useful for the youngest, beginner groups. They are enjoyed primarily because, for many children, they are the first books they have ever read. However, they are very limited in scope as far as interest is concerned!

Table 4.6 Phonetic elements

Consonants	Vowel sounds	Sight words
h	a (cap)	is
c	i (pig)	a
d	u (cup)	the
f		to
g		and
etc.		etc.

'Breakthrough' books

Breakthrough books, published by Longman Schools Council Programme in Linguistics, are comprised of some 26 books. Both illustrations and print are clear. The books are principally aimed for use by children who have begun to construct sentences. One slight problem is that books in the Yellow series have no capital letters other than the capital I – although this seems to make little difference to the children's enjoyment of them. These books contribute to a widening range of early readers.

'Fuzz Buzz' series

The *Fuzz Buzz* series, published by Oxford University Press, is comprised of some 20 different titles with colourful and vibrant pictures to accompany the text. The series centre around the Scottish character, Fuzz Buzz. The print size changes as the books increase in difficulty. The books are, in the main, phonetically based. In the easier selection of books various tasks are asked for. For example. 'Draw the tent and colour it in' and 'Write [copy] a short sentence'. These books positively cry out to be read. The request is always answered, and we find the younger children enjoy them immensely.

'Shorty' and 'Rescue Readers'

Ginn publish the *Shorty* series by James Webster. The series comprises two other series, namely *Rescue Stories* and *Rescue Reading*. The *Rescue Stories* are extremely well illustrated with sensitive use of pictures to add excitement and reality to the short stories. The vocabulary is quite advanced, because the books use a 'whole word' approach. The phonetic element follows the main text. This series enables the beginner readers, who have progressed through mainly phonetically oriented books, to 'have a go' at reading normal text. Direct speech is coloured red, which helps considerably, especially when teaching the formal concept of direct speech. Some six books make up the *Rescue Stories*.

The *Rescue Reading* books are graded according to reading age. They range from 5;6–6 years to 9–9;6 years. Each group of books in the range is made up of between 6 and 12 books depending on reading age.

'Starpol' series

Ginn publish the *Starpol* series. This series is comprised of books that pay attention to the idea of space travel. The books are very well illustrated, with considerable attention to detail. Both colours and illustrations are dynamic, and favoured by boys and girls alike. The text is modern, and the language used calls for fairly sophisticated reading skills. The idea of these books is to have high interest, low reading – although some of the words are rather advanced. What makes these books so popular is, without doubt, the clever use of colour in the illustrations, combined with contemporary text.

Other titles

The *Collins English Library* is comprised of a whole series of graded readers for students of English as a second language and for, as the introduction states, 'reluctant native readers'! Certainly the books provide a useful means for the children to get to grips with reading books that have a high interest level but which, in their original form, would be too difficult for them to enjoy at this stage. Some of the books are based on classics such as *King Solomon's Mines*, which have been abridged and simplified. The text is just the same as any paperback book but there are the occasional black and white illustrations. The illustrations seem to be very old fashioned and in need of an update.

The whole concept of high interest, low reading age is crucial for dyslexics, and Learning Development Aids (Wisbech) have a whole

Table 4.7 The reading schemes used at East Court. Interest ages are shown in brackets

Reading Ages in years & months	5-5.5	5.6-5.11	6-6.5	6.6-6.11	7-7.5	7.6-7.11	8-8.5	8.6-8.11	9-9.5	9.6-9.11	10-10.5+
Bangers and Mash (5-10 yrs)						—					
Collins English Library (10-16.6)											
Headwork Readers (11-15)		—									
Fuzz Buzz (8-14)	—										
Heinemann Readers (11-16)					—						
Primary Phonics (5-6)	—										
Ginn Rescue Reading (8-14)	—										
Ginn Reading 360 (5-12)	—									—	
Ginn Starpol (8-14)											
Trog Level 1 (7-11)					—		—				
Wellington Square (7-13+)				—							

range. These include the books by one of the authors (Michael Thomson – the *Castle of Grom* and *Space Pilot* trilogies, which are based on an adventure game book format but with a controlled reading age). Many of the children enjoy these as well as the spelling task adventure stories, *Book of Letters* and *Word Quest*.

By the time the children have a reading age of 9;6–10 years they are on their way to full control of the reading process. Of course, they will need a lot of help and encouragement, and to these ends a good deal of time is spent in reading sessions with the children.

We have all, we suspect, raised our eyebrows mentally to the earnest comment, 'I have read such-and-such a scheme', the implication being 'Therefore I can read and now I want to move on', when in fact the individual had done little more than struggle through a whole series of books without the satisfaction of actually 'reading' as non-dyslexics do. For these children, they have more accurately survived the experience but gained little. Yet, the implication is that they are ready for even greater challenge and confusion, and so the sorry saga continues until such time as child, inexperienced teacher and parents are all colluding in the sham of 'reading'. It is, therefore, a brave and skilled teacher who questions the process and brings sense and reality to the fore. To go back is depressing and substantiates the failure which haunts the child. A negative feeling can predominate. Yet, it need not. Especially when dealing with dyslexic children, truth is vital, as without it one supports a system which is based on 'cover ups'. It is therefore vital that when a child is failing to read, one must ask the question 'is what I am doing not relevant for the child at this time? Can I teach the child in the way he or she learns, rather than **make** him/her learn the way I teach?' Recently, a PhD student who was dyslexic wrote a piece for a journal about what it is like to be a dyslexic, particularly focusing attention on the style of her learning and making the point that dyslexics do have strategies of coding information, be it visual or auditory, via their own systems which can be quite different from the accepted orthodoxy and which will vary in both style and success depending on the day and their dyslexia level. Clearly, then, we have a duty to listen to dyslexic students and learn from them how we can become more effective teachers.

Equally, one must have a clear rescue package up one's sleeve. It is therefore important to have a clear reading scheme which allows for 'rescuing the floundering child'. It must be a scheme which is new to the child and have an interest level match, otherwise you are wasting your time. It is important to refocus after the discovery of non-reading. We will not dwell on exactly what non-reading is, but we all recognise the syndrome. It needs our specialist help, and we must not fail the child.

The child who does not make the jump from non-reading to reading along with his peers, say after one year, clearly needs specialist help and guidance. Of course, we would expect in the normal course of events that a failing child would be picked up before then. It is the individual who appears to be reading, certainly having a 'real go' at individual words, but who is unable to manage the higher level reading tasks, who may slip through the net. We should add here that we really do not subscribe to the concept of 'free reader' once a child has acquired the basics. This applies particularly to the dyslexic student, who left to his/her own devices at this early stage will probably flounder. We support the concept of maintaining continuing support, certainly until such time as it is clearly apparent to everybody that reading has become a joy – evidenced by the fact that every spare moment is spent deep in their book. In our opinion the dyslexic is not a 'free reader' until such time!

All too often, we are depressed by our visits to schools where an inflexible reading scheme is in evidence. The child follows in sequential order, and in rigid progression, a whole series of schemes which are narrow in the extreme and do not allow either breadth of passage of fluidity and are aimed at moving the child in a speedy progession from one reading scheme to the next without thought or clear monitoring of how the child is progressing, if indeed he is. Targets are the be-all and end-all. The child's actual ability to read, absorb and, most importantly, enjoy the process of reading comes a long way down the list of priorities.

Equally, library periods provide the children with an understanding of how libraries work and, importantly, allow them access to the reference section. The use of reference books is now so important a part of any child's education that to ignore the valuable contribution that these books make is unforgivable. Yet, at East Court we are faced with many children who have never had the workings of even a simple library explained to them, or how books can provide us with so much information. Figure 4.3 gives a diagrammatic presentation of how a library may be used both for fiction and non-fiction and reference books.

As reading skills develop so do other related skills which allow the child to make use of books, not only for reading enjoyment and the expansion of the child's imagination, but also for the development of written skills. The child increasingly patterns on the style, vocabulary and sentence structure of the books which he reads.

Finally, by the time children have progressed through the wide range of reading schemes, they are normally proficient enough to use the library. This does not mean that children are kept rigidly to reading graded text and working their way slavishly through the whole range of books; rather the reading scheme underlies the widely based approach at East Court to the teaching of reading. As the child progressively masters the reading process, so he has ready access to a wide range of books. However, it is important to underline the necessity of teaching the child the reading process so that he can enjoy using the library and reading books.

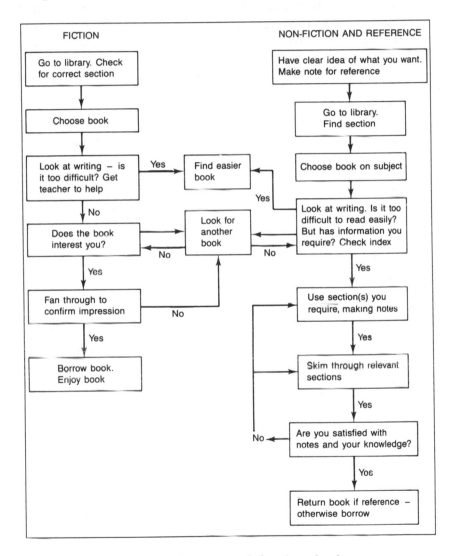

Figure 4.3 Diagrammatic flow diagram to aid choosing a book

I Can Read books, published by Young Puffin, provide interesting books based on two characters – 'Frog' and 'Toad'. These books aim to provide 'proper books' (whatever they are?). The pictures in the books are, like most, attractive and the text is large and easily read whilst the vocabulary is controlled to provide a set of books that are much enjoyed by the children at East Court.

Some of the 'Young Puffin' books are classics in the making. The books by Maurice Sendack are of particular note. However, these books are best enjoyed by children who are well on the road to reading success. The 'Young Puffin' range of books is extensive, and it is beyond our brief to review them. Needless to say, books by Roald Dahl, Rosemary Sutcliffe, Alan Garner, whilst not forgetting the classics of C.S. Lewis, are all eagerly read by the children. However, the reader is referred to the many catalogues available from publishers which all vie for our attention.

Chapter 5
Spelling

Introduction

Although both reading and spelling are part of the written language process which we teach, it is useful to provide additional teaching information under two separate headings. This is because reading and spelling require some different skills. Spelling makes different demands on cognitive subskills depending on the context in which it is used. Spelling individual words out of context requires either accessing and assembling sound–symbol relationships or, in some cases, accessing a whole word image. This must then be output to the speech or writing system. Spelling in sentences or in written work also requires those higher order semantic and syntactic skills required in reading.

Many of the approaches discussed in this book can help spelling, but it is also necessary to focus on specific techniques for the spelling process. Many non-dyslexics seem to generalise quite readily from reading of the occasional spelling word list to the whole process of spelling. If only that were the case for the dyslexic! In this chapter some procedures are outlined for the teaching of spelling. The particular technique chosen will depend on the level of written language competence, the particular learning style of the child and the type of material to be learned.

Teaching Techniques for Spelling

Written language structure

Although we shall be relatively brief here (having discussed structure in Chapter 3), this is perhaps the most important approach with dyslexics. The ability to apply alphabetic or phonemic skills (whether grapheme–phoneme or phoneme–grapheme) will enable the spelling of regular words. A thorough grounding in phonics, as discussed in

Chapter 3 and elsewhere, is a crucial component in the basics of spelling. Much of spelling involves the access of a word, whose sound can then be 'disassembled' or analysed into its constituent parts. Each sound unit, whether it is a syllable, vowel sound or consonant blend will have a matching group of letters for its spelling. These are often exclusive, thus (br) is always spelt 'br' in English. (The problem for dyslexics is of course homophones, spelling choices and irregular words!)

Although described elsewhere, it is worth stressing that following speech, sounding out of letter groups and use of regular phoneme–grapheme links are necessary. For spelling of large words children can be encouraged to sound out the beats in words, and undertake a syllable analysis. Appendix VI gives lists of multisyllable regular words that can be used for spelling exercises. It is helpful for some children if they write down the syllable as they spell the words. Thus if the teacher says magnificent the child can write 'mag'nif'i'cent'. This is done by the child repeating the word, syllable by syllable. As each syllable is said, it is written down; thus 'mag' is said and written mag, 'nif' is said and written nif and so on. This breaking up of the words into smaller units draws attention to the fact that each syllable is in fact easy to spell. This is a tremendous boost to confidence. The younger children at East Court in particular love spelling longer and longer syllable words. The cry 'Can we do a 10 syllable word?' is often heard! If these words are dictated syllable by syllable they can be spelt correctly even by severely dyslexic children – a great source of pride and amazement (even a way of generating extra pocket money!). The syllable analysis and exercises mentioned in Chapter 3 (page 88) and Chapter 4 (page 112) are very helpful for spelling.

Multisensory techniques

'VAKT' approach

It is a basic tenet of teaching the dyslexic that multisensory techniques should be used. These are based on the integration of sound, vision and touch. *Multisensory* teaching involves linking the three perceptual modes in the teaching of reading, spelling and writing. *Visual* shape of letter, word, sentence – visual perceptual skills required. *Auditory* sound of letter, word, sentence – auditory perceptual skills required. *Kinaesthetic* muscles in talking and writing – motor skills required. A typical diagram showing these 'linkages' is given in Figure 5.1. It is proposed that difficulties in any of these linkages can create problems in written language. The teaching techniques developed are those used by Gillingham and Stillman (1969) and Hickey (1977) and are sometimes referred to as VAKT (visual, auditory, kinaesthetic and tactile). Basic routines from these approaches are given below.

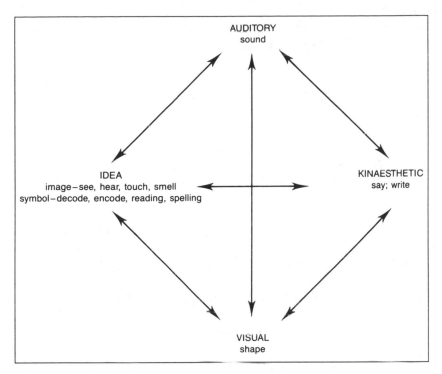

Figure 5.1 Linkages for multisensory teaching

The Gillingham and Stillman technique involves learning phonograms by eight linkages. These are given below.

Linkage 1
A card with a letter is presented: pupil looks while teacher gives the name of the letter; pupil repeats. Once the name is known the procedure is repeated but now the teacher gives, and the pupil repeats, the sound of the letter (visual–auditory : auditory–kinaestheic).

Linkage 2
The letter is made by the teacher. Its orientation, where to start in writing and the direction of movement are discussed; pupil then traces over the letter, copies, writes it from memory and then with eyes averted (visual–kinaesthetic : kinaesthetic–visual).

Linkage 3
The letter is shown; pupil names; teacher may move pupil's hand passively to form letter (visual–auditory : kinaesthetic–auditory).

Linkage 4
Teacher dictates the letter name; pupil writes (auditory–kinaestheic : auditory–visual).

Linkage 5
The letter is presented: pupil gives its sound (visual–auditory). This is the important linkage for reading.

Linkage 6
Teacher gives the name of the phonogram: pupil gives its sound (auditory–auditory).

Linkage 7
Teacher gives the sound, pupil gives the name of the phonogram (auditory–auditory). This is the important linkage for oral spelling.

Linkage 8
Teacher gives the sound, pupil writes it (sometimes with eyes averted) and gives the name (auditory–kinaestheic : auditory–visual). This is the important linkage for written spelling.

There are a number of basic drills that are aimed at reinforcing these links. Another example of multisensory techniques is the British adaptation of the above approach by Hickey (1977), widely used in the UK particularly by the Dyslexia Institute, an organisation having a number of assessment and teaching branches throughout the country. It should be pointed out that this is only a sample taken from the spelling pack; the programme is very detailed and structured, and indeed it is recommended by Hickey that the teacher undertake a specialised course in its use. The course is based on the teaching of phonograms or sound–symbol pattern(s) in a systematic way.

The spelling pack consists of 50 cards whose purpose is to present the written sound so that the learner can listen to them and spell them, if necessary in their several possible ways. The teaching procedures are as follows, for the sound ($\bar{\imath}$):

Teacher or learner reads the sound aloud	Learner: eyes averted
	Listens to the sound ($\bar{\imath}$)
	Repeats the sound ($\bar{\imath}$)
	Spells the sound by naming the letters i, y
	Writes the letter(s), naming each one just before writing

Later, he may add the irregular spellings 'igh' and 'ie' to the (i) card, noting their correct positions.

The pupil has multisensory practice for spelling.

Auditory	He listens to a sound
Oral	Speaks the sound aloud, links to the name(s) of the letters in its possible different spellings

| Kinaesthetic | Uses movement to write correctly the spelling alternatives, naming each before writing |
| Visual | Sees the spellings he has written and learns their different positions in words or their order of probability in words |

Further procedures are described for spelling, and the above example is mainly concerned with learning basic sound–symbol correspondence or individual letters. The same kind of approach would be undertaken with more sophisticated spelling patterns, suffixes or blends. Another important component is syllabification. This teaches various kinds of patterns, such as vowel/consonant/vowel or vc/cv, v/cc and so on. Indeed the child is encouraged by exercises to learn the forms of short and long vowels in respect of syllables, and this particular aspect of written language is made explicit.

Simultaneous oral spelling (SOS)

This is really an offshoot of the above, and used in the 'VAKT' programmes. There are a number of different versions of the technique, but the following are the important components

---

SOS methods for learning spelling

1. Teacher (or another) says word, this engages listening skills.
2. Child repeats whole word, reinforcing sound and enabling the following of speech.
3. Child names letters or sounds in the word. This helps mapping of sound–symbol correspondence and reinforces sequential letter combinations.
4. The word is written, each letter being named as it is written. This provides a motor or kinaesthetic memory, mapped onto the sound and shapes of the letter.
5. The word is read out loud, reinforcing visual to-auditory component, following speech and letter–sound correspondence.

At East Court our own particular method of SOS involves the children themselves working in pairs. This requires some initial training of the children in the procedure, and close supervision at first. Each child is given a 'difficult word list' of 10 words. These are chosen for each child. Sometimes they might be particular language structures, e.g. all CVC words, or light, flight, plight etc. Alternatively the words could be key basic words, either regular or irregular, or the words might be taken from the errors made in essay or other written work. Examples of key word lists are given in Appendix V, and a typical word list is shown in Table 5.1; it is a set of CCVC (consonant blend) words.

The word list is used daily, each child taking 5 minutes at the beginning of each English lesson (the procedure takes longer at first). This is the protocol for two children called, say, Bill and Michael. Bill takes out his word list and gives it to Michael. Michael reads out the first word and then Bill repeats the whole word aloud, and then spells it out letter by letter (names), Bill then says the whole word again. Thus, Bill says frog, f–r–o–g, frog. Michael then says 'yes' or, if the word is incorrect, makes Bill repeat and spell until it is correct. Bill then writes the word down, saying each letter *as he writes it*. Bill then reads the word out loud. If all is correct, Michael puts a tick in the appropriate box for that day (Table 5.1 shows 4 days of word list work), and goes on to the next word. An error is given a cross. This is done for all the words. Bill and Michael then change roles. The procedure is repeated every day for 10 days, representing two working weeks. Any words with one or more crosses go on to the next word list. If a word has 10 ticks it is deemed 'learned' (although we know with dyslexics that is may well be forgotten later!). We make a point of having re-tests of words already learned every few weeks. Normally these take the form of class challenges. This is where every child's list is read out and points can be gained for the correct spelling of 'own words' and 'other words'.

Table 5.1 Simultaneous oral spelling word list (difficult word list)

	1	2	3	4	5	6	7	→ 10
frog	✗	✓	✓	✓				
grin	✓	✓	✓	✓				
plan	✓	✓	✓	✓				
ship	✗	✗	✓	✓				
chop	✓	✓	✓	✓				
slug	✗	✗	✗	✓				
stem	✓	✓	✓	✓				
thin	✗	✓	✓	✓				
crab	✓	✓	✓	✓				
smug	✓	✓	✓	✓				

The above procedure covers many of the subskills mentioned previously and is a useful ongoing programme to develop spelling.

'Fernald' Tracing Technique

The Fernald Tracing Technique is similar at first glance to the techniques described above. However, the difference with the Fernald Tracing Technique is that it is essentially a modified 'look-and-say' method. The additional element is the tracing involved. Here the child learns a whole word, rather than any kind of phonic analysis and synthesis of the word. The Fernald Tracing Technique is particularly useful when teaching words which are irregular or new words that need to be learned quickly, and is also very useful for words that are required frequently but cause difficulty. In practice the method is slow, but it provides a method of whole-word learning for the child to whom 'sounds' mean little. A detailed description of the Fernald Tracing Technique now follows, taken from Myers and Hammill (1976) and Cotterell (personal communication).

Stage 1
(a) The word required is written for the child, regardless of length, with a wax crayon in large print on a strip of paper (e.g. 2½ x 12 inches or 6 x 30 cm).
(b) With finger contact, the child traces over the word, saying each part of the word aloud as naturally as possible as he does so. He repeats this as many times as is necessary until he is able to write the word on a scrap of rough paper, saying it, without looking at the original copy. (If he looks to and fro, he breaks the word up into small meaningless units.)
(c) The word should always be written as a whole unit from the beginning, in the case of interruption or error it should be started again.
(d) When the word has been written correctly in rough, it is written in the story, under a picture etc., the child saying it quietly as he writes it.
(e) Several words can be taught in this manner, and the child can start to make his own book about anything of interest to him. Working through high interest is an important feature of this method and motivates the child.
(f) Whatever he writes should be typed out by the teacher so that it is read back in print the next day.
(g) A word file is needed to hold a child's words. This should be alphabetically indexed (an old shoe box makes an excellent word file). In filing his words, he learns to identify the initial letter of a word and it is excellent training for later use of a dictionary.
(h) Words learned should always be used in context so that they are experienced in meaningful groups.
(i) The amount of tracing necessary per word depends on the child and the length of the word being learned.

Stage 2
This is the same as stage 1 but tracing is no longer necessary. After a certain period the children can learn a new word simply by looking at it, saying it over to themselves as they look and writing it without looking at the copy, again saying each part of the word as they write it. They should always read back what they have written afterwards, and the 'printed copy' next day. When vocalising a word it should not be a stilted, distorted sounding-out of letters and syllables so that the word is lost in the process. It takes a little practice to get the connections

established between articulation of the word and the hand movement. Children should stop tracing when they seem able to learn without it and it should be dropped gradually. First there is a decrease in the number of tracings, and then certain words are learned without it.

Stage 3

Children learn directly from the printed word without having it written for them. They merely look at it and say it to themselves before writing it.

'Visual inspection' methods

Many non-dyslexic good spellers tend to check whether a spelling is correct or not by looking at the word. They know what the word *looks* like. Unfortunately this strategy does not apply to dyslexics – in fact most, if asked to re-read a sentence, will read what they think they have written, rather than what is actually there! Expecting dyslexics to proofread their own spelling is therefore an unrealistic goal. It is a pity that most teaching procedures for learning spelling rely on visual inspection methods. A typical framework is given below (from Reason and Boot, 1986).

Visual inspection method for learning spelling

1. Look – try and remember it. Pronounce it carefully; look at the difficult bits. Are there any clues?
2. Cover the word – think of the spelling
3. Write – write it correctly without hesitating. Does it look right?
4. Check that it is right

Repeat the process until you are sure of the word

Each of the above stages (1–4) presents a number of problems for the dyslexic:

Step 1 The word has to be read correctly; the dyslexic needs to know what are the difficult bits, i.e. what is unusual or irregular orthography

Step 2 The word has to be remembered correctly – visual memory for the look of it, and auditory memory to remember the sound–symbol correspondences

Step 3 Requires further load on short-term memory systems and there is no on-going check at this time. If the wrong word is written this incorrect word can become part of the motor memory. Thus the incorrect spelling is being taught!

Step 4 Matching check required, dyslexics may make errors here

---

It may be seen from the box that many of the dyslexic's weaknesses are the very skills required by this method, and no additional help is given in the form of alternative strategy or rubric. It is not surprising that dyslexics find this type of learning very difficult and we do not recommend it. In one of our evaluation studies we found that non-dyslexics matched on spelling age were able to use both an 'SOS' method (see page 119) and a Visual Inspection method; whereas our dyslexics made no improvements with a 'Look-Cover-Say' approach, only with a multi-sensory approach (Thomson, 1991).

Mnemonics

Mnemonics can be a very useful tool for the spelling of those difficult words that are resistant to learning any other way. They can also be helpful for learning key words for certain subjects at school, or words particularly needed by that child. Of course it is unrealistic to learn all words this way, and some children are better at using them than others. Overloading children with hundreds of mnemonics is unnecessary, but a lot of fun may be had in providing them. Many children love producing their own mnemonics, and these are often the ones they remember best. One word of warning – do make sure that the children understand the principle of mnemonics. One of us can clearly remember telling his younger group that 'Eat Apples Up' will help you remember how to spell beautiful. Whenever one of the children in the group spelt beautiful he would write one of his usual wild guesses. Fortunately, before patience was entirely exhausted it became apparent that he had not realised that the clue sounds E(at) A(pples) U(p) were the letters in the difficult, irregular part of the word beautiful. Explaining the connection improved the spelling of the word dramatically! Mnemonic connections must not be taken for granted, and will often need explaining in detail for some dyslexics. Some of the favourite mnemonics at East Court are shown in the following box.

Some mnemonics helpful for spelling

Beautiful	Eat Apples Up or Everton And United
Necessary	Never Eat Cheese Eat Salmon Sandwiches And Remain Young
Hear (heard, hearing etc.)	You hear with your ear
Because	Big Elephants Can Always Understand Small Elephants
Tuesday	You (u) Eat Sweets day
Thursday	You (u) Are Silly day

Examples of deliberate mispronunciations to help spelling

Don't say friend say	'fry–end'
Wednesday	'Wed – ness – day'
Blancmange	'blank – man – ge'
Does, goes	'do – ez', 'go – ez'
Machine	'maxh – high – nee' or 'Mac-hine', famous Scotsman
Salmon	'sal – mon'

Spelling Rules

Spelling rules are a collection of short sentences that aim to give the children a logical strategy which, when mastered and applied, allows them to spell hundreds of words. The advantages are that they allow the dyslexic to apply logic. After all, Crystal (1987) quotes from one USA study where a computer analysis of some 17 000 English words showed that 84% of words were spelt according to a regular pattern. Only 3% were so unpredictable that they had to be learned totally by rote. It seems that the generally accepted figure, often quoted, for English words is 75% regular. However, of the 400 irregular words, it is observed that they figure frequently as words used in our everyday language. This, in effect, means that the dyslexic will need to make use of a large percentage of irregular words and will, like most of us, perceive that our spelling language is essentially irregular. It is as though our English orthography is 'An impossible code devised by a learned committee whole sole aim was to confuse as many people as possible'.

It is in an attempt to regularise spelling that spelling rules have been devised. Certainly, they receive a lot of attention in programmes devised for dyslexic children. They remove, to a considerable degree, the apparent illogicality, irrationality and arbitrariness of spelling. Taught prop-erly, they can act as a powerful means of helping the dyslexic child. The proper teaching implies that the rule is *not* just written on the board to be copied then applied for specific examples before moving on to 'more important things'. This kind of approach leaves so many questions unanswered that it adds to a general sense of confusion. It is often contended that rules turn what is a natural process for the children into a dry, boring, systematic process. This may be the case for many children who come naturally to reading and spelling and who have never experienced any kind of real failure in their acquisition of English. For the dyslexic, however, the spelling rule acts as a lifebelt. Let us consider the analogy of the 'lifebelt'. For non-swimmers, the lifebelt acts as a life-giving support and allows them to remain afloat and to make progress towards safety. For the swimmer, the lifebelt acts as an unnecessary hindrance. In many ways, spelling rules offer dyslexics a means of support that allows them to remain afloat. Of course, our aim is to encourage dyslexics progressively to master a given rule as a stage in their development towards understanding of the underlying process. This will, it is hoped, allow them to bypass the cumbersome rule and automatically spell the word correctly. This does happen progressively, but not, in our experience, without the proper teaching of the rule.

Some rules, devised by non-dyslexic helpers, seem to us to defeat the whole concept of rules i.e. a simple structured and logical approach to building words by applying rules. They are so complicated and obscure that they do not work. Even simple rules, like 'i before e except after c' can be so confusing for the dyslexic that they are self-defeating. The idea of 'i before e except after c' expresses the concept of position and sequence as well as exclusion. This must be attended to by the dyslexic in the middle of actually spelling a word which potentially contains an 'i. .e..' spelling pattern, e.g. receive or believe. The fact that the word will, in all likelihood, be in the middle of a sentence further underlines the developing complexity of the process. For the dyslexic faced with these tasks, it is little wonder that they find what initially appears as a simple aid to spelling incomprehensible. It is for this reason alone that it is vital that any rule must take into account that, to be of any help, it must be easily understood and must have clear examples which fully illustrate the action of the rule. Further, considerable overteaching must be undertaken until the process of step-by-step analysis and application is second nature.

Later in the text some of the processes will be analysed which the dyslexic is faced with when he attempts to acquire a spelling rule. However, before doing so let us consider some of the disadvantages which attend a rule-oriented approach. In the first place, the concept of overloading the dyslexic appears to be implicit because some of the rules are quite long, e.g. rule 10: possessive from the Gillingham–Stillman manual.

The singular possessive of nouns is formed by adding 's to the singular: Tom's knife, the child's toy.
The plural possessive is formed by adding an apostrophe to a plural ending is s: The boys' knives, the rabbits' burrow; and by adding 's to a plural not ending in s: men's voices, women's work, children's laughter.

The possessive of personal pronouns does not require an apostrophe. The form of the word indicates possession: his, her, their

The possessive form of an indefinite pronoun does require an apostrophe; one's, anybody's, nobody's, everybody's, somebody's.
Anyone's, no-one's, everyone's.

Certainly, as far as we are concerned, the above is somewhat obscure and long-winded! Yet for some pupils, it can act as a valuable reminder of a concept. Naturally, each stage or segment of the rule would need to be taught as a unit and it subsumes that the underlying process, i.e. the concept of singular, possessive, noun etc. will have been mastered prior to teaching the rule. We might add that we do not teach this rule!

Another criticism is that of the idea of learning by rote. This is easily dispelled by the application of mastery of each stage and part, the idea being to gain mastery of the process rather than learning the actual rule 'warts and all' by rote. Another criticism often made is that rules ignore the irregularity of our language. This is certainly true – but then, as we have indicated, some 75% of our English language is regular, and we are attending to three-quarters of our spelt language. Irregular words need another form of attack. We find mnemonics help here, especially if they are made up by our children! (See page 145.). Equally, deliberate phonetic mispronunciation can help, e.g. 'do – es', 'go – es', 'clim – b', 'lam – b', 'tom – b'.

Some English teachers cannot see the point of rules. They rely on the osmotic process and general teaching. Now we know that this works for many: equally we *know* that it does not for the dyslexic! One of the criticisms which seems at first to be eminently sensible is that spelling rules stultify the child's creative writing. Indeed, rules can result in a non-thinking approach. We support the general principle of encouraging freedom, diversity and creativity. Yet, the fact remains that without the crutch, aide memoire or spelling rule, the dyslexic child would be floundering. Finally, it is often contended that spelling rules are taught slavishly, then not used and are soon forgotten. Certainly this can be the case, and then criticism is fully justified. However, used properly, fully explained, frequently referred to and, most importantly, understood by the child who has to use them, spelling rules can be a lifebelt.

The reader is referred to Appendix VII for a listing of spelling rules used by us. However, we shall make mention of some of them by way of introducing them and explaining how we go about using them. We make use of the Gillingham–Stillman manual as our course book for spelling rules, but note that there are a whole range of teaching books which list spelling rules. It is refreshing to note in their introduction to spelling rules first published in 1960, some 30 years ago, they make comments which appear to be as fresh as the day they were written. The words of advice refer to prerequisites which we have, in many ways, reiterated here.

> Better never to teach a rule at all than to leave it a memorised statement without an established habit of use.

> A rule may be memorised in a lesson (sic) but the fixing of habit to ensure its foundation requires weeks, perhaps months during which the pupil encounters numerous unexpected situations where it must be applied.

Below are listed the first three spelling rules that we teach, and comments about their use.

Spelling rule no.1: The f, l, s rule (known as the flossy rule)

Words of one syllable, ending in f, l, or s after one vowel, usually use ff, ll, or ss.

> *Example*; fluff, pull, fuss.
> The cli<u>ff</u> is ta<u>ll</u> and covered with mo<u>ss</u>.

Simple spelling tests help anchor the rule into long-term memory.

Equally, writing of sentences supplements the process, e.g.
1. The clock fell off the wall.
2. The pig had a stiff leg.
3. The brass ball fell from the hall wall.

As soon as the child has gained an understanding of the rule and can apply it with a good chance of success, then we introduce exceptions. Normally, some 'clever clogs' will have immediately made mention of this and bus being exceptions!

Exceptions: if, clef, pal, nil, gas, this, as, us, yes.

'If', 'yes', 'us' and 'this' occur every day and are not normally a problem because most children either spell them correctly or soon gain mastery.
There are, of course, many words that we find as exceptions but that are not really used frequently, e.g. soul, deaf and err. Our aim must be to establish a system that deals with the majority of words. After all, we are not attempting to provide the children with every exception to a rule. Rather, we are aiming to give them a thorough grounding and a means of survival.

Spelling rule no.2: double the final consonant

This is perhaps our most popular rule. It appears to be a valuable rule which is relatively easy to understand. It is helpful and easily remembered by the children. It is known as the 1,1,1 rule.
Words of one syllable ending in one consonant, after one vowel, double the final consonant if the suffix begins with a vowel. Do not double if the suffix begins with a consonant.

> *Example*:   big, bigger, bigness.
> run, running
> step, stepping, stepped
> wet, wetter, wetness

The method of teaching this rule is described on pages 78 and 79. Naturally, it follows that a thorough understanding of both the terminology used as well as the concept of the rule is fundamental. Because dyslexics tend to be disorganised in their approach to spelling, relying very often on inappropriate or inefficient strategies to aid them, e.g. visual recall to decide how a word is spelt, it follows that rules allow for a logical, systematic, reliable approach to aid spelling. It is important that a system of teaching is utilised that calls for a 'concrete' checklist which will aid the dyslexic child. To these ends a number of aids have been developed to help. These ask for a considered approach and encourage analytical thinking. This does away with many of the early, inappropriate learned strategies of self-help.

Rule no.3 in the Gillingham–Stillman manual calls for analysis of accent patterns in the last syllable, e.g. be – gin = beginning, but o – pen = opening. In our experience, this calls for subtle phonemic awareness and the ability to differentiate where a stress is placed in a multisyllable word. This ability is entirely lacking in many of the children we teach. This is not a reflection on IQ, rather it calls on a skill that a majority of dyslexic children do not master until they are much older. Some never acquire this ability, and it is unrealistic to ask for it; therefore we do not teach this rule until much later.

We teach the magic 'e' rule, as it is easily understood and soon mastered and is easy to recall. This is knows as spelling rule no.3 at East Court.

Spelling rule no.3 (known as magic 'e' rule)

Words ending in silent e drop the e before a suffix beginning with a vowel, but do not drop the e before a suffix beginning with a consonant.

Example: hope, hoping, hopeful

The few exceptions to the rule are soon mastered, normally as they occur rather than making a point about them.

Exceptions: Words ending in -ce or -ge retain the e before a suffix beginning with a or o, e.g. peace, trace, change, charge – (able).

These three spelling rules are the mainstay of our spelling rule teaching. We expect the children to have a thorough understanding and be able to recall what each rule is about as well as being able to apply the rule. To these ends we have a number of worksheet checklists that test them. Of course, it does not follow that the children will always slavishly apply the rules in the right situation! However, we have found that automatic application of the rules does appear to be evident in the majority of cases by the time the child leaves us.

Other rules that we have found useful, and use as the need arises, are rules which cover regular plurals, plurals of nouns ending in -s, -x, -ch or -sh and plurals of nouns ending in -y. This gives us six rules to use in the normal course of events. Other rules can be used if they are found to be useful, but it is our experience that long lists of rules defeat the whole point of the exercise. By the time any dyslexic has used all 17 spelling rules he will be well on the way to becoming two things: (1) a theoretically perfect speller; (2) overloaded and confused by the sheer weight of the information! Clear classroom reference material should be presented on the walls.

Naturally, some of the many rules may well help the older dyslexic –
indeed, it is our experience that they can act as a very useful reference
source together with a good dictionary and the *Pergamon Dictionary of
Perfect Spelling* to boot. More will be said about the older student in
Chapter 7 (page 175).

Using Dictionaries

Dictionaries are reference books that list words in alphabetical order
and provide information about spelling, punctuation, grammar, meaning and use. It is a book second in importance to the Bible and held in
respect by most people, yet for the dyslexic it is a 'closed' book, a book
of unfathomable mystery. It is held by both teachers and parents as the
child's saviour. The problem for the dyslexic is that many of the things
the dictionary does so supremely well can only be utilised by an individual with certain skills in written language. These are the very skills
the dyslexic uses supremely badly, e.g. alphabetic order. The word listings and individual letter order that seem so logical to a non-dyslexic are
a complete mystery to the untutored dyslexic. The dictionary has minimal letter change together with considerable written information which
all too often completely overloads and confuses the dyslexic. The
spelling problems of the dyslexic child are too often answered by the
well-meaning, but misguided, response of 'use your dictionary'.

As we have been at some pains to explain, the dyslexic does not automatically assimilate our written language – in many respects written
English must be learned almost as a 'foreign' language. Its inherent
structure, pattern and rules must be taught together with the finer styl-
istic points which make our language both an endless challenge and a
delight.

It follows that the ability to make use of dictionaries allows the user
access to a rich source book. However, before dyslexic children can, as
it were, join the 'club' they must undergo an apprenticeship. This
implies that they first understand the code or alphabetic system, sound-
to-symbol correspondence and sequencing; have visual and auditory
awareness; and can discriminate pattern and sound, sound-blending,
letter ordering and letter patterns.

Alphabet

The question posed is 'Where do we start?' The answer is really in the
form of another question: 'What does the child know?' Assumptions
about what a given dyslexic knows must be treated contemptuously –
they are dangerous. First make sure that the alphabet is known and can
be repeated – not just the rote repeating. Individual alphabet letters in
wood or plastic can be a very useful resource – indeed, great fun can be

had using them to learn and master the alphabet. We use the words 'learn' and 'master' as two distinct concepts. To learn implies a process that will ultimately lead to understanding and mastery. For the dyslexic, learning is fraught with many pitfalls and understanding may not automatically occur. We all note the child where 'the penny drops' after learning. Often this does not happen for the dyslexic, but it is assumed to have done so. Mastery occurs when the process becomes automatic. A simple way to start alphabetic work is to spread out letter cards in a semicircle. Then begin the process of dividing into quartiles etc. Of course, sequencing of letters is a vital prerequisite to mastery of the alphabet and the ability to alphabetise. These specific subskills need to be mastered before the children stand any chance of becoming proficient at using their dictionaries.

Simple computer games beginning with serialisation and sequencing of the alphabet work well to these ends. Equally, random ordering of letters which have to be alphabetised can be incorporated to good effect. We have devised a number of computer games that employ the idea of task-specific learning, i.e. we have a clearly defined target to aim at – e.g. mastery of sequencing of the alphabet. One of our games requires the children to complete a named sequence of letters. The teacher can decide on letter sequences that he or she wants the child to learn, e.g. a, b, c?. The child types in the missing letter to complete the task. Alternatively, a random sequence can be chosen, e.g. j, k, l?. The number of letters in the sequence can range from two to five. Equally, the number of letters missing from a sequence can be decided on at the outset by the teacher prior to the child having a go. Say a sequence of five is chosen with three missing, then something like this would appear on the computer screen: C – – F – . The child is required to put in the missing sequence of letters against time. Time record is made by a bleep sound. When a given series of sequences is completed then the game is finished and the time taken to complete is presented on the monitor to the child. This is a very popular game. A task has been taken which, done on paper without the time element, could become boring. The 'gadget effect', as we term it, means that invariably the task is enjoyed. Games are a vital tool in our armoury. Following on from this, other ways of alphabetising using cards or worksheets can be utilised.

The youngest children are expected to begin a 'lifelong friendship' with the dictionary right from the start. After gaining mastery of the alphabetic sequence, quartiles are introduced as important markers. The mnemonic 'Elephants make Squirts – EMS' is taught. The pivotal point is noted, e.g.

A	E	M	S	Z

^

Experiments to verify this are conducted, followed by a game of 'target practice.' This involves the child with graph paper. Essentially the child draws as shown in Figure 5.2. At this stage only the key letters are looked at, not the whole words, e.g. 'C'. The aim is to find the place in the dictionary that contains 'C's. It will be noted that in the game 'target practice', letters are plotted up the left-hand side of the graph paper whilst the number of attempts is plotted along the bottom (left to right). The aim is to try and get a bullseye or direct hit on each 'go'. There is no time limitation at this stage. The child is encouraged to think carefully, using the quartile strategy taught to aid accuracy. Give this game prior to specific teaching of quartiles and then after, for a dramatic demonstration of increase in skill ability. Self-confidence increases by the minute! Follow this, for example, by reducing the number of moves to find a given letter. This will lead to careful consideration of where a given letter occurs in the dictionary before a move is made. The challenge, then, is for the child to gain the least number of moves to find a given letter. A numerical score can be arrived at (number of 'goes' to target). For example: letter aimed at – C; letter found – E; score 2. Letter aimed at – C; letter found – C; score 0. The lowest scorer at the end of the game is the winner.

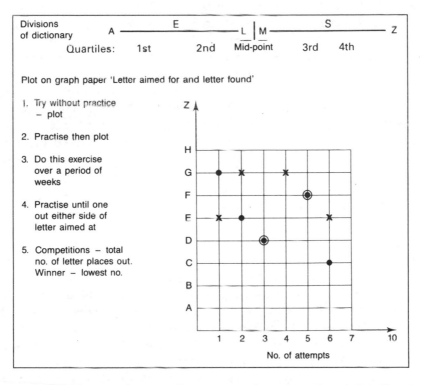

Figure 5.2 Dictionary techniques: ● Letter aimed at; x letter found; ○ bullseye

This may be followed by finding simple words such as 'cow', 'dog', 'mat' etc. The word will be copied from the board by the child, e.g. (1) look, (2) say, (3) write. Naming the letters as the child writes, finally, (4) read. Try for three letter words to begin with.

It is at this juncture that 'key words' are introduced. These are the words at the top of the page of the dictionary in bold type which indicate words to be found on a given page, and the individual letter range. Key words need explaining carefully, e.g. 'key words' indicate the first and last words on a given page. The letter sequence can be used logically to arrive at a given word. With practice it is possible to use these 'key words' as useful markers on a given page. Many children take some time to master this stage. Once mastered, it makes word finding much easier, because the child can use the 'key word' to target a given sequence of letters prior to finding the word. It cannot be emphasised enough that mastery of the process really does open up the dictionary for any child, and it is well worth the investment of time to securely establish this skill.

Once the sequence of the alphabet has been mastered, then it is time to teach the attendant skills of alphabetising. This is the precursor to full use of the dictionary. For many dyslexics, the idea of alphabetising does not come naturally – indeed, it is a skill, like learning the alphabet, that calls upon memory areas such as sequencing, temporal ordering, directional movement and short-term memory which the dyslexic has a particular difficulty with. The structure will need to be learned carefully, and clear explanations and demonstrations will have to be given. It is important to guide the children through the process and allow them plenty of practice (the idea of overlearning). Given this, the concept of alphabetising is soon understood, but practice in ordering whole words, both monosyllabic and polysyllabic, is called for. Old telephone directories can be used to these ends to make the point clearly and allow initial 'fun' practice before the full dictionary is used. Children see a practical use of alphabetising in using the telephone directory and yellow pages, whilst mastery of the dictionary is the ultimate goal. Full mastery of a dictionary is the objective for the dyslexic. It is for this reason that we encourage a large measure of fun in this discipline. To these ends we often introduce the whole process of dictionary practice under the guise of 'Sherlock Holmes', i.e. we, the children and the teacher, act as detectives questing for logical clues in the process of solving the dictionary riddle. Props such as a deerstalker, pipe and magnifying glass can be used. We are detectives looking for the 'Red acid drop' (clues), i.e. the targeted word! As skills progress so the speed element is introduced. Speed of word finding is vital if the children are in any way going to compete on equal terms with their non-dyslexic peers. The game of 'Cowboys' is introduced at this stage – see the box on page 155.

It must be realised that some words – those that have silent letters, e.g. ptarmigan, euphonium, Europe, gnat – or have difficult letter combinations, e.g. blancmange, pneumatic, salmon – or some homophones such as sun/son, rain/reign etc. – or phonetically confusing words such as pheasant/phone – will be very difficult to find. A dictionary which we have found useful and is much used by children at East Court is the *Pergamon Dictionary of Perfect Spelling*. This dictionary contains a listing of words, many of them commonly mis-spelled, with the phonetic mis-spelling, e.g. fesant, fone, in red with the correct spelling in black presented beside them. We have one in each classroom and they are well-thumbed. Another useful dictionary like this can be found in the Franklin Spellmaster, a pocket computer.

Cowboys – a dictionary game

The aim of this game is for two 'cowboys' to find chosen words in their dictionaries in the least possible time. Two words are chosen at random by their teacher and written on the board e.g. 'cat, dog'.

Two cowboys are chosen and issued with dictionaries.

Two assistants (seconds), who act as referees, are chosen. They check that no cheating takes place. They cross over to the enemy cowboy and stand close by to check that the word found is correct.

The two cowboys face each other across the room, dictionaries held like guns. Quips like 'This room ain't big enough for both of us' etc. (as used in all good cowboy films!) are encouraged. Either cowboy 'draws' to start game. The cowboys then search through the dictionary to find the first word.

The first cowboy to find a word is checked by his assistant, and then allowed to 'shoot' the opponent. However, both words have to be found to win the game. The aim is to put two 'bullets' into the opponent and despatch him to Boot Hill. If the wounded cowboy can find the first word (e.g. cat) before his enemy finds the second word (e.g. dog), then he shoots, and both are then wounded. The first to find both words wins by shooting his opponent twice. The cowboy shot twice dies dramatically and is carried off to Boot Hill. The next two cowboys begin play. This is a great competitive game and much enjoyed by all ages – even played in our children's own time!

Some time has been spent on the importance of careful learning of specific skills that will allow access and positive mastery of the dictionary. Having mastered these skills, i.e. the ability to find any word and to make use of the information contained in the dictionary, it is a sad fact that approximately 80% of people never read the important information sheets that begin all dictionaries. These few sheets contain clear information as to how the dictionary should be used to best benefit the user (Crystal, 1987). It is well worth extracting the main points from these opening pages so that the salient information can be explained to the children. Equally, dictionaries have extended use as vocabulary builders, and a few minutes spent regularly teaching vocabulary is time well spent. Some time ago a vocabulary exercise was given to some of our children. One of the words was 'entrail'. An enterprising boy wrote the following: 'I had to go into hospital to have my entrails out.' In many ways this sentence reflects the slight difficulties many dyslexics have with the use of language – they make a slight misuse of words in text. We should say that the vocabulary exercise required the child to find the word and write the page number prior to using the word in a complete sentence.

For the older dyslexic, *Roget's Thesaurus* is a real 'goldmine', and a companion book to the dictionary. Used properly, the Thesaurus aids both word finding and spelling.

Vocabulary development is concomitant with language development. It is for this reason that we never talk down to the children. If the word to be used is appropriate then it is used – followed by an explanation as to what it means. Many children enjoy extending their vocabulary, and make gallant attempts to use newly acquired words in written communication. Often these words are easily learned and retained. After all, they have the strategies needed to learn the words and the maturation. It is the older, first-learned words – such as they, were, there – which were confused at the outset and as a result still cause confusion long after the child has gained mastery of much more difficult words!

Chapter 6
Writing

There are a number of guides to the teaching of handwriting, and it is not the purpose of this section to provide a detailed description of, for example, direction of pen movements, paper positioning or writing patterns. The reader is referred to *The Handwriting File* (Alston and Taylor, 1988) for these details, or Aubrey et al (1982) and Smith (1977). Our purpose here is to make some specific comments relating to teaching handwriting to the dyslexic, to outline what we think are the important considerations, to make some suggestions as to how speed of writing could be evaluated, and to describe the teaching of essays/compositions.

Handwriting

Identification and assessment

We are great believers in 'getting on' with teaching in the classroom, and we would apply this maxim particularly to handwriting. It is usually fairly obvious when a child had handwriting difficulties – the writing is unreadable! It is sometimes more difficult to tease out the reasons for it. Not all dyslexics have problems with writing by any means, and if a child's handwriting is legible and reasonably neat and tidy, there does not seem to be any point in changing writing style. We are not in favour of teaching all dyslexics the same writing style – there seem no educational or psychological reasons for this. However, a number of dyslexics do have problems with handwriting. One reason is, of course, poor fine-motor control or 'graphomotor' problems. The aetiology of this is not clear, but basically implies that the movement control, or kinaesthetic skill, required in letter formation is weak. This might be due to 'neurological problems' or to maturation delay – it might equally be a result of the child never having been taught how to write properly! It certainly cannot be assumed that dyslexics have gained sufficient of the fine-motor control normally found in younger children.

The apparent cause is not as simple as this, however, because it is not always clear where the exact deficit lies. For example, there might be problems in gripping the pen, in arm movement, in visual perception/feedback in checking the letter shapes, or in kinaesthetic control movements. There are also other features to be taken into account. These include:

1. 'Deliberate' small or poor writing to disguise poor spelling.
2. Writing too fast and 'carelessly', either to disguise poor spelling or as response to pressure of being labelled 'lazy'.

Both of these seem reasonable attempts by the dyslexic to 'mask' their underlying difficulties and inevitably lead on to the third factor, i.e.

3. Repeated failure in all aspects of written language – lacking confidence and low self-esteem.

Our view is that it is better to focus on a particular weakness in the writing procedure itself, and try to remediate that. There are many 'check lists' of observations that provide guides – Table 6.1 shows an example.

Table 6.1 A check list for observation of handwriting subskills

---

Pencil grip: holding, pressure, smooth strokes
Positioning: paper, non-writing hand; body/desk
Letter and number formation: names/sound, start/finish position, shapes
Writing patterns: push/pull movements; vertical/diagonal patterns, circular movements
Presentation: relative size of letters, spacing, shape, line use, capitals

---

From Alston and Taylor (1988)

This is adapted from *The Handwriting File* published by Learning Development Aids, which provides more detail and a framework for the assessment of these features, followed by teaching points for each.

Handwriting style

We are not great believers in there being only one correct style for the dyslexic. The major criteria seem to be neatness and legibility. If a child has a good writing style it seems pointless to change it, or put him through a whole series of writing exercises to 'improve'. Whether the child has a cursive, italic, 'copperplate' or other style is secondary to the purpose of handwriting – clear communication.

However, if a child has difficulties in handwriting, such as poor legibility, writing that deteriorates under pressure, or is slow, we do teach a particular script. This is shown in Figure 6.1. This has the clarity of italic script with the fluency of cursive writing in aiding the production of 'joined up letters'. Once again, we would stress that we only teach this to those whose handwriting is at basal level.

Laterality

It frequently happens that teachers and parents are faced with the problem of a left-handed child starting school in a 'right-handed' world. Because the written forms of language scan from left to right in English-speaking (and many other) countries, it would seem that the left-handed child is at a disadvantage in acquiring this one-directional skill. He will have a motor tendency in the first place to write from right to

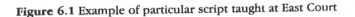

Figure 6.1 Example of particular script taught at East Court

left on the page. Then, when writing in the *required* direction, a left-handed child will be obscuring his line of text as he writes, thus depriving him of some continuity of experience.

There will also be conflicts of direction, both perceptual and motor, and therefore a tendency to regress, or make non-fluent movements or inconsistencies in the slope of writing. Sometimes a left-handed child is also left-eyed and will be visually scanning the material from right to left. Consequently, spelling patterns become disturbed as well as the arrangements of words in a sentence; in fact, he will have difficulties with fluency of reading and writing in general. Because of these ambiguities in direction, work is slowed down and undue time has to be taken to complete the ordinary demands of prose writing.

What advice could be given, therefore, to help a child with these left-sided tendencies in a right-sided world?

It is very difficult to generalise about modifying the left/right motor/directional biases of each individual child, as each one has a different underlying constellation of laterality ('sidedness'). The *total* behaviour of the child must be observed very closely as he uses hand, eye and foot for all the activities of the day. If the left hand is used continually for all the finer movements of writing, cutting (scissors), painting, spoon, knife etc., it would appear that there is a strong organisational (internal) preference for 'leftness' in motor tasks. In this case it is best not to seek to change to right-handed mode. If, however, the child uses either hand at random for both fine and gross movements and is having severe directional problems in writing and reading, a programme of specific help could be devised starting from a physiological level, which could mean emphasising *right*-handed motor activity in a left/right direction. These children seem to be rare, however, among the total population of ambilateral people (many of whom, although not seeming to have established a hand or eye dominance, in the final analysis prefer one side or the other for motor movements).

Because handedness is a part of an underlying complex organisation in the brain, our advice would be, in the main, not to change children except in the rare circumstances mentioned above (especially over the age of 7), but to give them strategies within their own patterning for dealing with the demands of school learning. These would include, of course, many left to right type patternings, tracings, always starting from a brightly coloured margin on the left (helping the child to notice differences in direction, especially in letters, words, sentences etc.) and using a book marker, both for drawing along the line during reading, and also for moving down the page on the left indicating the beginning of each line of text. Directional awareness can be reinforced in other activities, e.g. arrangement of tools, pencils, play equipment, table placings and everyday objects in life.

Teaching procedures

Assuming that there is a problem with handwriting, it is often necessary to start with the basics. These include discussing the place to start on the page, the notions of left/right or up/down in relation to layout and the concept of these terms. After that, one approach is to take the areas outlined in the checklist and provide teaching in each of them as appropriate to the child's need. Children having difficulties with pencil grip can be encouraged to vary the size of pen, or use special pencil grips to improve holding. The use of carbon paper, to encourage the heavy writer *not* to make a copy or the light writer to *make* a copy, is also useful. A generally relaxed approach is also helpful, as well as correct positioning. A comfortable upright posture is necessary, the paper anchored with the non-writing hand, enabling the writing arm to move freely. The paper may have to be taped down for fidgety children!

Formation of shapes may require practice, with detailed help in the formation of letters. This would include the direction of movement, with arrow cues on large letters, e.g.

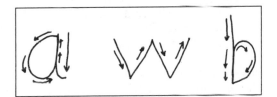

Many children are helped by verbalising letter formation; this can be varied in terms of:

1. Visual (show letter pattern) – auditory (verbal description of movement) – visual–motor (watch and imitate).
2. Kinaesthetic (child's hand guided while eyes closed) to visual–motor (open eyes and repeat).
3. Kinaesthetic – auditory – visual–motor (same as (2), but verbalise).

There are many writing patterns that can be used as precursors to cursive writing, for example

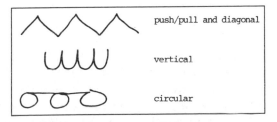

The above are only examples; there are many other teaching points that will be familiar to most teachers. The reader is again referred to Alston

and Taylor (1988) for a thorough and comprehensive review. It would be more helpful here if focus was more specifically on the dyslexic. 'Calligraphy' is taught as a subject on its own at East Court. For the child with good handwriting this involves illustrating their work, or 'illuminated manuscripts' or similar pieces of work. Those with weak handwriting receive specific teaching for writing. Our guidelines for these lessons are given in the box below, and we should like to share them.

Suggested structure of lesson for younger pupils

1. Children to sit comfortably within clear sight of whiteboard.
2. No clutter – files deposited at side of room.
3. Materials – pen, pencil, red pen, ruler, *thick* pad well positioned.
4. Check that all who wear glasses have them.
5. Check that all have all the materials they need (no biros, broken pens etc.)
6. Heading up: Name, capital letter to start, written just inside margin. Date – start in the middle of the sheet and write out in full, i.e. Monday 25th May, 1988. Underline in red. Be very particular about all this, as children continue working well if they have started out on the right foot. Write 'calligraphy' on board for all to copy, carefully and slowly, two or three lines down the page in the middle. Emphasise that they have plenty of time for all this, and reject anything that it not well done. Set a high standard and expect it.
7   Discuss capitals and lower case, shape and direction of letters as the opportunity arises.
8. Break lesson up into two or three parts.
9. Teach a letter or group of related letters. Children to watch formation, copy in air verbalising their actions using stiff arm, repeat on paper. Or teach a 'chunk' of a word, i.e. atch, etch, itch, otch, utch, and move on to related words, match, fetch etc. Make this as multisensory as possible, i.e. visual – watching the shapes; auditory – making the sounds and naming the letters; and kinaesthetic – large arm movements, smaller hand movements and writing.
10. Either children invent sentences using the words they have practised and illustrate them.
11. Or provide related work sheet to copy
12. Alternatively, poems and literature can form the basis of the lesson to copy.

Note: Those who still need to trace should be provided with individual work, i.e. some writing patterns and then written tracing, preferably linked to their interests.

Guidelines for the older pupils' lessons

Generally the older classes can be given a worksheet to copy after the same initial heading-up procedure as the young ones. Those who need special help can be dealt with individually. Pinpoint their needs and give them work to practise before going on to a work sheet. It helps if they watch you write 'chunks' or words for them to copy, discussing the directions, movements, positions and shapes as you do so. Be an encouraging friend rather than a judge. As they will have spent time on individual work, you would not expect them to complete a whole work sheet as well. Emphasise that quality is the aim, not quantity! This is difficult for some of the older children to adjust to when the rest of their school day is geared to high output.

Older children who write well get much satisfaction from the chance to produce a sheet of beautifully written work, decorated and illustrated. Those who really do not need any help, yet would benefit from extra time spent completing spelling work sheets or reading, can be given work of this nature. As with the younger pupils, do not accept anything but their best efforts. It is surprising how much pride children gain from completing a piece of beautiful written work. After all, normally they are struggling under the ever-present pressure of completing work against time.

The end product of the above may be a set phonic work written out well, or an illustrated picture/handwriting of, for example, the Jabberwocky or part of the Ancient Mariner. The former shades into structured written language work, the latter into art. In order to link to other aspects of the curriculum, work sheets can be made using material that covers other aspects of English work: extra English, drama, maths, science, history etc. Any material that lends itself to repetition or sequencing is appropriate, e.g.

Days of the week
Months of the year
Numerals .... also, sixth, seventh, eighth etc.
Alphabetising
Poems and rhyming word sequences
Colours
Singular and plural words
Gender
Names of animals and their young
General knowledge
Vocabulary lists etc.

Calligraphy lessons can give opportunities for the dyslexic's need for over-learning. The poem they read in extra English, the vocabulary they came across in spelling lessons or geography can be seen again and copied.

Writing speed

Writing is, of course, not just handwriting, letter formation and motor control. Written expression, particularly essay writing, will be considered later. There is, however, a midway point between handwriting and written expression. We have called this 'writing speed', and it involves speed of handwriting and also 'thinking' time. The thinking time might be creative in the sense of producing stories, poems or essays, or it might involve manipulating words or ideas already given. Many dyslexics are daunted by the thought of writing, and often will only write a few lines. Dyslexics can be helped to write much more (by the time the children leave us at 13 years old they are capable of writing three A4 page size essays in an hour!). How is this achieved? Perhaps the most important component is essay planning, which we discuss in the next section, but writing speed is also important.

The first is to evaluate the child's writing speed. One way of doing this is to undertake a set piece of writing from which a score can be obtained. This can be done by writing 10 words out at the top of a piece of paper. These should be at the child's reading and spelling level. The child is told that these 10 words must be used to write 10 separate sentences. He should also be told that neatness, capital letters and full stops are important, but that they will be timed. Then time him for 10 minutes. If a child uses up the 10 words, provide more at once as it is the timing which is important. Once the 10 minutes are up, simply add up all the words and divide the total by 10 to give a words per minute score. The above is adapted from Bramley (1984) by Mrs J. Jeffery, one of our past English specialists.

Table 6.2 shows two examples of the exercise undertaken by the same child about a month apart. In the first instance his speed was only 2.9 words per minute, but in the second instance this had increased to 6.0 words per minute. Although only a rough and ready guide, this system does provide the child, parents and teacher with a standard piece of work in a timed situation. Improvements that occur can be a real motivator and booster of self-esteem to the child, as well as a useful record of improvement in evaluating teaching. Re-testing can also be compared with other pieces of work showing improvement in grammar, neatness, sentence construction and time. The exercise can also be repeated as often as necessary, and more complex words can be used to stretch the child's ability in sentence construction and fuller sentence writing.

A number of exercises and ideas for teaching can be used to help this development; some of those used for the case illustration shown in Table 6.2 are described below.

The major technique to develop writing speed is self-dictation. A passage is chosen by the teacher, and the child dictates it onto a tape. The passage must be recorded in phrases or short sentences, with pauses for writing down the dictation. The length of pause is determined by the children, who leave a big enough gap to write down the words. This is done for the whole passage. When the tape is played back as a dictation exercise, the children are not allowed to stop the tape but can only use the pause to write down the particular phrase! Inevitably the first attempt is a complete failure as the children do not leave a long enough pause. This teaches the children a lot about their own speed; the slow-

Table 6.2 Two examples, a month apart, of 'writing speed' exercise*

Example 1

from those who click move stood garden sort cloud dry

I got a letter from someone in my old school.
Those people were beating me up yesterday.
In games I click my knee badly, so I retired hurt.

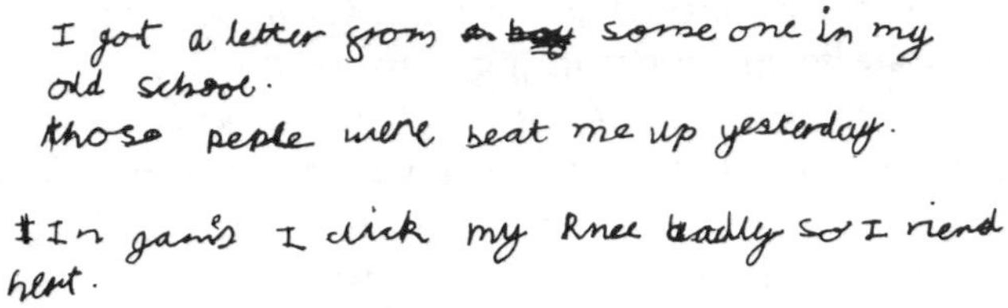

[handwritten text]
I got a letter from ~~a boy~~ some one in my old school.
Those people were beat me up yesterday.

‡ In games I click my knee badly so I riend hert.

Total: 29 words, 2.9 words/minute

Example 2

plastic dentist weather pencil soft book tree trainers rat queue

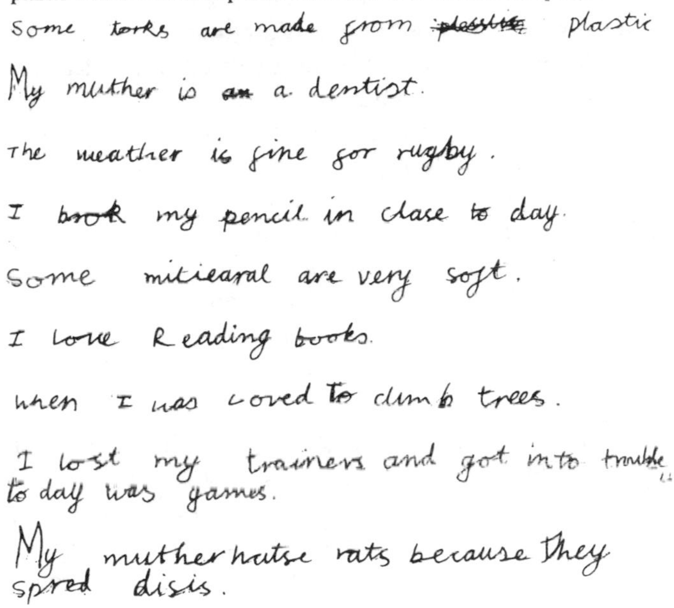

[handwritten text]
Some forks are made from ~~plastic~~ plastic

My muther is ~~an~~ a dentist.

The weather is fine for rugby.

I brook my pencil in clase to day.

Some miticearal are very soft.

I love Reading books.

when I was coved to climb trees.

I lost my trainers and got into trouble to day was games.

My muther hatse rats because they spred disis.

Some forks are made from plastic.
My mother is a dentist.
The weather is fine for rugby.
I broke my pencil in class today.
Some materials are very soft.
I love reading books.
When I was loved to climb trees.
I lost my trainers and got into trouble today was games.
My mother hates rats because they spread disease.

Total: 60 words, 6.0 words/minute

*All spelling has been corrected, but grammar and choice of words is original.

ness of their writing is always a surprise and sometimes a shock! When the exercise is repeated, they will leave longer pauses (usually not long enough again). The exercise can be repeated many times, and without realising it the children increase their speed of writing in order to fit into the pauses. They become very aware of their own limitations, and self-improve.

The above exercise has additional advantages. It can be used as unsupervised work, separate from others in a group for any length of time required. We do not advocate spending long on this task at any one time; rather regular practice is the ideal. The passage can be geared to the child's own reading and spelling, and might even include particular letter patterns to reinforce phonic work. It is also a lot of fun for the child and can boost confidence, self-esteem and motivation. Improvement is self-monitored and becomes obvious.

Another technique is paragraph-writing. Here the teacher chooses a topic, and the child is required to write a paragraph of about 100 words, and times himself. When he finishes the number of words the time is recorded, and his own words per minute worked out. Again this is very much a self-monitoring and awareness exercise. The self-monitoring with a stop watch makes it a 'fun' way to improve competence and develop speed.

Before moving on to essay planning we might also help the child to realise that a one, two or three page essay is not impossible in terms of actual writing speed. This will be discussed in the next section.

Essay Writing

The student's ability to communicate ideas via the written word is all too often taken for granted by teacher and lay person alike. Yet, for the dyslexic, it can be an impossible task. Verbally proficient, they are able to communicate spoken ideas without difficulty, yet getting their many ideas down on paper is all too often an insurmountable task. As we have indicated, much of our time at East Court is spent trying to overcome this state of affairs. Particular emphasis is placed on the formal acquisition of skill development which will lead on to the ability to write formal essays, especially for children of 12–13 years of age. The development of essay writing techniques is actively taught. Fundamental to this is our ability to help dyslexic children organise their many thoughts into a coherent pattern and to give them the ability to marshall and structure their ideas. As has already been mentioned in earlier sections, development of underlying skills will progressively allow the children to communicate ideas via the written word. This is encouraged from an early stage. By the time the children join our leaving group (12–13 years) they will be reasonably proficient but essay-writing skills will need further honing. The suggestions in the following figures, however, apply also to older age groups.

An early introduction to the notion of 'thought plans' is made. Of particular use is the notion of key words. The following box presents one way of approaching this, and we often discuss this as a way to begin any essay topic with the children.

Thought plans

Key words
1. Brainstorm – think of *anything* to do with the topic. Write down key words
2. List key words – write down key words in order of importance, reject irrelevant words. Prepare to rearrange order
3. Organise words – mark off into paragraphs
4. Clothe words – put words into sentences and fill out

Another way of organising ideas and essays is to develop them graphically by linking up boxes. This is preferably used for the auditory dyslexic as it allows the stronger modality, i.e. visual, to be utilised in an attempt to help the dyslexic. This is particularly useful with children who are doing flow diagrams in computer work, and links well with the idea of bringing the computer into everyday work. Figure 6.2 shows examples of this, and is based on the essay title 'The hunter' and shows some ways that ideas can be organised into two different ways using 'flow diagrams' or 'spreading root' formulation. Because of the difficulties in organising sequence and getting the order of ideas right, we normally opt for a

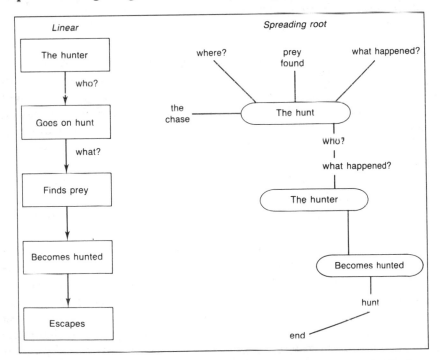

Figure 6.2 Organising by flow diagram or spreading root for the essay title 'The hunter'

linear plan with the children at East Court. The following box details our introduction to essay planning.

Essay planning – Groups I and J

Linear plan (following a line)

The idea is to develop a logical and systematic plan. Starting at the beginning and developing, in a sequential manner, towards the conclusion or end.

A. *Detailed* planning is important.
B. *Logical* progression in sequence must follow.

Ask these questions

1. How long have I got?
2. How many pages are needed? (My speed of working.)
3. Can I, at the start, see my way to the end?
4. How many paragraphs to a page? How many sentences to a paragraph?
5. Begin working on plan – spend approximately 5–8 minutes in 60 minutes.
6. Draw 'Linear plan' outline, e.g. division of line into pages, paragraphs.
7. Jot down ideas; 'sketch out' aim for 'key areas', words, major heading.
8. Fill in paragraph headings.
9. Remember – *Intro*: 'setting scene'
              Development: 'Expansion'
              Conclusion
10. Don't panic! Remember that you are attempting to paint an accurate picture using words.

The aim is to get the children thinking carefully about the task in hand. Considerable discussion will take place during which the 10 points will be discussed at length. It is quite useful to aim for a target number of pages that a child will write. Normally the children are given a timed session in writing for 1 minute. Here any subject is chosen; it may be chair, box, table etc. – this is not important. Our aim is to see how many lines have been written in that time and then calculate from this sample how long it will take the children to write one, two or three pages. It is surprising how many sentences can be written in this 1 minute. Children are very surprised just how much time they do have, even including time for planning and thinking. By the time they leave us, the children are writing three pages of A4 essay within an hour. This is no mean achievement for a non-dyslexic child, let alone for the dyslexics at East Court! We insist that every child undertakes a plan. In a three page essay they divide their plan into three pages. Each page is then divided into paragraphs (say three or four paragraphs per page). Each paragraph must have a key word associated with it, and then that paragraph or key work linked to a number of ideas, either further key words or sentences. The essay must then be written by following that plan, including those key words or ideas that are linked to the plan. There is usually a line written down from start to finish. Figure 6.3 gives you an example of a model plan: the essay title was 'The wreck on the Goodwin sands'.

Page	Paragraph		Sentence plan
		Start	
1	1	Introduction	Set sail, the ship (description), coaster left Ramsgate, Nov. 15, stormy day, cargo
	2	Storm	Storm, dark clouds, rain, wind, waves, lightning strike, navigation out of order
	3	Wrecked	Low tide, pushed onto sands, ship broken up, self rescue, all safe
2	4	The wreck	Find old wreck on sands, tide coming in, climb mast, fear, flash back to good times
	5	Tide in	Cling to mast, see ship go by, signal, don't see you
	6	Tide out	Explore wreck, find skeleton, find gold
3	7	Ghost	Head sound, see 'ghost', really wind blowing skeleton with telescope
	8	Rescue	Sun comes out, dries wood, use glass from telescope, made fire, see helicopter
	9	Take off	Winched up, have share in gold, a tale to tell
		End	

Figure 6.3 A model plan for the essay title 'The wreck on the Goodwin sands'

Initially, the children find the idea of planning an alien one, because they erroneously believe that, given some 60 minutes or the like to write an essay, they will need to begin writing immediately. This is an inappropriate strategy and leads to the discovery, normally within 10 minutes or so, that they have ground to a halt and cannot think of what to write next! However, given instruction on how to go about planning a linear essay plan and then how to apply it, the children soon come to appreciate that we are giving them a foolproof way of writing a good essay. The initial complaint of spending time on planning is soon forgotten in their newly found skill area. To have a plan which allows the child to write following a structure without having recourse to stopping and thinking every few minutes helps no end. At the end of the year, prior to moving on to their senior school, when we discuss how they have perceived our help (or hindrance!), essay planning figures large. Another example may be in a discussion essay. Figure 6.4 shows an example of a 12 paragraph plan for an essay on 'Capital punishment'. Typically, this would involve a discussion in class, and then the class would all think about the paragraphs and put them in order. Finally, they would produce their own plan as a result of this discussion.

Paragraph	(Page 1)
	Start
1	What is capital punishment and for what offences?
2	In what countries is capital punishment still used? Give brief examples
3	What is the situation in the UK? Brief history
	(Page 2)
4	Introduction to arguments: for/against
5	Deterrent: 　　examples to others 　　make you think twice 　　police/terrorists
6	Punishment: revenge by society
7	Stops offenders doing it again. Early release from prison
	(Page 3)
8	Do deterrents work? 　　evidence of history 　　why people murder
9	Mistaken conviction (Guildford Three)
10	Rehabilitation/insane people
11	Uncivilised: religion
12	Sum up arguments: own opinion

Figure 6.4 Essay plan for 'Capital punishment'

Particularly useful in completing linear plans is linking, as said before, with computer program planning. Arising from this there can be a number of activities, e.g. linear plan in terms of logistics, i.e. planning a course of action etc. An example of doing this is to get the children to give instructions to an alien who has arrived on planet Earth and has the language and meaning, but nothing else. They will follow the instructions exactly. We ask the children to give instructions for putting a record on a record player, or making a cup of tea. One of our favourites is getting them to explain how to tie a tie. This involves careful, ordered thinking, as well as providing us all with great merriment when we try to follow the instructions. Exercises like this help with organising thought processes and the sequence of events. Similarly, computer programs such as 'Story writer' (ESM)', or others that enable stories to be built up in a sequential linear way are also useful if linked at the early stages of development in essay plans. Of course, getting the order of events, the plot and having sequential plans right are not the whole story. Writing should be rich and create an interesting and vivid description. This of course implies not only to teaching simile and metaphor, but also to introducing how things could be described. We often use the term 'painting with words'. One way of doing this is to read examples of good prose to the children, asking them to close their eyes while we read. Although we may not all be able to write at this level, we can all appreciate good writing.

With regard to metaphor and simile, we make the point in discussion that our language is rich because of metaphor and simile. Put simply, a metaphor is a figure of speech in which a term is transferred to something it does not literally apply to, e.g. a heart of stone, feet of clay. A simile compares one thing with another and is normally prefixed by 'as' or 'like' e.g. as green as grass, as black as night, a head like a sieve. Just asking a child to describe an activity normally involves the use of simile and metaphor. To supplement this we have work sheets – an example is given in the box.

Work sheet using metaphor

Use a *metaphor* to describe the scenes mentioned.

For example: The moon on a stormy night as 'The moon was a ghostly galleon tossed on cloudy seas'.

1. Waves on a windy day.
2. A boat in a storm.
3. A fire in a dark hall.
4. A daffodil in a green field.
5. A dead tree on a hilltop.

Now make up five of your own scenes, and make metaphors for them. Write these on a sheet of paper.

Below are examples of 1–5 from our leaving groups.

1. The sea was a cavalry of dirty white chargers galloping towards the cliff.
2. The boat in the storm was an acorn in a raging sea.
3. The fire was burning red devils licking the wall of the darkened hall.
4. A daffodil in a green field was a beautiful lady dressed in yellow dancing on green silk.
5. The dead tree was a petrified giant silhouetted against a crimson sky.

Figure 6.5 gives an example of how key elements can be used for attaching description. This essay is normally given after we have dealt with metaphor and simile. The example is taken from an essay about a 'swamp beast' and some similar 'pegs' can be used to describe 'swamp' and 'beast' as illustrated in the diagram.

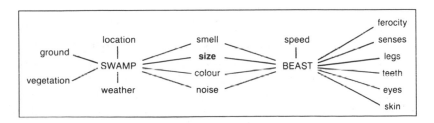

Figure 6.5 Descriptions for the 'Swamp beast'

Use adjectives	Set scene	Description
Alternative words, e.g. hot, boiling, burning, frying, sizzling, scorching, dehydrating, scalding, sweaty	Enter desert	Heat Sand Wind Distance
	Encounter	Colour Vileness, Shape, horror Smell
	Storm	Clouds, flood Cold, rain, sand
	Salvation	Hot again Oasis, cool, green

Figure 6.6 Description, based on an essay 'In the desert'

It is not enough just to give vivid descriptions, it is also necessary to discuss how the child can go about doing this. Again, reading from good English prose tends to make the point. Figure 6.6. shows another example that is based on an essay 'In the desert'. Here it is necessary to introduce alternative adjectives as well as setting the scenes: entering the desert, encountering a lizard (this is part of the essay story) and possibly a desert storm and so on.

Mention of comprehension strategies, an equally important area, is perhaps pertinent here – because the concept of planning is implicit. Many of the children at East Court require careful help to enable them to analyse what exactly is wanted by way of the questions. So often, by misreading a simple verb, they can completely miss the point of the

---

Comprehension notes

1. Read the front (first page) *very carefully*. It contains vital information:
   (a) *Time allowed*
   (b) *Basic instructions*
2. Make sure you read the italicised 'lead in' to the passage
3. Read through the first passage quickly – so you get an idea of what is contained in the passage
4. 'Scan' the questions, noting the marks
5. *STOP!* Now ask yourself the following questions:
   (a) what is the passage about? – think 'linearly'
   (b) what do the questions ask?
6. *NOW* read the first question very carefully – what is wanted? Are there parts to the question – if so, how many?
7. *READ* VERY CAREFULLY the part in the passage where the information is contained. (Normally, but not always, the early questions will be concerned with the first part of the text)
8. *ORGANISE* your thoughts – *REMEMBER* full sentence answers, with proper 'lead in', unless told otherwise
9. KEEP AN EYE ON THE TIME. DON'T PANIC!

question and produce what, on analysis, is a reasonable answer given that the question was slightly different, yet carries no marks because of a simple misreading error. Equally, it is very easy to misunderstand what the question is about because it is phrased in an unusual or ambiguous way. The box on page 172 details one of our overhead projection slides which we use as a basis for discussing techniques and strategies to deal with comprehension exercises.

Grammar

The teaching of 'grammar' to dyslexic children is a vexed question. Our own view is that the teaching of formal grammatical systems, parsing and parts of speech is to place too great a load on the child already in difficulties with the basics.

There are, however, a number of features of grammar that must be learned if literacy is to be acquired. For the dyslexic these need to be *taught* – they will not be acquired from general exposure to literature or reading. In addition, assumptions must not be made about what a child might or might not know. There is no harm in going over what might be old ground with dyslexics. It can always be undertaken in the guise of 'revision' with older pupils, anyway.

The box on page 174 presents a summary of the basic grammatical information required by dyslexics. Anything further can result in overload and frustration for teacher and pupil. The items described use approximate descriptions, as there are often no agreed definitions. For example, 'sentence' has about 200 definitions according to Crystal (1987). It is this very complexity that makes our point concerning the difficulties of teaching grammar to dyslexics. In the items described, it is necessary to teach what the grammatical unit is, and when it is used.

It will be observed that grammar, especially parts of speech, is essentially an abstract, theoretical concept. The dyslexic must have a very firm grasp of the concept before he stands any chance of correct sorting. Parts of speech change with different usage; equally, muddle ensues when every word should be capable of labelling by the child. The complexity of the process is beset with difficulties which the dyslexic unfortunately all too often finds perplexing at best, incomprehensible at worst!

Basic English grammar for the dyslexic

Structure of language

Sentence	In general a set of words linked to form a sense of its own. Operational definition for written work – 'begins with a capital letter and ends with a full stop'
Paragraph	A set of sentences with a similar set of ideas or theme. Starts with the first word indented. Operationally about three to four paragraphs per A4 page
Phrases and clauses	Parts of a sentence
Tenses	Past, present and future

Punctuation

Full stop	Marks the end of a sentence, or for abbreviations (e.g. prep.). Used to separate a sentence, and to pause for breath in reading
Question mark	Expresses a question, indicates intonation for questions in reading
Apostrophe	Used in contractions, e.g. I am – I'm; will not – won't; or to indicate 'ownership', namely the cat's breakfast, the boy's ball etc.
Exclamation mark	Indicates surprise or other exclamatory force
Comma	Many uses! Marking grammatical units, lists etc.
Direct and indirect speech	The use of 'speech marks' or inverted commas to identify the beginning and end of speech. Each new speaker to be given a new paragraph. Distinguishing between this (direct speech) and reported (indirect) speech is difficult for the dyslexic, e.g. 'Come and play', shouted Mark, against Mark asked me to come and play

Parts of speech (word classes)

Noun	Name of person, place or thing
Adjective	Describes a noun (what is it like?)
Verb	'Doing' word (also associated with first, second and third persons, and tenses)
Adverb	Describes a verb (how was it done?)

Chapter 7
The Older Student

Choice of Course

Before we look into study skills we feel that discussion on choice of course to follow must be made. Most schools follow a core curriculum, e.g. English, maths, science, chemistry, geography, history or computing, with a choice having to be made soon after the child has reached his or her fourteenth year. In some cases, specialisation takes place at even earlier ages. There are both advantages and disadvantages associated with this, particularly for the non-dyslexic. However, inevitably for the dyslexic there is considerable disadvantage. Specifically, it pushes them into having to make choices before they are both developmentally and academically ready. Given that the dyslexic will often be a late starter, it follows that skill levels, particularly in core subjects of English and mathematics, may well still be below their full potential, especially at the crucial age when they have to make a choice of subjects. This choice will, in many respects, 'close doors' for good. Once specialisation is followed, they will find it increasingly difficult to change courses. The National Curriculum encourages a broadly based approach and it is hoped will allow students defined as having special education needs under the 1981 Education Act access to specialist help and advice so that some of the pitfalls associated with the wish to promote specialisation at an early age will be overcome. Certainly, consultative documents indicate that help, both in the form of modification of curriculum and increased awareness of condition, will benefit the dyslexic.

GCSEs are normally based on a central core selection with choice being made beyond that. The core subjects are always English, maths, science; choice is normally made regarding geography, history, physics, biology, computing, Craft design and technology (CDT), art etc. English language is often a real stumbling block because the dyslexic is being examined in the formal use of English and little or no allowance is made for his or her dyslexia – the argument being that to do so in this subject would be unfair and would invalidate the whole idea of the examina-

175

tion, i.e. a test of formal, written language (see page 182). Experience tells us that the dyslexic often finds English literature a considerably easier examination. Certainly, examination success is much higher. A number of factors cause this result. First, with literature, the student has a text to read, study and learn, with definable concrete facts from which to hang information. Secondly, there is a finite area of study, with considerable weighting given to sensitive interpretation of text. Thirdly, the student can prepare for the examination by study of the facts. Fourthly, there is a structure within the course books which can be used as a basis for further study and as a means of structuring study aids. With English language, the dyslexic has to face unfamiliar text which must be quickly read and questions answered. Further, essay titles require a particular approach – again starting from scratch. These are all areas in which the dyslexic's handicap is highlighted.

Study Skills

It seems strange to us that study skills are often perceived as something which is not specifically talked about until the student is approaching a senior position in his or her school. It is somehow seen as a disparate skill which, at a certain stage, needs to be attended to – a 'bolt-on accessory' – when the reality is that every child has the right to receive specific study skill teaching right from the first day of entry to school. Indeed, it could be argued that study skills are life skills and strategies of efficient learning should be encouraged at pre-school level. Why there is this delay in teaching 'study skills' at schools until the children are a good way through the educational system is a mystery to us!

Good teachers will of course encourage specific study skills training from the child's first day at school. They will in many cases explain specifically how a child can profit from applying a particular approach to learning a given point. This in many ways emphasises the concept of stage and process; yet it comes as no surprise that there is evidence to suggest that study skills are not seen as a specific area, rather as an adjunct to the process of learning.

In this section we shall stick to the remit of study skills for the older pupil, but we want to emphasise that these skills can and should be capitalised on by many younger groups of children. We shall confine ourselves specifically to the dyslexic, but would add the rider that what works for the dyslexic in many cases works very well for the non-dyslexic. The reverse arrangement, however, as we have been at pains to note, does not work!

Central to study skills for the older pupil is the idea of organisation. Without this vital ingredient, disorganisation and chaos reign supreme. With the best will in the world to 'really study hard', the dyslexic student is, without organisation, skating on thin ice. The ability to see clearly what has to be done in such and such as assignment – to plan a logical approach to the many problems – is implicit, and without it the student is lost. One of the specific problems facing the dyslexic is that of temporal organisation, i.e. organisation of time. It is known that decreasing time coupled with increasing work load can result in information processing problems, i.e. inefficient use of memory and other mental processes. We note that the personal 'walkman' can aid focus of attention for some children when completing homework.

Organisation

Organisation of self is vital. In a school or college setting the students will, in many respects, be left to their own devices; they will be expected to plan their time in an efficient manner. This will range from self-study times or private study to timetable planning as well as organising library visits to gain reference books and to access information generally. Implicit with this will be the need to organise friends. After all, group pressure is a powerful influence and it is important to link study where practical. This may be via paired or shared learning. A group of students contract to complete a given set of study notes, each student being responsible for studying the agreed area in depth and then supplying each member of the group with a set of notes. In this way cover of an area is in depth and everybody can benefit. Of course, it is important that trust in each other's ability to produce useful notes is accepted prior to this kind of arrangement.

Where lists of information have to be rote learned, a system of paired revision works well. We encourage this system at East Court. Equally, talking to an expert in a chosen subject can be most beneficial, especially for the dyslexic who is weak at taking notes. Of course, to do this effectively implies that the questioner has prepared a set of questions which can be given to the expert. Here, taped notes can be used to good effect. Students often overlook the expert information programmes which are produced via TV and radio. Such programmes can make clear a point which has long been puzzling a student. After all, TV and radio have the very best presenters with unimaginable resources as back-up. A video recorder can be of particular use, as it allows the concept of overlearning to be applied. The student can re-run a point on the video in an attempt to make clear a part that he has misunderstood. The reference library is another useful source of information, but it is important that the students are taught how to use it for best results. Equally, a visit to an exhibition can make clear a confused point. An example of this being done is visits we arrange to places such as the Maritime Museum or the Imperial War Museum. Time is well spent on visits to such places, as they allow ideas that have been taught and may well still be free floating to fall into place. Of course, implicit in such visits is the requirement of organisation in the production of sensible and challenging worksheets. The instruction 'write an essay on your visit' will not do!

It is surprising how the idea of chronological time causes many dyslexics confusion – yet concrete examples, i.e. Maritime Museum and Imperial War Museum, 'earth' and make clear the relative time position for many because the information is presented via concrete examples and exhibitions.

For many sixth form dyslexics, time allocation will be a real problem. They will be held responsible for organising their timetable in an efficient manner. All too often, no help or guidance is forthcoming. Coffee breaks of increasing time duration can become the order of the day. Therefore, it is important that some form of help and guidance is given to the dyslexic. The non-dyslexic may also benefit from this.

A clear demarcation of work and free time needs to be made, and then stuck to. We can all recall the students who appear to be working hard, hour after hour – indeed, they are found sitting at their study table with books strewn all around. They are exhausted by the process, yet little tangible evidence of the sweat of their brow is forthcoming. They are in the 'spiral' of working to a point of exhaustion but having little to show for their efforts. Often they are highly motivated. The problem is one of not knowing how to apply study skills. As a result, actual work output is limited and time is wasted through no fault of their own.

It is for this reason that study skills must be taught. Luckily, many dyslexics will have had the benefit of learning skills being taught to them as they progress through a programme of help.

Strategies for working

The idea of 'strategies for working' seems obvious. The first thing to be attempted is to analyse exactly what is required, the objective, the 'target' which we are aiming at. This will imply that the 'target' is known, i.e. what exactly is wanted and when. It will pose the question: 'Which route is the best to take, and how long is available to reach the objective?' A plan of action needs to be arrived at which takes into account these points. Many dyslexics find a diagrammatic approach useful because it allows a clear statement of aim as well as providing a visual prompt.

Forward planning is vital for dyslexics, as experience tells us that cramming everything into the last few hours invariably results in chaos for them. What started out as a good account deteriorates into a sketchy work which is lacking in structure, organisation and fact. A proper plan of action which is realistically related to the timetable and free time available allows the student to gain required information from further reading of reference material. Equally, it allows note making towards the formulation of a well-planned and executed essay.

Having organised a timetable for work sessions, it follows that a degree of self-discipline must be imposed. It is therefore very important to stick to the plan of action. This will involve having to say 'no' to spontaneous impulses, invitations from fellow students and temptations to do 'exciting' things. However, if the students can master their own time, then they are in a position to apply a number of specific strategies to aid their working potential and output. The idea of switching 'off' and 'on' is one which we foster at East Court. We ask that our children work what amounts to a 5-day week, 9 am–5 pm or thereabouts. Lesson time is seen very much as time for serious work. This does not detract from the fact that our lessons can be great fun, but it does work on the assumption that 100% effort is being applied for a number of short periods during every lesson. Break time is a time when the children are encouraged to switch off, relax and change activity. This does away with boredom and allows the children to recharge for the next session of work.

For the older student, often anxious to do well, the fact remains that they often mix up the idea of work and play. This can be quite disastrous, and does not come to light until the end of the first term. We all know logically that we are incapable of working for hours on end at any one task which calls for a multiplicity of hierarchical skills, especially when learning is also involved. Yet, we have all seen students grind themselves into exhaustion by missing this important fact. Our suggestion is that the day be divided into sessions. A change of subject or area is called for, certainly at hourly intervals. This may mean, in essay or project work, that a slight shift of focus can result in the type of change required.

Given that a reference requires researching, then it follows that there are many routes to be used. These may include reading text and making notes. The making of notes calls for special skills. These will include the ability to perceive exactly what the author is saying, particularly the salient points and can be seen as the skeleton. Each sentence would contain a fact; however, the 'fact' may not always be pertinent and will only add a flavour. It is important to impress on the students that, in examinations, facts equal marks. It is no earthly good spending half a page on one point to find that each point, or fact, carries only one mark. Rather, it is better to concentrate on noting down facts, even in a shorthand way. Paragraphs invariably contain a set of facts which go towards forming a major point. One of the problems in making notes is to become sidetracked by the reading process. Reading can, in some circumstances, become a purely mechanical act, i.e. one is only going through the act – no monitoring at a higher cognitive level is taking place. Facts are being missed and precious time is being used up. In some cases the notes made are really a shortened form of essay. This defeats the whole point of the exercise. The student ends up with reams of notes that are far too cumbersome to be of any use in either writing an essay or revision. The secret of note-taking is to fillet the piece of writing for the facts it contains. These are the 'nuts and bolts'. It is easy to clothe them with words once the student has the bare information.

Note-taking

The key is to note facts down in a way that is easily used and understood by the writer, e.g. they must make sense, be reminders of the facts and, most importantly, act together to form a coherent 'whole'. Notes are, in effect, the dehydrated essential information which can be rehydrated by words to form the full picture.

Reductionist approach

It may mean that initial notes need to be précised down to form core notes. This process follows the idea of a reductionist approach because an attempt is being made to lessen the load in short-term memory store, and yet still to allow information to be filed away in long-term memory for retrieval later by a series of key words. An example of this type of approach is used in our essay planning lessons, and this has been covered in Chapter 6. The act of trying to reduce notes concentrates the mind wonderfully and is a learning act in its own right. Given that a string of ten facts has to be learned, then it follows that perhaps a simple mnemonic may help. The idea is to use the mnemonic to aid memory retrieval. An example of this process follows. Moh's scale of hardness used in geology lists ten minerals which are used as indices to the hardness of a given mineral. The mnemonic is:

'The Girl Can Flirt And Other Queer Things Can Do'.

This gives a clue as to the index minerals:

1. The = Talc
2. Girl = Gypsum
3. Can = Calcite
4. Flirt = Fluorite
5. And = Apatite
6. Other = Orthoclase
7. Queer = Quartz
8. Things = Topaz
9. Can = Corundum
10. Do = Diamond

Each key mineral can then be logged, expanded on as to its chemical formula, usage etc. Ten 'bits' of information are held in memory store as keys that further unlock information which can be elaborated on ad infinitum!

Card index

A card index can act as a means of storing information in a logical and systematic way. Having written an essay, the bare bones are filed away on a card index ready for the next call. Of course, it is vital to have a system of card index organisers which follow the agreed original form of course study. This may be alphabetically, or by subject. Card index cards offer a ready means of carrying information around. Every odd moment is important for learning or revision, especially for the dyslexic. Waiting for a bus, queuing for lunch etc. is time that can be profitably used for revision. After all, the dyslexic has to work two or three times as hard as his or her non-dyslexic peer to keep at the same level.

Large wall posters of important facts can act as a constant reminder of things to be learned. These are, in many ways, a larger extension of the card index idea. Certainly, in our experience they work well. The use of different colours also helps to lessen the load and break up the information. Equally, the colours act as a visual clue reminder.

Speed of working

Speed of working can be a real problem. It is for this reason that strategies of self-help are important. Making known the fact that a particular student is dyslexic and explaining some of the spin-offs of this can be of considerable help. Equally, forward planning can help to lessen the workload. Given that the student is slower than his peers, it does not necessarily follow that this is just a fact and nothing can be done about it; rather it suggests that there will have to be a different approach to the work. This may take the form of using a shortened form of work, where lists of information are produced without the endless pages of general waffle which some students seem to delight in producing. Sketching out the plan or route is beneficial in two ways:

1. It enables the student to formulate a brief plan – visually presented.
2. It lessens the load, reduces confusion and aids the student to keep to the point.

Because of short-term memory problems, it often transpires that the student says the same thing in three different ways, thereby wasting valuable time and effort in the process. A plan helps to overcome this weakness.

Reward for effort is a useful idea because, having worked hard for a given period – say an hour – on a particularly difficult part (or even a whole day or a week), it seems a good idea to reward oneself for having achieved a tangible result. We are not suggesting that this be done each day, otherwise it loses its effect, but only when a goal has been achieved.

The reward may be a cup of coffee or reading a favourite book. It need not involve financial expenditure!

Examinations

As well as the basic difficulties facing the dyslexic individual in written language, one of the most daunting prospects is examinations. Examinations are important in their own right, but also the dyslexic individual finds certain qualifications difficult to obtain, such as GCSEs for vocational training courses or other forms of higher education. Examinations in particular demand a high level of written language skills. Thankfully, the old examination system of imposing formal, and in many cases , artificial, trials of memory, has been modified. Many examination boards have an enlightened approach to examinations. The idea of 100% continuous assessment has been adopted in some cases. This seems to many to be a much more appropriate and realistic means of assessing the true ability of a student. After all, few of us face examinations beyond school, yet it does not impede upward progress through a chosen career. Indeed, continuous assessment seems to be, in many cases, a far more effective way of measuring a person's true ability to access and use information. However, the formal initiation rites of our society/education system still apply in the majority of cases. In reading before the examination, the individual will find that lack of fluency and accuracy will make it difficult for him or her to obtain information from set text books. This means that it will take longer to acquire knowledge, and in many cases to read at a level appropriate to the forthcoming examination. Even if the individual has overcome the basic reading accuracy difficulties, fluency and ease of reading may lag behind. Similarly, meaning may get lost due to difficulty in the actual 'techniques' of reading. This is particularly frustrating where 'skimming' is needed for the great amount of literature to be surveyed prior to examinations. In many cases, the dyslexic individual reports that he has to read material two or three times – once for reading accuracy, a second time to obtain some kind of comprehension, and a third time, to try to remember the material. Reading will also obviously affect the actual examination performance. The individual will be handicapped when it comes to reading questions, particularly those questions that require a considerable amount of interpretation, such as English language or literature. Spelling will also present a major difficulty, as very poor spelling will give a false impression of retarded scholarship – the reader focuses on the spelling errors and does not observe the actual content in respect of understanding, or knowledge, of subject matter. This is important in terms of general written language but particularly in more technical subjects. Not only do spelling errors make a very poor impression on the examiner, but they also slow down the rate of work output due to the constant checking required by the examinee. It is for this reason that we advocate the learning of subject-specific spellings.

As well as spelling and reading, other more subtle written language difficulties present themselves. These include inappropriate punctuation and poor grammatical structure, which combine to give the impression of a less able student. Finally, the obvious lack of fluency in writing will handicap the individual considerably. This inability to organise thoughts in written language is one of the greatest problems for the older dyslexic. It results in a tremendous gap between oral comprehension and its written form, which will apply to writing essays, reports and projects as well as in the examination itself.

Even in higher education a tutor can sometimes receive a piece of writing more typical of a child than of a very able engineering or physics student. This incompatibility between thinking power and effective problem-solving, on the one hand, and immature spelling and writing, on the other, is a source of great frustration to the able student. Even worse, it can result in a potentially very able student being refused entry to a higher education course. An interesting observation is the success intelligent dyslexics have in subjects such as geology, science, computing, CDT, engineering/technical drawing, pharmacy, art, photography or geography, if support and understanding are given by the institution to reading and writing difficulties. Such topics would appear to reflect the 'spatial' nature of the skills involved (as opposed to sequential, symbolic systems like written language). Often familial skills reflect these occupations, e.g. engineering, surgery, draughtsmanship, design, athletics and architecture.

Examination preparation

In preparation for the examination it is essential to select examination topics with great care. This applies to GCSE, 'A' level and institute examinations, where time must be spent on considering a collection of five or six of the best probabilities. This will entail discussion with the head teacher and subject teachers, as the combination of subjects chosen might not be the traditional or usual one for a particular school. It has been found, for example, that in some comprehensive schools where children begin to specialise in the third year, they are placed in 'courses' from which subject change is difficult. Parents of dyslexics should be particularly aware of this probability so that early discussion can be held with the school. It is hoped, of course, that wherever possible the difficulties in English language (which present a very special problem for the dyslexic) have been recognised earlier in the school career and some intensive specialist teaching provided. This recognition and special help, together with a report from a qualified authority, will help here. Although individuals are advised to avoid subjects that require a tremendous amount of written language and are very 'literacy' based, this is something unavoidable due to the tremendous interest an individual has in a particular subject. English language, however, is often a requirement for acceptance on training courses, or further education. This presents and invidious difficulty to many dyslexics. Many examination boards will provide allowance for some examinations (see below), but are reluctant to make allowance for English language, their argument being that spelling, writing, syntax and so on are all part of the English language component. It is sometimes possible to obtain a waiver for English language in some higher education courses, if evidence can be provided of dyslexic difficulties, but in many cases the individuals are resigned to having to take English language GCSE a number of times.

Another factor to consider here is the proportion of continuous assessment against examination. It is not advisable to opt for a major continuous assessment option if appropriate tutorial and planning support is not available to the dyslexic. 'Continuous assessment' sounds like the better alternative, but in reality is not always easier than examinations. The former requires a consistent, all year round effort, and unless work is carefully presented and well organised it will present as poorly as a badly written examination paper.

Examination concessions

After selecting the topics with the above criteria in mind, the examinee will need to develop strategies for the actual undertaking of the examination. In the initial stages (preferably at least a year before the actual event), it is important that cooperation is maintained between school, parent and possible relevant authorities. The first step is to check the particular examination board's attitude to written language difficulties. This establishes what kind of allowance it is prepared to make, and in what subject areas. Ideally this checking should be done through the school, which may be able to advise on alternative boards. In some school situations, however, where there appears to be a lack of sympathy for this specific difficulty, it may be up to the parent to instigate inquiries via the school as to the possible attitudes of examination boards.

The next stage is to obtain reports from teachers and an educational psychologist. Any reports can be submitted to the examination board prior to the examination answer scripts, or continuous assessment submission. The report should be as recent as possible, certainly no more than 12 months old, and should normally be sent by the school, or the college or authority where the individual is studying. In addition to a report from an independent specialist, a report from the school is also helpful. This should indicate that the individual has a good ability in the subject area, has produced good projects in oral work and in the class and, in the opinion of the teachers, is a candidate who would normally pass and do well in the examinations, were it not for the written language difficulties.

There are certain important aspects to the report that are worth considering. It is not enough simply to obtain a report saying that an individual is dyslexic. This may not be accepted by the examination board – one reason being that some examination boards do not fully understand the implications of 'being dyslexic'. Further information is required if they are to make a fair assessment of the allowance that is to be made for that individual. Examination boards have standards to maintain, and are particularly concerned that an 'excuse' for poor ability in the subject is not used, or that the individual just does not happen to be particularly good at essay writing as opposed to having a specific learning problem. Typically, they require a report from a psychologist with some kind of reliable measure of intelligence. This is particularly important, as it will indicate that the individual's problems are not due to low ability.

As well as an objective measure of general intelligence, the report should include some measure of current reading, writing and spelling performance. This is important also for the kind of recommendations that should be made to the examination board. For example, if the individual is hardly able to write or spell at all because of a gross or fine-motor control problem, or has very severe reading difficulties, one might want to recommend that either a teacher reads the text and questions to the student, or an amanuensis concession be granted. However, if the problem is less severe, involving difficulty in expressing ideas fluently in written form, one might want to recommend simply that allowance be made for spelling, punctuation, graphic style, and that marking is for content or knowledge of the subject matter.

Specific examination strategies

More specific advice for the examination itself follows. These comments would be helpful to many students, but require even more consideration for the dyslexic.

1. Specific preparation for examinations can take place at least a year before the actual event. This preparation could take the form of practice in short, weekly sessions, in writing answers relevant to the subject being studied. It is necessary, therefore, to obtain copies of previous examination papers. One question per week can be chosen, and a 'model' answer prepared. A teacher (or parent/friend) can go through the answer, checking obvious things (punctuation, capitals, spelling, sentence structure etc.), discussing the answer and fostering care and fluency in expressing ideas. This provides an opportunity to find the relevant content of the subject in question. Another

exercise is timing the answer, as during the examination it is important to allow only a limited time for each question, and it is essential to answer the correct number of questions. (See also Writing speed, page 163.)

2. Develop appropriate study techniques (see page 156).

3. The following strategies for answering questions might be addressed to the student:

   (a) Read the question three times: (i) to check the actual words and ensure correct readings; (ii) to read it for understanding: 'What does it say?; (iii) to read it finally for what question/problem it is posing: 'What does it ask?'

   (b) After making quite sure what is asked, jot down quickly on spare paper all the words, names, ideas (and dates) associated or linked with the question. Anything at all that can be remembered about the topic can be jotted down. Once one or two words are down on rough paper, these in turn will suggest more associated thinking, until between 10 and 30 words are on the rough paper.

   (c) Next 'order' these words into some hierarchy of importance, writing them as a list, with the most important idea or name etc., first. Develop the ability to make meaningful 'sequences' of ideas, names, examples etc., perhaps in their importance to the subject or the steps and stages of the problem: but first, just a list of key words.

   (d) Begin the answer by rephrasing the question in some way, as an introductory sentence. Writing has now commenced on the answer paper! Take key word no.1 and 'clothe' it in a simple sentence or two. Try and write a 'link' sentence to key word no.2, and so on. It is useful to prepare a few typical 'link' sentences to use in answers.

   (e) When the words have been exhausted, write a 'summing up' sentence or two, a conclusion or a short discussion. This will require reading through what has already been written.

   (f) Read through the completed answer, correcting any errors, omissions etc. that are noticed.

   (g) Do not attempt to write too lengthy discussion essays. Use diagrams, flow charts, graphs or block designs whenever possible. Concentrate on making a plan, and writing short, clear sentences that relate directly to the question. Then read the question again; and read the answer so far; finally write a concluding, summing-up sentence.

4. These strategies can be practised on questions some time well before the examination. These 'practice answers' can form very good revision material if they are kept. Begin by writing short answers. Time the answer and, spending 10 minutes or so initially, gradually make

your answers longer. Aim to bring the plan and writing within 35 minutes. It is essential to read the whole paper through first and choose the easiest question for the first answer. Be sure to answer the correct number of questions. This means taking time for at least some writing on the questions that appear more difficult, or less interesting, but which must be answered to complete the requirement.

5. When the examination day arrives, the candidates should be more confident after a year or so of experience of this kind. They will have accustomed themselves to their 'examination strategy' and will know that they will be able to sit down and tackle the questions immediately.

Chapter 8
Computers and Dyslexia

This chapter has required a complete revision, because computer technology has changed so rapidly and, as a result, how we can teach children using computers has inevitably changed in terms of its emphasis. Indeed, we have been forced to change our terminology – now we must describe computers as 'Information Technology'. We expect that within a few years of this edition being published, computers will have changed yet again out of all recognition and what we have written here may seem a little dated. However, there are still some universals, and some of the things we said in the first edition still apply so we have included them in this chapter.

The first of these is that we need to select carefully elements of the computers that we want to use with dyslexics. They need to be relevant to dyslexics' needs and fit into an overall curriculum geared to developing their reading and spelling process. It is not our intention here to describe a general IT curriculum (although we shall use our use of computers at East Court as an illustration), but to focus on those particular things which are relevant to dyslexics.

We should like at this point to draw attention to the excellent series of booklets produced by the British Dyslexia Association, and the Dyslexia Computer Resource Centre, based at the Department of Psychology, University of Hull. They produce a number of booklets including *How Computers Can Help*, *Word Processing and Spell Checking*, *Dyslexia Exams*, *Word Processing*, *Maths Programs*, *Dyslexic Adults and Computers*, as well as specific booklets on particular kinds of computers. We have unashamedly used parts of those booklets in some of our comments and we would urge readers to look at them as they do provide excellent source material.

Using Information Technology in a Specialist School

We have tried to incorporate computers or information technology both as a 'distinct entity' i.e. with a computer room where children are taught IT, as well as integrated within the classroom. We have achieved this by having a computer in every classroom in the school. This is inevitably expensive and something which not all schools would be able to do, but we feel that there are very worthwhile benefits. Not least of which is that it demystifies computers, providing relevant day-to-day work – another tool to use with the children – and provides immediate access and use of computers when required.

We have Archimedes machines, but they could equally be PC or AppleMac compatibles depending on what the school's particular policy is. All the computers have hard disks, printers, word processing software and other general IT software. In addition we have an IT room which has seven networked computers. This enables the room to be used to teach IT, as well as being booked up by other staff to work with their English or maths groups.

Computers are often used as a 'distinct' entity, i.e. with a computer room where children are taught 'computer studies'. The other approach favours the 'integration' of computing within the curriculum. Table 8.1 shows the strengths and weaknesses of both approaches. Obviously the comments can be applied to any educational situation, but we felt it helpful to make these points as an introduction. We shall now turn to the specific use of computers with dyslexics.

Table 8.1 Computer as 'integrated' and 'distinct' elements of a curriculum

Element	Advantages	Problems
Integrated	1. 'De-mystifies' computers 2. Relevant to day-to-day work, another 'tool' 3. Immediate access and use when required	1. Major staff/child training in simple use 2. Expensive or inconvenient (many computers needed, or must be moved around) 3. General curriculum will need new emphasis/re-thinking
Distinct	1. Easier to set up (less cost) 2. Less staff training 3. Less travel time in moving computers about	1. Subject 'boxing' – no cross-curriculum teaching and lack of integration 2. 'Mystique' of computer room and specialists

Computers in the Classroom

The most important use of the computer within the classroom is as a word processing tool. This might be using a talking program, producing a fair copy of work, editing work and the other important elements of using word processing which are described later. Sometimes individual children undertake their classwork on the computer, which can then be printed out. At other times a computer may be used to run particular programs which are aimed at reinforcement and/or teaching, see comments later on using a computer with dyslexics.

If you are using a computer in this way as a classroom tool it does require a good deal of staff training. It is important for each teacher to be aware of using the computer in his or her day-to-day curriculum and lesson plan.

All the children in the school have their own floppy disks. These include word processing and IT disks. Many children bring their own additional disks and/or laptop computers, and we provide a number of laptops in the school as well. We describe the use of laptop computers and some of the important elements which are required later (see page 201). As far as our own school is concerned, all our children have a typing lesson once a week in order to develop keyboarding skills. This gives them a general overall development of typing skills. Some schools like to give the pupil an intensive burst of two or three weeks typing to develop up to a certain number of words per minute in order to help them use word processors and laptops appropriately. At all stages we should emphasise that careful thought needs to be paid to the time constraints and demands of using computers. Children will need to be directed and helped as to when and where they are going to print their work. We have twelve printers around the school (with approximately twenty computers) and this is for only 68 children. There are an additional two printers in the study and the office where one of the Principals or the office staff may be persuaded to allow them to be used for printing out children's work. However, children can still turn up after a homework or essay writing period having failed to print their work out. It is important for the school timetable to take into account times when children can print out their work. One also needs to be aware that sometimes printers will not be working and there can be endless difficulties at times in getting work into hard copy. We cannot overemphasise the need for a 'whole school and staff approach' to the use of word processors and laptop computers in the school.

Information Technology Curriculum

All our children undertake at least one lesson of IT a week. The IT room is also bookable by English or any other staff. Typically, an English group of six may go in there to undertake punctuation exercises, word processing work or other English-oriented programs with the whole group. We have a networked computer room which helps children to learn how to 'log on' and undertake some of the basic interactive requirements, important for dyslexics, as some of the basic routines and sequences required can be quite difficult for them. We cover the normal range of IT which is given in Table 8.2.

Table 8.2 IT curriculum

1. *Word Processing* – Loading up a word processor, getting text on screen, editing, using spellcheckers, printing (see detailed curriculum page 197)
2. *Desk Top Publishing* (DTP) – This looks at ways in which children can use word processors and DTP programs in order to integrate text and pictures. It looks at the way pictures can be positioned, placed on text, how text can be changed in terms of colour, graphics can be used to develop things such as newspapers, poems, illustrations and so on. This work is a natural extension of word processing and we find the Archimedes computers particularly lend themselves to this. We use a program called Impressions.
3. *Database* – This is creating databases, including how to put data into the computer, organise it, search for specific items, print out graphs and generally do analysis work.
4. *Spread Sheets* – Linked to this is looking at how to perform mathematical computations data, but also collation and manipulation of numerical data. One of us (MET) finds that using one of the spreadsheets to keep records of children's housepoints is a very useful way of introducing them to using spreadsheets – particularly as collecting housepoints can give you a biscuit at the end of the week!
5. *Graphics* – This is both importing graphics from 'clip art', colouring, changing as well as developing other graphics from paint and draw programs.
6. *LOGO* – A programming language which broadly creates graphics. See comments later on LOGO.

All of the above are important elements of using IT, but we would like to turn now to more specific details of those things which are important for helping dyslexics.

Using Computers with Dyslexics

Written language activities

Most of the later items we discuss such as word processing, talking computers and so on are written language activities, but here we mean specifically activities which are often used within an English class. A number of programs are used for the overlearning essential with dyslexics. These range from practice drill programs, including ones that we have devised ourselves, to programs that teach particular spelling rules. Typically, children may be taught specific patterns in class and then, to reinforce an exercise, in a work sheet and also on a computer. For example we have a program that practises the 'doubling rule' (swim, swimming, see page 149). The child has to land a space ship in the correct place depending on whether the letter is doubled. There are many practice/reinforcement programs like this. In addition, a computer can be used in planning essays. An example is the use of the program 'Storywriter' (ESM). This enables the construction of story 'paragraphs' that can be read to create different storylines due to branching options. This can be linked to flow diagrams and linear planning (see page 167), adventure game story books and logical sequencing of ideas. For reading, there are a number of programs that produce the so-called 'cloze' procedures e.g., 'Tray' or 'Copywrite' (ESM), which enable us to make text on screen, and which the child has to recreate using guesses from context. The particularly useful feature of the latter is that the teacher can create his or her own texts. A number of appropriate texts can be created and stored on disk. Children can also make their own text, to challenge others. The texts made can be matched to the child's reading level, ranging from one or two simple sentences to a complex text. Material can also be adapted from the child's reading scheme (providing this is for your own classroom use only!). In 'Copywrite' the text is read by the child, the timing being controlled by the teacher. Then the text is wiped out leaving dashes for each letter, and punctuation. The task is to recreate the text. Words are typed in and, if correct, appear at the right point in the text. Words not appearing in the original result in a 'bleep' and points being taken off. The program therefore uses memory, spelling and contextual comprehension skills of children. Points are given for each word, and clues can be given (less points are given if clues are asked for). This can also be used in game format by getting two children, for example, to compete with another pair to see who gets the most points. (Match the children carefully!)

There are many other programs with spelling or reading drills but space prevents us from reviewing them all (see BDA software review). Each English classroom has a number of disks containing these written language programs, which can be used in tutorials with one child on the computer, one being taught. Sometimes they might be used in small groups, or as a 5 minute 'reward' at the end of a lesson. Each child has his or her own disk for written language and word processing work. The self-discovery of the systematic approach needed in keeping records is important. The children realise they cannot rely on short-term memory (weak in their case anyway!), and this helps reinforce the importance of writing.

Adventure games

We find these very useful for the children at East Court, both as a general stimulus for comprehension and written work, as well as for their dyslexic difficulties. Typically each teaching year has an adventure which they do during the year. The titles change from year to year as software changes. There are a number of reasons why we find these (or similar) programs useful. Initially, they provide useful reading practice – they are text and graphics programs, so the reading is limited to a few lines of text at most. The children soon find that if they do not take notes, they will lose their way and not progress! This underlines the importance of keeping logical notes to aid memory. The problems that need solving in the adventure require a logical approach, which helps thinking skills. The adventures also benefit from the construction of maps, useful for directional skills. Perhaps the most important feature is their stimulation of written work, essays or stories based on the text. Also useful are the keeping of log books or diaries for recording progress, as well as having useful links to other areas of the curriculum such as art or music.

Word processing

It is a truism that word processing will be helpful for dyslexics, but it is quite important to be aware of what modifications to the curriculum are necessary and also how one is going to train dyslexic children to use word processing appropriately. Again, the British Dyslexia Association computer booklets are excellent for this, but our own experiences may also be a starting point. We are including a brief case history and the word processing curriculum that appeared in the first edition of our teaching handbook, we well as some other comments, but we are adding further comments on the use of spellcheckers, laptops and talking computers in particular. Often when using a simple typewriter or even writing, one has to arrange text correctly, spell words correctly as well as choosing the actual words used for an essay or the piece of writing that one is working on. The information processing capacity of dyslexics is notoriously weak and expecting them to do all of these things, particularly with problems of sequential order memory, results in quite a considerable overload. How often do teachers comment, 'You can spell when you don't have to write an essay', or children themselves say, 'If only I didn't have to think, write, spell and set out all at once'. Owing to this 'multi-tasking' nature, word processing can help by enabling the writer to concentrate on a small bit or work at a time. In addition, if a dyslexic child is tired he/she can save the work and continue it at a later time.

Keyboarding skills

There is no point in teaching word processing skills, an important skill for life anyway, without some minimal keyboard awareness. This implies at least being familiar with the layout of the keyboard, and 'hunt and peck' typing skills. We expect a lot more, and each child is given a formal typing lesson once a week. We also encourage practice outside the formal curriculum, and that letters or other personal matters be typed or word processed and printed. Although some children will undertake 'typing' on the computer from time to time, the formal typing lessons are on manual typewriters initially. This helps the children develop strength in all of the fingers, especially the ring and little finger. The children can then graduate to electric typewriters or computer keyboards. We are not expecting fluent touch typists, but many children become really quite competent. The teaching also helps alphabet skills, sound–symbol associations and organisation, particularly if exercises are given following their phonic work. We do not use 'concept keyboards' or similar non-standard layouts, as the reality is a 'QWERTY' keyboard, despite its many faults.

Fair copy work

An important part of word processing is to put essays, poems or other special pieces of written work onto the computer. Often the 'reward' for good work is to 'put it onto the computer'. This can be printed out, and copies made to be filed, put on the wall, given to parents or sent to relatives in Australia! Sometimes, particularly for younger children, it can be very time consuming to type all of the work on, so that, for this element of word processing, the teacher can type some of it onto the computer, perhaps taking turns.

Editing

This is a major component, and is linked to the 'fair copy' work of course. Here written work can be corrected and developed from the 'first draft'. This can be done via tutorial, working with the child on the computer, or by correcting the original (or subsequent printouts), for the child to edit himself. The most obvious points are to correct punctuation and spelling, but development of vocabulary, description or sequence of ideas should not be ignored. Punctuation may be added, words deleted, whole paragraphs shifted around to make the sequence of the essay or written work more logical. Systematic spelling mistakes may be corrected by use of commands that change the spelling throughout the text and layout can be improved by justification, use of margins and tabulation. We have found that many of the children take a great deal of pride in producing their work on the word processor and, surprisingly to us, they have no difficulty in translating from upper to lower case and vice versa. Figure 8.1 and the following series of boxes give examples of editing a simple piece of writing.

The writing in Figure 8.1 was produced by an 11-year-old dyslexic boy, after deciding to write about the placement of the telephone box in his village. The first stage involved copying the text onto the screen.

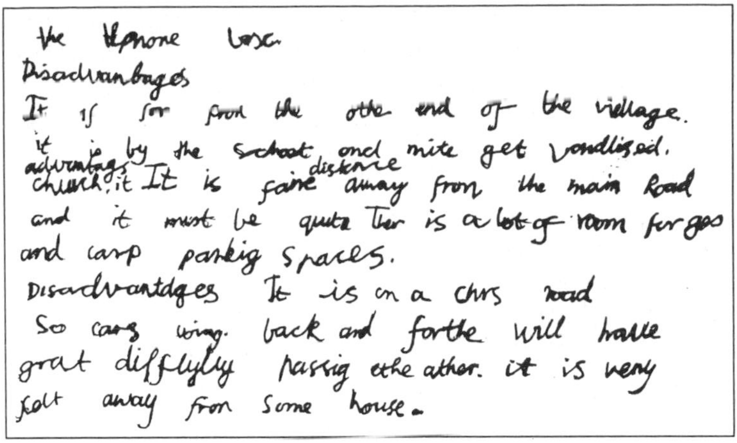
the tlphone box.
Disadvantages
It is for from the othe end of the village.
it is by the schoot and mite get vandlised.
advantags distance
church. it It is faire away fron the main Road
and it must be quite Ther is a lot of room for gps
and carp parkig spaces.
Disadvantdges It is on a chrs road
So cars wing. back and forthe will have
grat difflyly passig ethe ather. it is very
falt away fron Some house.

Figure 8.1 Writing used for the word processing exercise

Spelling was corrected by use of 'type over', 'delete character' and 'insert' (to accommodate new text without losing old). Systematic errors were corrected by use of 'change' or 'replace', e.g. 'fron' changed to 'from' throughout.

VERSION 1

the tlphone box
Disadvantages
It is far fron the othe end of the villeage,
it is by the schoot and mite get vandlised.
advantage distance
church. It is a faire away fron the main Road
and it must be quit: Ther is a lot of room for gps
and carp parking spaces.
Disadvantages It is on a chrs road
so cars eoig back and forthe will have
grat difflyty pasig ethe ather. it is very
far away fron some house.

The punctuation was then tackled using 'swap case' for capitals as well as insertions. The headings were removed and, by the use of markers and the 'Move Block' key, the 'floating' words and the odd sequence of ideas ('disadvantages – advantage–disadvantages') were rearranged. Some words were also changed to improve the sense.

VERSION 2

the telephone box
Disadvantages.
It is far from the other end of the village,
it is by the school and might get vandalised.
advantages distance
church. it is far away from the main Road
and it must be quiet: There is a lot of room for groups
and car parking spaces.
Disadvantages It is on a cross road
so cars going back and forth will have
great difficulty passing each other. it is very
far away from some houses.

VERSION 3
the telephone box
It is far from the other end of the village,
It is on a narrow road
so cars going back and forth will have
great difficulty passing each other. It is very
far away from some houses.
It is by a school and might get vandalised.
It is a far distance away from the main road
and it must be quiet. There is a lot of room for
car parking.

Finally, the grammar was polished up by using linking words and the whole text neatened up by use of 'Justify' and 'Format Block'.

VERSION 4

The telephone box.
The telephone box is far from the other end of the village and it is on a narrow road so that cars going back and forth will have great difficulty passing each other. Another disadvantage is that it is by a school and might get vandalised.

On the other hand, it is a far distance from the main road and it must be quiet there. There is also a lot of room for car parking.

The above example was undertaken by tutorial. Appendix XIV shows examples of prepared work sheets on punctuation, précis and 'expansion' that can be used with the word processor.

All of the above does of course imply skills in word processing. These need to be taught, and are undertaken both by the English teachers and the computer studies teacher. A detailed curriculum outline is given below. We happen to use 'View' and 'Folio', but the actual system is not crucial. We feel that one simple and one more complex word processing system is helpful, for younger and older children respectively.

Curriculum Outline for Word Processing with Dyslexics

Children are taught basic *skills* in using word processing, supplemented by *activities* to develop these skills. Word processing is linked to both English and computer studies curriculum, although the word processing is seen increasingly to pervade all areas of the curriculum.

Objectives for children leaving East Court

- To be familiar with the concept(s) of word processing systems.
- To be familiar with keyboard layouts and have basic typing skills such as paper loading, positioning, line spacing and correct fingering.
- To be able to load, save, print out and access our word processing systems.
- To use word processing for simple editing, planning and structuring of written word.
- To be aware of, and have used in some cases, applications of word processing (e.g. developing of work sheets, writing letters, standardised addresses etc.).

Skills and activities

Skills (1)–(9) below are hierarchical in order of difficulty. Activities are linked to other curriculum work (especially English but not exclusively).

Skills	*Activities*
1. Familiarity with computing system. Using disk and word processing system, saving, loading and writing text on screen.	Writing brief sentences on screen, or doing phonic exercises on screen.
2. Writing and simple editing, use of deletion, addition, insertion.	Changing spellings. Adding words/sentences to prepared texts. Preparing cloze procedures and (later on) punctuation exercises on prepared texts.
3. Writing and printing, using filenames. Storing text, printing hard copy, using printers (simple commands).	Printing out short stories/poems. Fair copy of 'star' work. Keeping own disk/data.
4. Searching through documents, finding sections for editing.	Finding target words/sentences in texts.
5. Splitting/joining lines.	Adding/deleting sentences to texts.
6. Screen modes 'wrap around' screen and printout.	Examining texts in different modes.

Skills	*Activities*
7. Formatting, justifying	'Tidying up' a text.
8. Presentation, layout, highlighting, printer codes. Type of print.	Simple changing layout of texts, changing typefaces of texts.
9. Shifting paragraphs, re-structuring text, use of markers.	Moving key words about, re-ordering sentences/paragraphs, expanding, developing ideas of text.
10. Systematic spelling errors.	Change in text.
11. Tabulation.	Re-tabulate/organise text.

Mathematics

The Maths Department has disks containing tables, games, puzzles, problems and tests at various levels of difficulty. Computerised records of each pupil's progress are also kept.

The programs cover such topics as number patterns, place value, problem solving, logic, coordinates, vectors, geometry, decimals, fractions and percentages. The levels range from 'Derrick the spider, who helps with band of 10' (i.e. tens and units), to 'Governing Britain and devising a Budget'.

These programs reinforce a class topic in a visual, colourful and often in a comical way. Thus the learning process becomes fun rather than a chore.

While some children work on these self-correcting programs, a teacher is able to give another child individual attention.

Games

Of course computers are always available for the children in their free time for 'Space Invaders', other adventure games, personal word processing, personal letters and as a hobby for them to use. The children may book their free time to play computer games. There is always a waiting list.

Staff implications

Before finishing this chapter we should like to emphasise the comments concerning teaching staff and computers. To use computers properly requires considerable staff training and effort. In our case all of our teachers have had training in the basics, i.e. loading and using programs. The English specialists have also had a thorough grounding in the word processing systems. We have regular in-service meetings where the computer specialist might undertake further training, or we look at a particular program.

Value of educational programs for dyslexia

The following four points are taken from one of the BDA booklets and summarises some general principles:

1. Motivation and reward
2. Illustration of new teaching point, as revisionary reinforcement for earlier teaching points.
3. Training in left/right directional aspects of literacy and accuracy in reading response.
4. Stimulus of group interaction.

Maximum benefit if the program is useful educationally, relevant to needs and current skills, foolproof computerwise, easy to use under the supervision of someone who knows the pupils and the programs.

Spellcheckers

We feel that it would be useful to make some comments about the use of spellcheckers. Obviously they are useful for dyslexic children, but cannot be used just without thought i.e. saying to a child 'go and spellcheck your work'. Spellcheckers do vary considerably in their efficacy and some are less suitable for dyslexics than others. Usually they give a series of alternative spellings for a child to write in. Dyslexics inevitably will find that equally as difficult as spelling the word correctly in the first place. Visual memory may be weak, and those children who have difficulty in self-correcting their own work i.e. not being able to recognise when a word looks 'wrong', will be at a loss to decide which word to choose as a correction. Homophones will not be picked up either, as usually the computer will think that these are spelt correctly. Care therefore needs to be taken not only in choosing an appropriate spellchecker, and again the BDA's booklets are excellent for this (booklet C2), but also in how one is going to help the child to use a spellchecker. Ideally this should be in tutorials, in a one-to-one, or certainly a very small group, situation.

Some of the difficulties can be illustrated by the following real-life examples from children* with quite severe dyslexic difficulties. Here are two sentences which the children wrote in answer to a comprehension exercise:

1. What to was is that on the thored day it lokt as if the see had carmed down and the pacenger frlt unconed and less wored and wear not sea sick any mour.
2. He lives in a pore home and lokt as if he was riring ript cles.

What the boys wanted to write was:

1. What happened was that on the third day it looked as if the sea had calmed down and the passengers felt unconcerned and less worried and they were not seasick any more.

---

* The boys who wrote the above have asked us to acknowledge the source, and we are happy to do so. Thank you, David Brenchley and Tom Moremont!

2. He lives in a poor home and looked as if he was wearing ripped clothes.

It is quite clear that a spellchecker would not be able to deal with the initial part of example 1, as it was all spelt correctly but due to omissions, odd grammar and peculiarities of expressing made no sense at all. Example 2 obviously reflects a slight 'w/r' problem in this particular child but is not atypical of many dyslexics.

Table 8.3 shows how various spellcheckers have dealt with these examples. We have divided these into so-called phonetic attempts, real words and omissions/unusual attempts. We have given the examples based on the system on the laptop we used (the Amstrad), the two word processing software packages we use on the Archimedes i.e. Pendown and Impressions Style, and a typical PC word processing software package (Word). It may be helpful for readers to have a go with these examples on their own spellcheckers and see what they come up with!

It is important, therefore, just to reiterate that a spellchecker only compares a word with its dictionary and will not indicate words omitted or added. If the alternative word given cannot be recognised, the spellcheck will not be particularly helpful and many spellcheckers are much better with near misses due to typing errors rather than words with a lot of wrong letters in them.

However, the spellchecker at least does point to words where there may be a problem and where one can go back to try and find the correct spelling, and are a very quick way of finding a word rather than looking it up in the dictionary.

Laptop computers

Over the last two years we have started to use laptop computers in the school. When we use the word laptop, we are really referring to a dedicated word processor such as the Amstrad NC100 (no longer produced) or the Tandy Dreamwriter. It is unfortunate that true laptops are very expensive because they are trying to emulate all the functions of a computer in a small machine, although we do have one or two children who use them. Laptops are often suggested in Special Educational Needs Statements for children who have handwriting problems and also where spellcheckers are suggested. These are often recommended very glibly without any expectation as to how they are actually going to be used, and there are many practical problems which need to be borne in mind. If these can be solved, however, a laptop can be a very useful addition to a dyslexic's armoury against the written language system!

We have approximately half of the school using laptops, some with their own and some supplied by the school for more specific tasks. Many children really do benefit from the independence of taking work around and they can be a very flexible way of undertaking work.

Table 8.3 Types of spellchecker and how they check words

	Amstrad Laptop	Pendown (Archimedes)	Impression Style (Archimedes)	Word (PC)
'Phonetic' attempts				
carmed	**calmed** carved harmed	**calmed** carted charmed	**calmed** warmed carved	**calmed** crammed carved
thea	**they**, then tea	**they**, tea tough	**they**, theta tea	**they**, tea then
mour	four, mourn	**more**, mare many	hour, moor pour	moor, move mourn
watshing	**watching** washing	**watching** wishing outlying	**watching** washing	**watching**
pacengers	no match	**passengers** peninsula	no match	no match
lokt	loft, loot	lost, lofty	loft, lout lost	lot, lost locket
ript	rift, rapt ripe	rift, ripple	rapt, rip riot	ripe, rip rift
Unusual/omissions				
thored	toured	toured thinned	whored	**third** thread
wored	bored wired word	**worried** worked orate	bored, work wired	**worried** world wormed
unconed	no match	uncommon unsigned	no match	unchained uncooked
cles	ales, clef clues	class, clues	clef, clues	clues, cells chess
riring	airing, hiring riding etc.	rearing, racily	hiring, tiring	riding, wiring rising
frlt	**felt**, fret	**felt**, fault fraud	**felt**, fret	**felt**, fret

bold = correct word offered

Power

A very important element of laptops in a school situation is how they are going to be used. Will they be battery operated, which implies that batteries may well run out quickly, or will rechargeable batteries be used? If this is the case, there will have to be a system thought out for how they are going to be recharged, At East Court we put aside our science room for the evening, and racks of laptops are laid out for recharging as appropriate. Using laptops from mains electricity in the classroom can prove difficult – fighting over the one plug in the classroom can lead to disrupted classes! All these things will need to be thought out very carefully.

Printing

It is very important for thought to be given to how work will be printed out. There have been so many times on a Wednesday morning after a Tuesday evening essay has been set for our older groups that children have said they 'did not have time to print out their work', 'there were no printers available', 'the printer in the study has broken down', and so on. One needs to be prepared for the frustrations of work not being handed in due to these difficulties! It is important, therefore, to have lots of outlets for work to be printed out and for these to be discussed carefully with the children, opportunities given for work to be printed and other staff members made aware that this is going to take place during homework sessions. This is not a trivial point as all the staff in the school need to be aware of these difficulties and co-operate.

Keyboarding skills

It is absolutely crucial, as in word processing in general, for children to have reasonable keyboarding skills. If laptop computers are going to be used regularly and the children carrying them around would expect to use them often, they will need to develop useful speeds in using computers. One option is for children to go in intensive keyboarding/typing courses in order to get their words per minute up to a certain level before they are allowed to use laptops; this is an approach that some schools have adopted. We tend to provide typing lessons once a week over a long period and encourage regular practice to get children up to speed.

The above are very important considerations. There have been many times when children have been given laptops or have asked to use them and the facility has fallen by the wayside as they have not been able to integrate all the above points.

The final point, of course, is how the children are going to carry them around the school. Insurance, storage, the particular set-up of a school are other important considerations if laptops are to be used widely around the school.

Talking computers

One of the things computers have lacked until recently is the ability to undertake true multisensory work, in particular the auditory component. At a special educational needs conference recently we were very impressed with dictation systems that allowed a person to speak into a microphone and words would appear on screen as if by magic! These are obviously very powerful tools and we are sure they will develop over the next few years so that they are available to all. With these one is even able to define 'macros' i.e. standard paragraphs such as 'address' which would then appear with one key word.

The dictation systems are currently very expensive and one needs a quite powerful computer. In addition, the computer must be 'taught' to learn your particular voice and to learn new words. We are in the process of trying out how feasible it is to use a computer like this in the school situation where dyslexics are producing unusual spellings and pronunciations for words and also whether a number of different children could use it at different times.

We currently use 'Talking Pendown', which in conjunction with the Somerset Program, is a very useful tool for our children. The Somerset Program involves a series of sentences which are graded from CVC words through silent e, consonant blends and so on. The child looks at the sentences, reads them out aloud, turns the card over and then has to type them in from memory. Whatever particular system one uses, they do show a number of benefits. One can use them either in a structured programme or just in terms of the child's own work.

Talking Pendown has a number of advantages in that it gives consistent and immediate feedback on what the child is typing in. This enables the link between speech sounds and written text, the most important element of teaching dyslexics, to be made explicit and reinforced. Sound/letter links are often linked. It also gives time for pause, reflection and sound awareness when a child is typing onto a speech system. It allows self-monitoring auditory feedback in conjunction with visual feedback as well.

Basically there are two systems for keyboard into sound. The first is where the computer gives feedback by converting text into speech. This can be done by synthesised speech which is rather robotic, although we have to say that we find many of our children do like the 'dalek' kinds of sounds and they take great pleasure in trying to produce words that the computer cannot pronounce or pronounces in a very odd way. The second, of course, is digitised speech which is based on the recording of somebody's particular voice. To make the computer talk when text is typed in is not expensive and can be done through quite reasonably-priced software which should include the following capabilities:

• Speak letters as they are typed in.

- Speak a word immediately after it has been typed by pressing the space bar.
- Speak a sentence on typing in, and also speak segments of words or words which are spelt incorrectly, or non-words.

In addition, some programs will be able to read portions of the text back, create word banks, speak dictionary and spellchecks and alter the pitch and speed of speech and use colour overlays.

(Another fun thing for children to do is to make up their own words and see how the computer pronounces them. All of these games are good ways of trying to develop links between sound/symbol systems and should not be discouraged.)

A talking computer, particularly one which can convert typed-in text into speech, is another useful addition to the teacher's armoury and something which children get great benefit from.

Interactive Books

Interactive books are a wonderful new field that is still in its infancy. Clearly, the development of computer graphics, voice chips and the like has enormous and exciting potential to help us in our quest for better results from our pupils. Having a computer which interacts with you is very exciting and, best of all, it is non-judgemental, has no hidden non-verbal communication systems or hidden agendas! It is able to speak, answer questions, highlight words, present facts, expand and project animations, give sound effects – indeed, all that we recall about that one special teacher who first seeded in us a love of books and their magic!

There is a growing library of interactive books which, we suspect, will progressively enhance the old and largely outdated perception of the 'dusty' world of libraries. Interactive books are an ideal way of giving the dyslexic child confidence in the reading process.

Every subject would benefit from this new approach, which integrates the best from all sources. Maths is an area ripe for this type of treatment, allowing children to explore, develop and clarify ideas. Interactive books encourage oral and visual perceptual skills, call for reasoning prior to activity, and extend vocabulary and word recognition. They also underline the importance of reading for meaning.

Clearly, every aspect of a child's reading development needs to receive attention. There are, as we have already indicated, a whole range of underlying skills which need support. Dyslexics have, generally speaking, a weakness in phonological awareness which centres around the various auditory components. Interactive books certainly have their place in any special needs classroom.

There are a growing number of suppliers of this software, amongst them Four Mation and Sherston Software.

Like anything new, there will be CD Rom publishers promising that their merchandise is the best, but who in reality will have little real concept of the needs of the school or specialist user. We advocate the judicious use of glossy magazines, to be found in most large bookshops. Titles like *CD Rom* and *What PC* give reviews aimed at the general reader. Equally, talking to others and consultation with your school library service to see if they can help, will pay dividends. The market and technology is now moving at such a pace that it is difficult to predict the future.

Clearly, CD Roms have advantages over some books in that they allow the student to delve even deeper into them with just the click of a button, rather than seeking information from reference books via sequencing alphabetically, recording in short-term memory, searching etc. prior to finding. Three dimensional images, music, video predictions and the like are all enhancers. A CD Rom takes less space than a book, is lighter and has the potential to ignite our children's imagination.

America is ahead of us in this field. Edmark, based in Washington, produce a whole range of interactive books. The child creates stories by building from various databases, selecting scenes, introducing characters and planning plots. He/she can add music, dialogue and sound effects. In the process wider learning takes place. The system requires 8Mb RAM and implies that an up-to-date computer is a prerequisite.

Appendices

Appendix I: Examples of Individual Education Plans (IEPs) – English

The general format of these IEPs is one that we use at East Court. They are examples from different teachers to give the reader a flavour of different approaches. There are, of course, other alternatives. Note that we test our children twice a year on some of the following: the Neale Analysis of Reading, British Ability Scales Word Reading, WORD Reading Dimensions, Vernon Spelling and BAS Spelling. This forms the basis for some of the criteria referred to.

EXAMPLE 1 General English IEP for one pupil – Individual Education Plan – English

Pupil's name FB

National Curriculum Targets and Stages

AT1 Level 5
AT2 Level 6 but contrasts with weak reading accuracy and cannot always access texts.
AT3 Level 3

Nature of the pupil's difficulty (Priorities and principal concerns of this IEP)

Strengths

Can read difficult texts well given time. Good comprehension.
Is beginning to use word processors well.
Great determination but ineffective study skills.

Weaknesses

Lacks confidence in his reading.
Slow and muddled essay writing. Spends hours at home working on essays. Difficulties in using linear plans.
Weak spelling of multisyllable words, poor syllabification skills.

Objectives

To allow FB to read more fluently, spell 3–4 syllable regular words, write 2-page essays in 1 hour from a plan and become more effective in study skills and output of work.

Action plan

Teaching arrangements and activities

Syllable analysis of multisyllable word lists.
Reading of selected lists.
Example essay plans discussed and developed.
Listening to FB read.
Paired reading.
Discuss ways of becoming a more effective producer of work. Graph of achievement.

English class and tutorial.
1. One to one tutorials.
2. Discussion with FB about ways to achieve greater output.

Resources
EC word lists. EC essay plans. Class and personal readers.

Monitoring
Success criteria

Correct spelling of multisyllabic words.
2-page essays in 1 hour.
Attainment testing in February.

Pupil's comments: I find story telling difficult, I prefer facts. I agree to the plan.

Outcome: This would be completed after the above.

EXAMPLE 2 Class Plan for English for one group of six children

CLASS/SUBJECT PLAN

Class B   **English**   **Autumn Term 1996**

Curriculum needs, including Key Stages/AT Levels

Key Stage 2
AT1   Level 2 working towards Level 3.
AT2   Reading strategies at very basic levels, need to build up sight
       vocabulary. Working towards Level 2.
AT3   Working towards Level 2.

Objectives, including IEP links

1. To encourage children to listen carefully to instructions and to listen
   to each other in discussion.
2. To build sight vocabulary and phonic knowledge for both reading
   and spelling.
3. To improve confidence and fluency in reading, writing, and speaking.

Action plan

Targets and stages

1. Give children opportunity to listen, discuss and plan weekly stories.
2. To teach sight vocabulary using key word list.
3. To teach phonic components, alphabet, consonants, short vowels,
   cvc words, (k) sounds, c, k, ck, initial consonant blends, consonant
   digraphs, triple blends, final blends, long vowels, open syllables,
   flossy words, closed syllables and one, one, one rule words.
4. To teach grammar, using full stops and capital letters in writing and
   to use punctuation, as means to reading with expression.
5. To teach about use of tenses and about nouns, verbs and adjectives.
6. To begin simple comprehension work.
7. To encourage the composition of simple sentences, leading to the
   composition of short stories.
8. To teach a cursive style of handwriting.

Activities

1. Individual reading books with associated flash cards, word lists and
   comprehension activities.
2. Group reading phonic texts. 'Royal Road' by Daniels and Diack.
3. Work sheets, word family spelling, flash cards, dictation, 'Somerset'
   spelling/reading, speed reading word lists, class spelling tests, reading and spelling games.

4. Daily spelling using SOS for individual spelling needs.
5. Comprehension exercises.
6. Alphabetical order activities and dictionary games.
7. Speed writing, simple sentences.
8. Story writing after discussion. When complete the children read their stories to me. I encourage them to edit their own work and put in any punctuation missed.

Resources

Individual reading books.
Speed reading lists.
My own flash cards.
'Alpha to Omega' Hornsby and Shear, Heinemann.
'Somerset' cards. Talking Computer Programme.
'Royal Road Readers', Daniels and Diack.
Dictionaries.
Work sheets.
'Dyslexia A Teaching Handbook', Thomson and Watkins, published by Whurr.

Monitoring

Success criteria

Mastery of sight word lists.
Speed read cvc word lists to at least 20 words in 10 seconds.
Read a prepared page of reading book with fluency and accuracy and answer questions about the story.
Listen to simple set of instructions and carry them out.
Listen and discuss ideas for stories with more confidence.
Write simple stories in time set, using full stops correctly and gradually spelling more accurately, particularly words containing phonic components taught.

Outcome

EXAMPLE 3 General written language IEP for a child

Pupil's strengths

Has good communication skills. Articulates well and is confident when speaking to the group.

Weaknesses

1. Lacks concentration – easily distracted.
2. Reading age 4 years below chronological age.

3. Structure of essays weak.
4. Spelling age 4 years below chronological age. Unsure of vowel digraphs.
5. Handwriting and presentation lack consistency.

Objectives

1. To help him to become more focused.
2. To raise the accuracy and speed of reading.
3. To improve his ability to write a more structured essay: full stops and capital letters, paragraphing, descriptive writing, more mature choice of words.
4. To continue phonic work, particularly vowel digraphs, and introduce -cle syllables.
5. To help him to be more aware of the importance of consistently neat presentation.

Teaching arrangements and activities (Group of 5 pupils)

1. Set targets of work to be covered – reward positive attitude with plus points. Seat him away from potentially disturbing influences.
2. Continue with individual reading at own level (ensuring success). Books chosen from Headwork Stories, Ten Minute Thrillers with follow-up work from copymasters. Group Reading Ginn 360 scheme – word lists presenting more difficult vocabulary prior to starting a story: using same word list for speed reading, comprehension, spelling, parts of speech. Hearing reading daily (paired reading, with teacher, group reading).
3. Essay writing – topics chosen for creative writing supported by written material from which simple plan is compiled. More creative writing using word processor with supervision by teacher editing and discussing sentence structure and punctuation. Excercises using prepositions and homophones.
4. Revise vowel digraphs by referring to wall charts, making cartoons illustrating sounds. Syllable analysis: cle syllables, display board demonstration and teacher-made phonic worksheets.
5. Encourage neat handwriting and presentation by awarding plus points.

Resources

Appropriate reading books, computer, flash cards, phonic work sheets.

Monitoring

Discussing work relating to reading during tutorials, discussing/editing work during computer lessons, testing phonic work (dictation).

Success criteria

Assess and discuss attitude; ambition for immediate future (i.e. Group for next year, G or H   possibly I or J?). Reading level evaluation at next monitoring.

Outcome

EXAMPLE 4 English IEP focusing specifically on aspects of reading

National Curriculum Key Stage and Attainment Target Levels

Key Stage 3
AT1 Level 4
AT2 Level 4 but reading accuracy weak.
AT3 Level 3

Pupil's strengths

Has good word attack skills for reading lists of words when untimed.
Enjoys writing stories.
Good writing speed.
Making good progress in comprehension.

Weaknesses

Slow at speed reading lists of words.
Very slow and hesitant when reading text.

Objectives

To improve reading speed (and accuracy).

Teaching arrangements and activities

To practise reading speedcard from Reading Workshop (Pink Box). Timed reading of card to be entered on graph, 4 times per week. Use of controlled word lists (EC lists). Time and accuracy measures. Reading and completing Reading Workshop comprehension cards. Library lesson, continue reading Five and Ten Minute Thrillers and other books at a suitable level. Library lesson and tutorial, read Somerset cards.

Resources

Speed reading cards.
Reading Workshop (Pink Box).
Five and Ten Minute Thrillers (LDA).
Somerset cards.

Monitoring

Success criteria

Improvement in reading speeds as shown on graph.
Improvement in reading speed and accuracy score at next test.

Appendix II: Phonic Work Sheets

Although we feel that the best teaching involves active participation and
should be dynamic, there is an important place for appropriate work
sheets. This is because dyslexics require overlearning, i.e. a great deal of
reinforcement of what has been taught. This is particularly important as
far as phonic work is concerned. We have a number of source materials
for work sheets, and many that we have devised ourselves. The latter are
on computer disk, and can be printed out when needed, with the added
advantage that they may be changed easily to suit the needs of individual pupils as they are on word processor. The computer disks reflect the
written language structure, and an example of each work sheet is printed out and kept in a ring file. Teachers may choose the one they want
and print out copies for their own use.

   We have about 10 or so work sheets under each of the following
categories:

  1. Individual letters and sequencing
  2. CVC, short and long vowel sounds
  3. Initial and final consonant blends:
         (a) sh, th consonant digraphs
         (b) consonant blends
         (c) nasal blends ng, nch, nk
  4. Long vowel sound VCE words
  5. Vowels with r, ar, er, or, ir, ur
  6. Double consonant endings ff, ss, zz, ll, ck
  7. The w rules – wa, war, wor
  8. The v rules
  9. Soft sounds – soft c (s), soft g (j)
 10. Wall words – gu, dge, tch
 11. Homophones
 12. Vowel digraphs:
         (a)   long (ā)   ai   ay
         (b)   long (ē)   ee   ea
         (c)   long (ī)   igh   y   ie
         (d)   long (ō)   oa   ow   oe
         (e)   long (ū)   oo   ew   ue
         (f)   (oy) oi   oy
         (g)   (ow) ou   ow
         (h)   (aw) au   aw

13. Compound words
14. Suffixes:
    (a) doubling the final consonant (spelling rule no 2)
    (b) drop the e before adding the suffix (spelling rule no.4), including the effect of soft c/g
    (c) change y to i before adding the suffix (spelling rule no.15)
15. Prefixes
16. Syllable division and word patterns
17. Plurals:
    (a) adding s
    (b) adding es to hissing words
    (c) plurals of words ending in -y
    (d) plurals of words ending in -o
    (e) plurals of words ending in -f or -fe
18. Silent letters
19. Grammar and general English:
    (a) punctuation
    (b) possessives
    (c) comprehension
20. Difficult words

All of these worksheets will not be presented – just a few to give a flavour of the type of exercise that is useful. These range from simple, 'mechanical' phonic tasks, to those involving higher order skills of comprehension or vocabulary. One or two examples have been taken from some of the above categories, and a range of exercise types chosen. Each of these could be adapted for any given word pattern or written language structure. We have made some comments concerning each example.

Example 1

This reflects the need for classification of sounds for the dyslexic. Here, simple CVC words are used and are required to be sorted by short vowel sound. The example below can be completed visually as well as auditorally. The words could all be given on tape to stress auditory classification, or the same format could be used with other sound patterns.

Classification of CVC words under short vowel headings

Read the words, then write them under the right vowel 'family'. The first two words have been done for you.
Words:
  mad, hop, fed, big, pig, cup, can, bin, ten, bun, pot, sit, pet, tap, ham, get, lid, dog, nut, box, fix, fat, wet, hug, fin, jet, fan, sum, cod, sad.

a	e	i	o	u
mad			hop	

Example 2

Another form of classification, or drawing attention to similarities among words, is visual matching. Again, introducing different patterns or a tape accompaniment can be used.

Visual matching of word families

What is the same about these words? Underline the bits that are the same in all three words.

(1)	where	(2)	sank	(3)	flake	(4)	swing	(5)	snail
	what		drink		cake		swop		snow
	who		link		shake		swipe		snag
(6)	wasp	(7)	fly	(8)	brown	(9)	wash	(10)	fresh
	clasp		flag		bran		fish		froze
	lisp		flower		bring		push		free

Example 3

It is also useful to link a particular letter pattern to sentence completion or simple cloze procedures. This can introduce comprehension, vocabulary and grammatical skills. The following example focuses on nasal blends or sounds at the ends of words, but in the context of sentences.

Nasal blends

Read the sentences; choose the correct words, then write them out.

1. I have (camp, cramp, clamp) in my left leg.
2. We crash into the stump with a (munch, lunch, crunch).
3. My best pal is a (blend, bland, blond).
4. Run it up the (ramp, lamp, stamp).
5. I cannot (bend, lend, mend) you the cash.

Now write some sentences of your own, using some of the words in the brackets.

1. ....
2. ....
3. ....
4. ....
5. ....

Example 4

The next example is similar, except magic or silent 'e' is highlighted, and the sentence completion task is more difficult, with a wider choice of alternative words.

Cloze procedure: choice for sentences using short and long u

Complete these sentences by choosing the correct words from this list.

June   tune   use   huge   must   shut   tube   cube   fuse

1. All electric plugs have a _____ .
2. I take one _____ of sugar in my tea.
3. Don't forget to _____ the windows before you leave the room.
4. You _____ clean your teeth before you go to bed.
5. I had to buy a _____ of toothpaste.
6. I had a very big meal in the cafe. It was so _____ that I felt ill.
7. The sixth month of the year is _____ .
8. We play the same _____ over and over again on the juke-box.
9. Dad told me not to _____ his pen.

Further examples of 'sentence completion' phonics follow. Example 5 follows the 'w rules'; in this case wa saying (wŏ), Example 6 draws attention to short and long vowels in the same sentence, using magic 'e'. Example 7 reinforces the notion of regular sound–symbol links by requiring new words to be produced by changing one letter. In addition the work sheet uses (or) spelt au or aw. The same sort of format can be used for any written language structure, depending on the needs of the child and the stage reached.

Example 5

Choosing 'w' words to complete sentences.

The 'w' rules

When 'a' comes after 'w', it says (ŏ) as in orange. Choose the correct words from the lists to fill in the spaces in these sentences.

1. swat swan
   Follow the path to the lake and you will see the _____ .
2. wanted swat swap watch
   He _____ to _____ his _____ for sweets.
3. smash squash watch
   He drank his _____ and ate his cakes for his break.

4. wasp   swat   quads

_____ the _____ with the newspaper.

5. want   watch   wand

I _____ to see the wizard use his magic _____ .

Now write a new sentence for each word you have used from the lists (nine sentences), using a separate piece of paper.

Example 6

Sentence completion magic 'e', using short and long vowels in the same sentence.

The short and long sound of i, o and u

The vowel in the first word is short (says its sound). The vowel in the second word is long (says its name). Put each word in the right place in the sentence.

1. hid   hide

I told my brother to _____ and he _____ behind the cupboard.

2. kit   kite

My father gave me a _____ to make a big _____ .

3. pip   pipe

She got a grape _____ stuck in her wind _____ . It made her sick.

4. bit   bite

You may have a _____ of my apple if you only take a little _____ .

5. hop   hope

'I _____ you win the _____ , skip and jump race', said Dad.

6. rod   rode

I got my fishing _____ out of the cupboard and _____ to the lake on my bike.

7. rob   robe

The man in the bath _____ attacked the thief. 'You won't _____ me.'

8. slop   slope

Don't _____ the water out of the bucket when you go up the _____ .

9. hug   huge

I gave my father a _____ _____ when I met him.

10. cubs   cubes

I went to see the bear _____ at the zoo. The keeper gave all of them two _____ of sugar.

Example 7

Sentence completion: creating new (or) words. Drawing attention to similarities in word 'families' or regularities.

Vowel digraphs

The (or) sound ('au' and 'aw'). Put the right word in the spaces in the sentences. Change the first letter of the word in dark letters to make a word that will make sense,

e.g. **code** Last week I **rode** to school on my bike.

1.	**dawn**	You should cover your mouth when you _____ .
2.	**drawn**	A _____ is a type of shellfish.
3.	**pause**	What is the _____ of all this noise?
4.	**taunt**	It is a ghost's job to _____ people.
5.	**fault**	Gold bars and money are kept in a bank's _____ .
6.	**trawl**	A baby must learn to _____ before it can walk.
7.	**lawn**	A baby deer is called a _____ .
8.	**brawl**	An American is often said to talk with a _____ .
9.	**haul**	_____ is a boy's name.
10.	**launch**	If someone has a big, fat tummy it is sometimes called a _____ .

Now use the old words in sentences of your own (10 sentences). Use a separate piece of paper.

An alternative form of work sheet is a more analytical type, that focuses on one particular aspect of phonetic awareness or skill. The next three examples illustrate this, taken from different parts of written language structure. Example 8 looks at magic 'e' from a different perspective, and requires a use of sound picture. Some teachers may feel that the teaching of (rĭp) and (rīp), for example, for rip and ripe respectively can be confusing, but we find that the children at East Court enjoy this way of representing *sounds* as opposed to *spellings* and it does encourage them to analyse words and syllables. Example 8 requires a table of spellings and sounds to be completed, whereas Example 9 includes a simple 'rote' recognition of sound and spelling. Example 10 requires more thought, but still uses spelling/sound picture distinctions.

Example 8

Using spellings and sound pictures to complete a table of CVC and CVCE words.

Magic 'e'

Complete the following table of short and long vowel sounds

CVC word	Sound picture	Word + 'e'	Sound picture
rip	(rĭp)	ripe	(rīp)
pip	(pĭp)		(pīp)
	(bĭt)	bite	
cap			(cāp)
	(scrăp)	scrape	
slop		slope	
not			(nōt)
cub			
		plume	
us			
		hope	

Example 9

Analysing vowel sound and representing by sound picture and spelling,
(ō) spelt oa and ow.

Read the word, make the sound picture, write down the spelling of
the vowel sound.

Word	Vowel sound picture	Vowel sound spelling
boat	(ō)	oa
coat		
goal		
groan		
show		
below		
soap		
crow		
snow		
throat		
oak		

Now write two sentences using some of the words, or any another
words spelt in the same way.

1.

2.

Example 10

Represent spellings of (k) by k or -ck using sound pictures.

Spelling of k

Complete the spellings of these words using 'k' or 'ck' and write the sound pictures. (Hint – all the single vowels at the end of the words given are short.)

Word	Spelling	Sound picture
ta	tack	(tăk)
ba		
plan		
as		
pa		
sti		
croa		
chee		
fli		
ne		
cra		
pin		
stan		

Further work sheets in the 'analysis' mode involve syllable division. Just two examples are given here. The first (Example 11) requires simple division followed by sound picture representation, whereas the second (Example 12) requires analysis into syllable types, with only four types being considered (see pages 88 and 112).

Example 11

Splitting two syllable words and representing by sound picture.

Syllable division

Divide word. Make sound picture. Read from sound picture.

Word	*Syllable division*	*(Sound picture)*
spoken	spo'ken	(spō'kĕn)
primate	pri'mate	(prī'māt)
genus		
agent		
unit		
profile		
craven		
tyrant		
tripod		

Example 12

Syllable analysis, using only four syllable types.

Syllable division

Copy the words below, then re-write them and divide them into syllables. Identify the syllables; vowel–consonant–e syllables = vce, closed syllable = c, open syllable = o, diphthong = dip.

	dip c		
soonest	soon'est	forgetful	resume
	o o c		
devoted	de'vo'ted	forgetfully	tendency
	vce c		
hopeful	hope'ful	stupidly	feeding
season		animal	silly
seasoning		acid	silent

recent	ailment	sailing
road	delay	dismay
floating	saving	astride
famous	hunch	David
amazing	astonishment	astounding

Spelling rules also lend themselves to analytical work sheets. Example 13 illustrates the '1,1,1' doubling rule at a fairly early stage of its teaching. Here, pupils are requested to tick one syllable, one vowel, one consonant and the suffix beginning with a vowel. If four ticks occur, double the final consonant. This is a fairly explicit, mechanical introduction to the rule, but is a good starting point.

Example 13

Teaching the 'doubling' suffix rule by explicit protocol.

Suffixes – the doubling rule (spelling rule no.2)

Root word	1 Syllable	1 Vowel	Ends in 1 consonant	Ending	Starts with a vowel	All ticks – double final consonant
shop	√	√	√	+ing	√	shopping
rust	√	√	×	+y	√	rusty
swim				+er		
bump				+ed		
big				+est		
hid				+en		
grim				+ly		
help				+er		
wet				+est		
skip				+ing		
trip				+ed		
stab				+ing		
sail				+ed		
plot				+ing		
stick				+y		
steep				+er		
wait				+er		
step				+ed		

'Search and discover' tasks are another useful format for work sheets. Here the task is to find and identify a particular letter pattern or combination. This aids sequencing, reading and tracking as well as teaching the letter group. Example 14 illustrates such a task for the (j) sound. This work sheet also requires some composition work.

Example 14

The 'search and discover' task for the (j) sound.

The soft sound (j)

Underline all the (j) sounds that you can find in the story below. There are 19 to find. Then finish the story in your own words.

> The people who live at the edge of the village said that a gentle stranger had been there. He had left a message, written in large letters on a piece of paper, pinned to a hedge. The message said, 'This is a magic page. Only use in an emergency'. Jack and John found the message. 'What sort of emergency?' said Jack. Just then, Jim came charging by on his bike, skidded and
> ....

The next two examples illustrate the introduction of a particular written language structure as part of a work sheet. In Example 15 a list of silent letters is given which are then used in sentences, and in Example 16 a number of homophones are given.

Example 15

Reference list of words given to use in a sentence.

Silent letters: kn, gn

When k and g come before n they are silent and only the n is sounded; here are some examples.

knack	knob	gnash	consignment
knee	knock	gnat	campaign
kneel	knockout	gnaw	foreign
knew	knot	gnome	reign
knife	know	sign	
knight	knowledge	design	
knit	knuckles	resign	

Complete the words with spaces in the sentences below. Choose from the words that are given above.

kn
1. My mother has the – – –ck of cutting herself whenever she sharpens a – – –fe.
2. I – – –w how to tie many different – – –ts.
3. The boxer sank slowly to his – – –es and then fell forward onto his face. 'It's a – –– – –out!' shouted the referee.
4. My mother polishes our – – –b and door – – – – –er every day.
5. My sister is going to – – –t me a new sweater.

gn
1. The man gave a sharp whistle which was a s——— to the dog that he could start to ———w his bone.
2. I like the des——— of that new for————car.
3. The Customs men found a cons————————of for————guns hidden in the hold of the ship.
4. Queen Victoria re———ed for sixty-four years.
5. Some people put tiny plastic —————s in their gardens.

Example 16

Giving examples of homophones to use in sentences.

Homophones

A homophone (same sound) is a word that sounds the same as another word, but is spelt differently, e.g. sea/see.

Copy out these sentences on a separate piece of paper.

Choose the correct word from inside the brackets. Use a dictionary to help you.

1. Can you (reed, read) this book?
2. There is cold water in that (pail, pale).
3. The tap has a (leek, leak).
4. He has a (pain, pane) in his neck, poor boy.
5. We lost our ball on the (beech, beach).
6. We had baked (beens, beans) for (tee, tea).
7. Can you (see, sea) the (see, sea) from (here, hear)?
8. She works on the farm as a milk (made, maid).
9. (Peel, peal) the orange.
10. If you don't eat your (meet, meat), you won't have any pudding.
11. Is this (meet, meat) (reel, real) (steak, stake)?
12. That house is for (sale, sail).
13. The sky is very (blew, blue) today.
14. He climbed to the top of the mountain (peek, peak). He is a (great, grate) mountaineer.
15. There is a lot of (dew, due) on the grass today.

Appendix III: Common Words for a Basic Sight Vocabulary

These words consist of those most commonly found in early reading schemes, and can usefully be used to form flash cards for a basic sight vocabulary. The words are divided into three lists, the most frequent being List 1. Once the words on these lists have been mastered, the child should be able to sight-read 50–60% of the words in early readers. Inevitably the words tend to be restricted in terms of vocabulary, with function words predominating.

List 1: very high frequency words

a	in	to	was
and	is	so	of
he	it	the	that
I			

List 2: high frequency words

all	be	has	not	they
are	but	have	on	we
as	for	him	one	with
at	had	his	said	yes
you				

List 3: further high frequency words

These words, together with those of Lists 1 and 2, form half of the words found in early readers.

about	by	did	go	just	much	no	our
some	wants	where	an	came	do	has	like
make	now	out	then	well	which	back	call
down	her	little	me	off	over	there	went
will	been	can	first	here	looks	must	old
right	this	were	with	before	came	from	if
made	my	or	see	two	what	your	big
could	get	into	more	new	other	she	up
when							

Appendix IV: Suggested Key Word List for Irregular Words

It is envisaged that these words would be taught early on in a teaching programme. A variety of methods could be used, e.g. words on flash cards, to recognise and read; simultaneous oral spelling or other multisensory technique; computer games; matching against words given orally; 'bingo' games.

The following criteria have been used in selecting these words:

1. Frequency counts of children's written language.
2. Words most commonly found in early reading schemes.
3. Sources of written language structure.
4. Words commonly mis-spelt by dyslexics.

Note that some of the words do have spelling guides or rules, for example the 'w rule' for was, want etc.; or even commonalities, e.g. come, some. However, as the words cannot be spelt by following speech using the most common alphabetic conventions, they count as 'irregular' words here.

Where words form a 'common irregular sound' they can be taught together. Words are listed alphabetically, except where they form groups of commonality (of sound, *not* visual similarity!).

Key irregular word list

above	of
all	one
always	once
any	other
many	mother
are	brother
beautiful	said
because	saw
come	son
some	they
could	thought
should	you
would	your
does	was
done	want
give	water
goes	were
gone	work
have	world
know	year

Appendix V: Key Word List for School Subjects

These lists provide words for various school subjects that can usefully be learnt by dyslexics. It can often mitigate against dyslexics if subject words are incorrectly spelt, whether it be examinations or irritated subject teachers!

Mathematics	Computers	Science	History	Geography
triangle	command	acid	reign	ocean
quadrilateral	mode	alkali	monarch	continent
perimeter	computer	combustion	battle	glacier
symmetry	switch	element	sword	city
diameter	disk	biology	castle	country
angle	drive	physics	plague	desert
subtract	screen	chemistry	armour	climate
multiply	printer	equipment	soldier	agriculture
divide	program	bunsen burner	torture	industry
acute	monitor	science	ancient	direction
obtuse				

Appendix VI: Word Lists

Note that these lists are grouped together conveniently by syllable length and are not necessarily in order of difficulty for an individual child. Teachers need to choose the appropriate list for their child.

The copyright for these word lists belongs with East Court School and permission for their use can be obtained from the authors.

Lists 1–5: one-syllable regular words

Lists 1–5 provide the teacher with sources for regular, one syllable words. 'Regular' refers to words that can be spelt by following speech and applying conventional or the most commonly used sound–symbol correspondence rules. They cover the basic CVC words, and the use of vowel combinations, consonant blends at initial or final positions and magic 'e' words. The words can be used for reading, speed reading, spelling, syllable analysis or vocabulary development where appropriate.

Lists 6–9: two-syllable regular words

Lists 6–9 provide sources of two-syllable words for teacher reference. As above, 'regular' refers to words following the conventional or most frequent sound–symbol, orthographic or alphabetic rules. The words can be sounded out, syllable by syllable, and spelt by these grapheme–phoneme conventions. Increasingly, the words given will be stretching the vocabulary of most children (and many adults!), so that vocabulary development and discussion will often need to go hand in hand with the use of the lists in speed reading, syllable analysis or spelling.

The reader's attention is drawn to comments made at the start of each word list. In order to provide specific source material, some of the lists have particular, or specific, syllable types used. Reference to pages 88 and 112 on syllable analysis will be needed for those readers not already familiar with the six syllable types.

Lists 10–14: multisyllable regular words

Lists 10–14 provide teacher references for three, four and five-syllable words. As before, 'regular' refers to conventional sound–symbol relationships, i.e. the words may be sounded out, syllable by syllable, and by following speech and using normal alphabetic or phoneme–grapheme rules, may be spelt. Inevitably, as the words become more complex, some of the conventions, whilst following 'regular' sound–symbol guides, are rather less frequent. Examples are -ture saying (cher) in lecture or -tion saying (shun) in station. It is assumed that these and other associations will have to be taught. It must be said, however, that the notion of 'regular' is being considerably stretched in some of the words!

The reader's attention is drawn to comments made at the start of each word list. In order to provide specific source material, some of the lists have particular or specific syllable types used.

Note that syllables such as 'tion' in station and 'tial' is partial do not fall neatly into the six syllable classification. They are called closed syllables because the vowels are short, a final consonant ends the sound, and the two vowels do not produce one of the vowel sounds defined on page 89.

East Court word list 1: one-syllable CVC words (closed syllables)

cat	beg	cub	pig
men	rid	pat	top
dog	rot	get	hut
pin	sum	win	nod
mug	had	box	lot
fog	but	ham	tip
sat	bit	rip	dip
gun	hug	bug	let
fox	pan	got	fun
can	dig	mop	bad
big	hen	hit	log
wet	cut	hid	peg
jam	pot	keg	fat
rob	men	nap	lad

him	ram	mud	bid
six	dad	mad	tub
hop	hum	did	led
cap	big	met	hid
red	tag	map	hog
rug	set	nut	ran

East Court word list 2: consonant blends (CCVC) words (closed syllables)

spin	blot	clap	shut
stop	glad	strap	spot
twig	spat	flip	glen
clip	trap	slot	strip
glut	trip	spit	grip
flag	twin	plot	swim
prop	prim	shed	slap
drum	step	stab	clam
smug	frog	from	grit
plan	clop	pram	flop
trip	shop	bled	stun
crab	snap	sprig	tram
ship	crop	grid	twit
slit	flap	slug	plum
chop	quit	glib	snug
grin	smog	glum	prep
scrum	chap	crib	clan
snip	bred	drop	trim
fret	plum	chip	drag
snag	slap	brat	strum
swot	plop	trot	slip

East Court word list 3: one-syllable consonant blends, CCVCC plus end blend words (closed syllables)

crust	crush	smash	twist
brush	crest	quest	thing
chest	string	frost	clink
crisp	swing	stink	stand
froth	blink	trick	crash
spring	shrink	cling	trunk
fling	stick	shack	drunk
spank	brand	stack	slick
bland	blush	splash	shock
crack	prank	slack	slung

stung	black	blank	stamp
drink	grand	cloth	gland
chink	think	brick	chunk
slush	slang	sting	plush
snack	truck	brush	slump
twang	flush	cramp	stunk
thick	drank	plank	smack
stock	chick	clamp	strung
slink	bring	swank	clump
slack	stuck	sling	shock

East Court word list 4: one-syllable magic 'e' (CVCE) words (vce syllables)

pine	ride	cube	hide
cane	bite	wine	tube
robe	pane	ripe	wire
hope	cute	mope	lame
cape	rate	nape	name
hate	tide	fire	tone
hire	same	made	game
fade	rise	wise	side
lone	came	dome	cone
nose	rose	bone	fate
nice	rice	mice	lice
gate	fine	rode	mile
life	mule	pale	fuse
make	time	mute	wave
sane	rule	take	vote
kite	lake	mine	pipe
joke	tube	like	code
wide	woke	tune	five
cube	dune	dive	tape
pose	home	wife	site

East Court word list 5: one-syllable vowel combinations (digraph/diphthong syllables)

All these words use the most common vowel combinations, and are 'regular' in that sense. However, it is assumed that the vowel combinations have been taught. The following have been used: (ā) ai ay; (ē) ee ea; (ī) igh y ie; (ō) oa ow; (ū) ew; (oi) oi; (ow) ou. The reader is referred to Appendix VIII for further examples of less common vowel combinations. Note that ow is only used as (ō), e.g. snow, in this list.

sail	mound	bay	pout
sheet	teeth	sight	lie
might	boil	feet	may
cry	dream	spoil	hound
boat	fight	shout	queen
stew	fly	coal	right
coil	way	tie	soil
day	join	ground	steam
team	play	road	hay
pie	crow	leaf	glow
snow	bright	joint	point
chain	paint	fray	pay
feed	die	street	lout
way	hoist	sighs	flay
noise	stout	groan	coin
found	clean	why	low
teach	tow	speed	knight
toad	laid	shoal	brain
stay	say	light	dry
night	bow	raid	beach

East Court word list 6: two-syllable words with VCCV (closed syllables only)

Note that the third column consists of words with double letters, and the fourth column consists of words with unusual or difficult meanings for vocabulary development with children requiring 'high-low' work.

velvet	atlas	puppet	rancid
tandem	nutmeg	traffic	sylvan
bandit	tinsel	offend	lintel
signal	tonsil	cotton	cygnet
magnet	ransom	flannel	candid
napkin	hectic	funnel	fiscal
dismal	pencil	happen	aspic
goblin	limpid	assist	syntax
contest	kidnap	attend	antic
cancel	muslin	fillet	lactic
sandal	piston	collect	jetsam
Hamlet	litmus	rabbit	raglan
system	trumpet	attempt	sampan
vandal	problem	rubbish	mantis
splendid	catnip	button	septic
dental	humbug	tunnel	dispel
goblet	subject	gallon	impel

until	dismiss	tennis	pastel
seldom	lentil	mutton	flotsam
insult	limpet	madden	embed

East Court word list 7: two-syllable – regular word structure

Limited to open, closed and vce syllable types only. No consonant blends in initial position.

final	inhale	nylon	invade
ugly	vanish	kingdom	vampire
student	imbibe	bagpipe	inside
poker	dentist	intend	confuse
dial	bucket	umpire	pilot
insult	duet	tribal	lazy
lady	inmate	legal	cutlass
litmus	tadpole	infant	intone
even	tonsil	alcove	disgust
poem	humid	basin	pistol
amuse	salute	content	polite
spider	duty	infuse	expand
bamboo	banish	bankrupt	pilgrim
expect	migrate	sunrise	exhume
simplest	belong	subside	icecap
insect	intent	unjust	contend
dilate	peckish	ignite	vibrate
depend	absent	constant	vantage
regal	demand	hundred	musket
poplin	finish	degrade	urchin

East Court word list 8: two-syllable words – regular letter structure

Using open, closed and vce syllables, but with r-combination or -le syllable types in each word.

Column 4 consists of unusual or difficult meanings for vocabulary development. Teaching note: CV + Cle is open syllable + -le, e.g. ta'ble, CVC + Cle is closed + -le, e.g. bot'tle.

hermit	able	ankle	firkin
castle	confirm	ladle	mantle
turban	maple	bottle	vesper
kettle	fiddle	buddle	nectar
verbal	disturb	banner	diddle
battle	huddle	gamble	baffle

doctor	ample	cuddle	concur
table	surplus	stable	waffle
turnip	babble	nipple	surpass
little	western	buckle	incur
circus	batter	beetle	mangle
murmur	unborn	hurdle	fertile
barter	partake	meddle	fable
apple	marble	rattle	adverb
corner	herbal	barber	assert
army	angle	staple	ajar
paddle	dabble	topple	mettle
further	muddle	rabble	averse
paper	toddle	handle	mottle
thimble	sparkle	minor	supple

East Court word list 9: two-syllable words – any syllable type

Every word contains a vowel combination (dip) syllable type. Column 4 contains unusual or difficult meanings for vocabulary development.

about	bedroom	baboon	voucher
window	seesaw	mountain	twilight
fountain	argue	goatherd	rowan
railroad	gauntlet	unclean	pauper
treatment	barmaid	gleeful	oboe
powder	pursue	leaflet	abstain
virtue	mermaid	amount	typhoon
greenhouse	typhoid	waiter	profound
spoonful	freewheel	laundry	adroit
maintain	stayed	keeper	subsoil
highlight	wooden	rightful	oaken
approach	indeed	footstool	audit
foolish	throaty	yellow	restrain
dainty	joyful	feeble	trefoil
downhill	needle	doomsday	plaudit
bargain	freedom	traitor	aloof
eagle	monsoon	daylight	parboil
crayon	easy	playschool	jaunty
boastful	creeper	crowfoot	heathen
tiptoe	auction	lighthouse	flounder

East Court word list 10: three-syllable regular words

Producing open, closed, CVC and r-combination syllables only. No -le or vowel combinations.

carpenter	Atlantic	candidate	investment
peppermint	September	habitat	cabinet
infancy	establish	capital	unwanted
turpentine	surrender	generate	saturate
abnormal	immortal	tropical	destitute
reporter	sarcastic	contribute	electric
important	contractor	introduce	remember
assassin	bombastic	lemonade	statistic
astonish	commandment	penetrate	terminate
thunderbolt	aggressive	tornado	demolish
underpass	committee	lumbago	dictation
mizzenmast	consultant	hospital	centipede
malcontent	passenger	projector	graduate
incorrect	inspector	undulate	hydroplane
October	separate	sycamore	November
personnel	intercede	marmalade	atomic
embankment	December	indulgent	dinosaur
fingerprint	castigate	circumvent	departure
fantastic	porcupine	important	kingfisher
underpants	scapula	computer	regular

East Court word list 11: three-syllable regular words

Any letter pattern and syllable type, except that each word has at least one 'vowel combination' syllable in it – 'dip' syllable type.

appointment	sunflower	underfoot	stowaway
wheelbarrow	unseemly	employment	alkaloid
foolhardy	audience	amorous	steeplejack
exhaustion	entertain	countershaft	streamer
avenue	housekeeper	royalty	remainder
unsightly	readable	reclaimed	pointedly
tremulous	tomahawk	plausible	outlandish
audible	revenue	teetotal	auspicious
powerful	unknowing	tantamount	infighting
overhaul	powdery	onlooker	thousandfold
empower	overleaf	arduous	soothsayer
neighbourhood	strawberry	toiletry	pedigree
nauseous	apportion	mispronounce	interflow
eavesdropper	disjointed	audacious	however
delightful	annoyance	teachable	gooseberry

bluebottle	nightingale	kedgeree	encounter
waterspout	loyalty	indiscreet	freewheeler
authentic	ungainly	highwayman	handmaiden
upheaval	interview	arachnoid	freebooter

East Court word list 12: four-syllable regular words

Open, closed, vce and r-combination syllables only. No -le or vowel combinations.

differential	appreciate	rhododendron	literature
temperature	adventurous	transportable	continental
interruption	television	imagination	repercussion
diminutive	attribution	resolution	repetition
institution	composition	dormitory	dictionary
preparation	distributor	solicitor	character
tolerable	perceptible	comprehension	despicable
vegetable	convertible	considerate	independent
inhabitant	consequently	pyrotechnic	non-conductor
penultimate	circumference	deprivation	originate
assimilate	demonstration	combination	chiropodist
magnificent	congratulate	calculator	radiator
automatic	capitulate	amalgamate	cybernetics
contributor	Adriatic	geography	togetherness
eradicate	dedication	curriculum	symptomatic
ventriloquism	uranium	thermoplate	retribution
panoramic	projectionist	overextend	experience
insulation	miscalculate	hyperactive	understanding
referendum	operatic	resignation	disrespectful
extinguisher	explanation	insomniac	dehumanise

East Court word list 13: four- or five-syllable regular words

Any letter pattern and syllable type, except that each word has at least one vowel combination syllable in it – 'dip' syllable type.

anonymous	treasonable	discontinue	reasonable
exploitation	mausoleum	tautology	influential
discountenance	disagreement	entertainment	anomalous
embroidery	counterbalance	superheated	augmentation
unseaworthy	buffoonery	overweaning	wicketkeeper
foreshadowed	authority	knowledgeable	unspeakable
goodfellowship	pronounceable	disembowel	automatic
autonomous	freemasonry	redeemable	unreadable
delightfully	disappointment	unemployment	available

East Court word list 14: five-syllable regular words

Open, closed, vce and r-combination syllables only. No -le or vowel combinations.

administrator	modification	intermediate	mathematical
inconsiderate	technicality	undergraduate	occasionally
originally	multiplication	ultraviolet	identification
pronunciation	privatisation	opportunity	particularly
terminology	articulation	vocabulary	extracellular
metamorphosis	exterminator	ectoparasite	gramatology
Echinococcus	macroglobulin	histochemistry	antependium
metalliferous	counteroffensive	metaphosphoric	crystalliferous
echolocation	ferromanganese	metencephalon	interpretation
irreducible	attenuation	pasteurisation	aftersensation
polysaccharide	countersignature	postmillennial	ferromagnetic
interoceptor	interpretative	metaphysician	expropriated
legitimation	lepidoptera	lexicology	manipulative
materialise	nationality	necessitated	palaeolithic
peculiarly	radiology	repatriation	Yugoslavian

Appendix VII: Spelling Rules

The following are rules taken from the Gillingham–Stillman manual, which we use at East Court.

Rule 1: *Words ending in ff, ll, or ss (the f, l, s rule)*
Words of one syllable, ending in f, l or s after one vowel, usually end in ff, ll, or ss: The cliff is tall and covered with moss.

Rule 2: *Doubling the final consonant (the 1, 1, 1, rule)*
Words of one syllable ending in one consonant, after one vowel, double the final consonant before a suffix beginning with a vowel, but do not double it when the suffix begins with a consonant: big, bigger, bigness.

Rule 3: *Silent e (the magic 'e' rule)*
Words ending in silent e drop the e before a suffix beginning with a vowel, but do not drop the e before a suffix beginning with a consonant: hope, hoping, hopeful.

Rule 4: *Regular plurals*
The most common way of forming the plurals of nouns is to add s to the singular: dog, dogs; elephant, elephants; table, tables.

Rule 5: *Plurals of nouns ending in -s, -x, -z, -ch or -sh*
Nouns ending in s, x, z, ch or sh form the plural by adding es to the singular: gas, gases; tax, taxes; topaz, topazes; torch, torches; thrush, thrushes.

Rule 6: *Plurals of nouns ending in -y*
Nouns ending in y after a vowel form the plural by adding s: boy, boys. Nouns ending in y after a consonant form the plural by changing y to i and adding es: lady, ladies.

Rule 7: *Plurals of nouns ending in -f or -fe*
Most nouns ending in f or fe form their plurals regularly by adding s: roof, roofs; fife, fifes. However, some of them form the plural by changing the f or fe to ves: leaf, leaves; knife, knives.

It should be noted that the rules do not follow the Gillingham–Stillman sequence.

Appendix VIII: Vowel Digraphs/Diphthongs

Note: there is some overlap between this and Appendix IX.

ā		ē		ī		ō	
ai	ay	ee	ea	igh	y	oa	ow
wail	day	three	eagle	might	cry	boat	snow
pail	way	speed	seat	fight	dry	coat	bow
main	say	beech	peat	sight	fly	road	low
rain	tray	seem	meat	bright	why	coal	glow
jail	may	teeth	peach	right	pry	moat	row
raid	gay	feet	beach	knight		shoal	crow
nail	bay	fee	least	night		croak	tow
laid	stay	cheer	steam	sighs		groan	
tail	hay	meet	clean	fright		moan	
wait	play	week	heath	slight		cloak	

ū		(or)		ow		oi	
ew	ue	au	aw	ou	ow	oy	oi
stew	glue	August	awful	sound	sow	destroy	boil
few	blue	saucer	saw	mound	cow	boy	foil
grew	flue	haul	paw	ground	cowl	toy	despoil
knew	cue	caught	thaw	found	town	joy	toil
blew	due	daughter	crawl	shout	crown	enjoy	point
chew	value	jaunt	draw	stout		alloy	poison
mew	argue	pause	awkward	grout		employ	joint
slew	revue	cause	shawl	lout			coil
		fauna	straw	astound			
		launch	gnaw	foul			

APPENDIX IX: Ways of Spelling

Ways of spelling (ā)

a	a – e	ai	ay	ea	ei	eigh	ey
BABY	SAFE	SAIL	PLAY	GREAT	VEIN	EIGHT	
lady	vale	bait	say	steak	veil	sleigh	they
shady	stake	jail	way	break	rein	neigh	obey
David	brake	vain	slay	yea	reign	weight	grey
data	flake	rain	dismay		reindeer	freight	
station	save	tailor	bray			neighbour	
basis	blame	raisin	pray				
gravy	male	mail	stay				
raven	pane	pain	ray				
hazel	lace	bail	gay				
radio	gale	paint	day				
baker	gate	wait	tray				
fable	made	trail	clay				

Ways of spelling (ē)

e	e – e	ea	ee	ei	ie	ey
RECENT	THESE	EAT	FEED	CEILING	CHIEF	KEY
Venus	scheme	sea	see	conceit	shield	valley
regret	breve	peace	meet	deceive	piece	abbey
pretext	intercede	meat	heel	receive	shriek	chimney
equator	athlete	weak	week	neither	field	money
neon	sincere	leak	speech	seize	brief	donkey
begin	delete	team	peel	either	priest	
legal	scheme	mean	feet	receipt	yield	
female	stampede	seam	seem		diesel	
decent	extreme	beat	need		belief	
	here	dream	three		pier	

Ways of spelling (ī)

i	i – e	igh	y	y – e
TIGER	PIKE	LIGHT	DRY	TYPE
spider	mite	fight	cycle	style
tripod	dine	might	cry	lyre
tiny	site	bright	typhoon	pyre
giant	recite	sight	tyrant	
diagram	white	night	pry	
tidy	pile	knight	why	
diamond	vice	sigh	fly	
item	smile			
title	provide			
Bible	drive			

Ways of spelling (ō)

o	o – e	oa	oe	ow
PONY	HOME	BOAT	TOE	SNOW
moment	joke	float	foe	low
Dover	rode	road	floe	blow
rodent	clove	coal	doe	glow
grocer	dome	moat	roe	crow
Roman	grope	boast	sloe	row
crocus	alone	coax	woe	borrow
trophy	dole	groan	hoe	shadow
polite	pose	toad		slowly
obey	prose	coat		throw
	wrote	soap		arrow

Ways of spelling (ū)

u	u – e	ue	eu	ew
MUSIC	MULE	RESCUE	EUROPE	DEW
bugle	cute	cue	feudal	chew
human	fuse	sue	pneumonia	new
student	tune	issue	neurology	stew
unite	duke	due	eucalyptus	curfew
uniform	dilute	argue	euphonium	blew
studio	volume	value		knew
cubic	mute	fuel		Jew
unit	cube	continue		few
usual	refuse	revue		grew
menu				view

Ways of spelling (ou)

trout	house
about	ounce
bound	mouth
found	loud
surround	proud
our	county
scour	thousand

Ways of spelling (ow)

how	flower
powder	rowdy
brown	endowment
drown	
crowd	
towel	
allow	

Ways of spelling (oi)

coil	point
toil	hoist
spoil	rejoice
join	poison
joint	exploit
moisture	

Ways of spelling (oy)

joy	employ
cloy	destroy
Troy	corduroy
enjoy	loyal
Savoy	royal
alloy	boycott

Appendix X: The Impossible Word List

transmogrification	chaos
anthropomorphic	gargoyle
carcinogenic	heuristic
mysticism	animosity
physiological	magnanimous
scepticism	ventriloquism
defenestration	synonym
autonomous	embellishment
ebullient	arachnoid
egalitarianism	capricious
pusillanimous	deny
deoxyribonucleic-acid	

Note: We only use this list after extensive training in the use of syllabification and the six types of syllables.

Appendix XI: Statementing

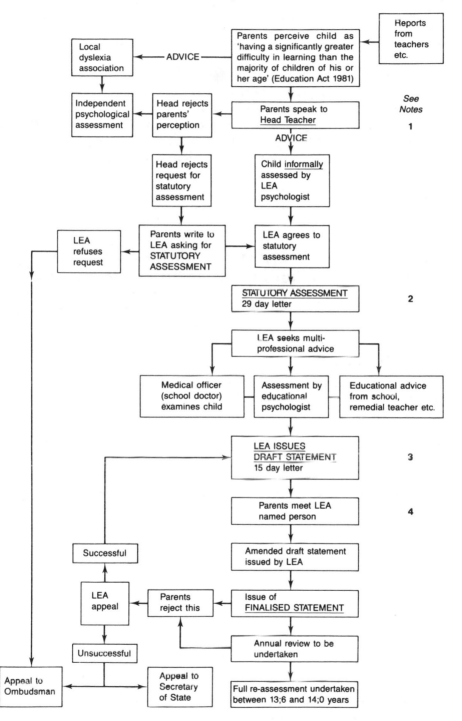

Action

Keep a date file

Notes
1. Write to head teacher:
   (a) formal appointment;
   (b) request help for specific reasons;
   (c) ask for written replies to all your letters.
2. Write to LEA asking for waive of 29 day letter. (This will allow time to gather advice etc.)
3. Write asking for 14 day 'stay'. This will allow time to prepare evidence.
4. Prepare notes for meeting. Try and foresee problems from LEA. Be prepared to talk. Do not lose control. Take and use a tape recorder.

Appendix XII: Using the Aston Portfolio for Prescriptive Teaching based on Error Analysis

Errors	Problem	Teaching cards (Aston Portfolio)
Reading – visual		
Reversals:		
dis/biscuit	Visual discrimination	Visual card 3/4
Omissions:		
lig/light	Visual memory	Visual card 4A
sum/summer	Sight vocabulary	Visual card 5 spellcards 8/9/10
dem/dream	Phonic patterns	Spelling card 3/4
	Analysis and blending	Auditory card 9
Substitution:		
read/road	Sound/symbol	Auditory card 8/10
by/bun	correspondence	
shop/shepherd	Visual memory	Visual card 4A/5
Visual similarities:	Visual memory	Visual card 4A
swimming/something	Sight vocals	Visual card 5
read/road	Analysis and blending	Auditory card 9
Spelling – visual		
Reversals: bot/dot	Visual discrimination	Visual card 3/4
Omissions: we/went	Visual memory	Visual card 4A/5
Sequencing:	Visual sequential	
Firday/Friday	sight vocals	
	Analysis and blending	Visual card 2/4A

Phonetic:

hey/hay	Sight vocabulary	Auditory card 10
cull/call	Phonetic patterns	
wic/week	Spelling rules	
wucs/works		

Appendix XIII: Some Examples of Minimal Pair Words (Southern British Pronunciation)

Vowels		*Consonants*	
seat	sit	pig	big
sit	set	bee	tea
set	sat	tin	din
cat	cut	din	kin
cut	cart	cap	gap
cart	cot	gag	hag
cot	caught	hen	men
cord	could	map	nap
pull	pool	sin	sing
pool	pearl	sink	silk
pearl	pale	lid	rid
day	die	red	wed
buy	boy	well	yell
toy	toe	you	chew
hoe	how	fat	vat
how	hear	thin	fin

There are others of course, as well as those contrasting larger units, e.g. frog – slog or hug – hung etc.

Appendix XIV: Word Processing Examples

In Chapter 8 a word processing curriculum was outlined. Many of the skills required need practice and exercise on the word processing system used. This appendix shows three examples of the way in which word processing exercises can be linked to other aspects of written work. In fact in these examples the word processing skills are implicit, i.e. they are necessary in order to fulfil the requirements of the task. In all the examples the basic skills of loading, saving and printing work are assumed.

The first example is one of a series of punctuation exercises. The purpose is both to revise the punctuation point covered in a previous lesson as well as provide practice. In this instance the exercise can be retained for reference. As far as word processing is concerned, all that is required is the addition of the punctuation, and perhaps formatting the text to tidy it up.

Word processing example 1: punctuation exercise on sentences, full stops and capital letters

1. Print the file PUNC2 from the course disk you have been given.
2. Sentences make a sense all on their own. They make a statement, give an instruction or ask a question. In the following passage you should finish the sentences with full stops, question marks or exclamation marks. There are four paragraphs. The first has been done for you. The number after each paragraph tells you how many sentences in each paragraph. Very short sentences are best here.
3. Read the passage, attend to sentences and meaning.
4. Edit, adding punctuation. Read again.
5. When you are happy about the punctuation SAVE (name) and then PRINT (name).

He took one more step. Watkin's mouth opened wide. He made a gasping sound. He slumped into the chair. (4).

Thomson jerked the gun out of Watkin's hand he stepped back quickly he had a gun now he must stop and think what he must do (4)

he could run for his life he could put Watkins permanently out of the game he could shoot him there and then he could kill him he could kill another human being he looked at the gun in his hand it was small and evil it could spit out death (8)

Thomson raised it he pointed it at Watkins could he do it could he steel himself to do it he squeezed the trigger gently nothing happened he checked the chamber the gun was empty Watkins had been bluffing (9)

The following two examples require rather more sophisticated English and word processing skills. Example 2 involves reduction and expansion in English. It requires word processing skills of word and sentence deletion; retabulating and formatting, adding words and sentences, and even shifting paragraphs. Example 3 involves similar word processing skills, but somewhat different English skills. The examples shown are difficult and would be used with older age groups and those with a reasonable level of literacy.

Word processing example 2: simplifying and adding to passage

LOAD SUM1. Print out a copy. Then use the word processor to edit and do this work on summary.

Often the main ideas in writing have examples or illustrations which are linked to the main idea. For example:

The amphibia, which is an animal class to which our frogs and toads belong, were the first animals to crawl from the sea and inhabit the earth.

This is saying – 'The first animals to leave the sea and live on dry land were the amphibia'. The part about frogs and toads is a detail.

Rewrite the next passage using only the main ideas. Edit out the details, examples and non-essential information.

1. It is often assumed that children who fail at school, and by 'fail' in British society we usually mean 'fail to pass examinations', do so because they are lacking the necessary intelligence. Nothing could be further from the truth. Some of the greatest characters in history have been total failures at school. Sir Winston Churchill is, perhaps, the best known such failure, but there are many others, especially in the field of art, music and literature. Many of the world's most successful business people admit to having spent most of their life at the bottom of the form. There are many reasons why children fail at school, not least of which is that they are too intelligent and, as a result, find their lessons utterly boring.

Now have a go at ADDING details, examples and non-essential information to this passage.

2. There are many causes of road accidents. Accidents can be due to vehicles. They can be due to pedestrians. In the end the causes are due to lack of consideration for other road users.

Word processing example 3: condensing passages

LOAD SUM2. Print out a copy of this. Then do the work. Then print out a copy of your edited work.

[Condensation]

'Condensing' a text means reducing it in length, yet keeping the main 'message'. One way of doing this is rephrasing the sentences, that is saying it in fewer words.

For example: 'There are some parents who, being extremely ambitious for their children, set out to pressure them to achieve in subjects and activities for which they have little talent and even less interest.' 32 words

You can express this more simply: 'Some children are pressured by ambitious parents to succeed in activities in which they are uninterested, and have little ability.' 20 words

Or, with some meaning missing: 'Some parents have unreasonable expectations of their children's achievements.' 9 words

So, rewrite these two passages with the same ideas expressed, but with fewer words. Put the number of words used after the changed passage.

1. Dr Thomson was a good squash player, but had a bad habit of arguing with the marker and the referee. Whenever a decision went against him he would immediately start objecting. He would argue and he would turn to the crowd and demand their support. It was not unusual for him to hold up the game by arguing for five minutes or more, and he kept on doing this again and again. (72 words)
2. The Blue dormitory was on trial for bad behaviour. Matron had reported that they had behaved badly during the night. Apparently they had been talking and making a noise late at night. Matron reported this late night talking to the Principals. Dr Thomson and Mr Watkins were investigating this behaviour and taking evidence from Matron, the duty teacher, the head of dorm and other members of the dorm. (68 words)

Appendix XV: Reading Game

'Difficult' words, e.g. words ending <u>TION</u>. Always aim for groupings.

EXAMPLE 1. FIXA<u>TION</u>
            2. EMANCIPA<u>TION</u>
            3. ELOCU<u>TION</u>
            4. FRUI<u>TION</u>
            5. ELONGA<u>TION</u>
            6. STA<u>TION</u>

△

STATION

1. Five packs of six cards are made.
2. Suites are shuffled and placed face up in the middle of the table.
3. Each player takes one card (in a clockwise order) which he has to read aloud.
4. If he cannot, he returns the card face up to a pile beside the main pile.
5. If the card is correctly read, then the player can keep the card and look at other players' cards which are kept face up in suites in front of the players.
6. If he can read his opponents' cards, he can claim them.
7. The winner is the player with the most cards at the end of the game.

References

Alston J, Taylor P (1988). The Handwriting File. Wisbech: Learning Development Aids.

Aubrey C, Eaves J, Hicks C, Newton MJ (1982). The Aston Portfolio. Wisbech: Learning Development Aids.

Backman F (1927). Uberkongenitale Wortblindheit (Angeborene Leseschwache). Abhandhungen aus der Neurologie, Psychiatrie, Psychologie und ihrem Grenzebieten, 40, 1–72.

Berlin R (1872). Eine besondere Art der Wortblindheit (Dyslexia). Weisbaden.

Bradley L, Bryant P (1983). Categorising sounds and learning to read: a causal connection. Nature, 301, 419–21.

Bramley W (1984). Units of Sound: Teachers Notes. Corsham: Units of Sound Productions.

Bryant P, Bradley L (1985). Children's Reading Problems. Oxford: Blackwell.

Burt C (1937). The Backward Child. London: University of London Press.

Chasty HT (1981). Dyslexia: Spreading word effectively. Times Educational Supplement, 13 November.

Chasty HE, Friel J (1991). Children with special needs; assessment, law and practice – caught in the act.

Cotterell G (1970). Teaching the dyslexic. In Franklin A and Naidoo S (Eds) The Assessment and Teaching of the Dyslexic Child. London: Invalid Children's Aid Association.

Cotterell G (1978). Checklist of Basic Sounds and Phonic Reference Cards. Wisbech: Learning Development Aids.

Crowther G (1982). Dyslexia Education, 20 August, 143.

Crystal D (1987). The Cambridge Encyclopaedia of Language. Cambridge: Cambridge Reference.

Cunningham A (1990). Explicit versus implicit instruction in phonemic awareness. Journal of Experimental Child Psychology, 50, 429–44.

Ehri L (1991). Development of reading and spelling in children: an overview. In Snowling M, Thomson M (Eds) Dyslexia: Integrating Theory and Practice. London: Whurr.

Elliott C (1983). British Ability Scales, Handbook and Technical Manual. Windsor: NFER/Nelson.

Fernald G M (1943). Remedial Techniques in the Basic Subjects. New York: McGraw-Hill.

247

Frith U (1985). Beneath the surface of developmental dyslexia. In Marshall JC, Patterson KE and Coltheart M (Eds) Surface Dyslexia in Adults and Children. London: Routledge & Kegan Paul.

Gillingham A, Stillman B W (1969). Remedial Training for Children with Specific Disability in Reading, Spelling and Penmanship, 5th edn. Cambridge, MA: Educational Publishing Co.

Goswami U (1988). Children's use of analogy in learning to spell. British Journal of Developmental Psychology, 6, 21, 33.

Goswami U (1994). Reading by analogy: theoretical and practical perspectives. In Hulme C, Snowling M (Eds) Reading Development and Dyslexia. London: Whurr.

Hall JV (1994). Oh, those vowels are walking! Australian Journal of Remedial Education, 26, 15–19.

Hamilton-Fairley D (1976). Speech Therapy and the Dyslexic. London: Helen Arkell Dyslexia Centre.

Hanna P R, Hodges R E, Hanna J S (1971). Spelling Structure and Strategies. Boston: Houghton Mifflin.

Hatcher P, Hulme C, Ellis A (1994). Ameliorating early reading failure by integrating the teaching of reading and phonological skills: the phonological linkage hypothesis. Child Development, 65, 41–57.

Heaton P, Winterson P (1987). Dealing with Dyslexia. Bath: Better Books.

Hickey C (1977). Dyslexia: Language Training Course for Teachers and Learners. Available from Dyslexia Institute, Staines.

Hinshelwood J (1917). Congenital Word-blindness. London: H K Lewis.

Hornsby B, Shear F (1974). Alpha to Omega. London: Heinemann.

Hulme C (1981). Reading Retardation and Multi-Sensory Teaching. London: Routledge & Kegan Paul.

Johnson D, Myklebust H (1967). Learning Disabilities, Educational Principles and Practices. New York: Grune & Stratton.

Johnson P (1995). Costing the SEN Code of Practice. Education, 26 May.

Lovett M, Borden S, DeLuca T, Lacrerenza L, Benson N, Brackstone D (1994). Treating the core deficits of developmental dyslexia: evidence of transfer of learning after phonologically- and strategy-based reading training programs. Developmental Psychology, 30, 805–22.

Miccinati J (1979). The Fernald Tracing Technique: modifications increase the probability of success. Journal of Learning Disabilities, 13, 3.

Miles E (1990). The Bangor Dyslexia Teaching System. London: Whurr.

Munro J (1995). Explaining developmental dyslexia: orthographic processing difficulties. Australian Journal of Remedial Education, 27, 1.

Myers PI, Hammill DD (1976). Methods for Learning Disorders, 2nd edn. New York: Wiley.

Naidoo S (1972). Specific Dyslexia. London: Pitman.

Newton M (1970). A neuro-psychological investigation into dyslexia. In Franklin AW, Naidoo S (Eds) Assessment and Teaching of Dyslexic Children. London: ICAA.

Newton M, Thomson ME (1976). The Aston Index. Wisbech: Learning Development Aids.

Olson R, Wise B (1992). Reading on the computer with orthographic and speech feedback. Reading and Writing, 4, 107–44.

Orton ST (1925). Word-blindness in school children. Archives of Neurology and Psychiatry, 14, 581–615.

Orton ST (1937). Reading, Writing and Speech Problems in Children. London: Chapman & Hall.

Reason R, Boote R (1986). Learning Difficulties in Reading and Writing: A Teacher's Manual. Windsor: NFER/Nelson.

Schonell FJ (1942). Backwardness in the Basic Subjects. Edinburgh: Oliver & Boyd.

Smith P (1977). Developing Handwriting. London: Macmillan.

Smith J, Bloor M (1985). Simple Phonetics for Teachers. London: Methuen.

Snowling MJ (1987). Dyslexia: A Cognitive Developmental Perspective. Oxford: Blackwell.

Snowling MJ (1996). Contemporary approaches to the teaching of reading. Journal of Child Psychology and Psychiatry, 37, 2, 139–48.

Steere A, Peck C, Kahn L (1971). Solving Language Difficulties. Cambridge, MA: Educators Publishing Service Inc.

Thomson ME (1984). Developmental Dyslexia: Its Nature, Assessment and Remediation. London: Edward Arnold.

Thomson ME (1988). Preliminary findings concerning the effects of specialised teaching on dyslexic children. Applied Cognitive Psychology, 2, 19–33.

Thomson ME (1989). Teaching programmes for children with specific learning difficulties: Implications for teachers. In Elliott C, Pumfrey P (Eds) Primary School Pupils' Reading and Spelling Difficulties. London: Falmer Press.

Thomson ME (1990). Developmental Dyslexia: Its Nature, Assessment and Remediation, 3rd edn. London: Whurr.

Thomson ME (in press) Subtypes of dyslexia: A teaching artefact? Dyslexia, forthcoming.

Treiman R (1983). The structure of spoken syllables: evidence from novel word games. Cognition, 15, 49–74

Vellutino F R (1979). Dyslexia – Theory and Research. Cambridge, MA: MIT Press.

Wechsler D (1976). Wechsler Intelligence Scale for Children – Revised. Windsor: NFER.

Wilsher C R, Atkins G, Manfield P (1979). Piracetam as an aid to learning in dyslexia; Preliminary report. Psychopharmacologia, 65, 107–9.

Index